Don't Get Too Comfortable

You don't know what's going to happen next!

To Bailey,
I ADDED A "Book Four
Skiing MADE ME DO iT," I Hope you
ARE Well & enjoy !.

Robert Emmet Buckley Jr.

[signature]

3/18/2019

Author, Bob Buckley, fly fishing near
Vail, Colorado in Cross Creek

Contents

INTRODUCTION

I don't know how many people really pay attention when the Public Service Announcements for the signs of a stroke are shown on their televisions. You are warned to think "stroke" when someone has a smile that droops, slurred speech, or difficulty raising both arms over their head. But even if you were listening to the announcement, you probably would not have had any clue that what was suddenly happening to me was a stroke. Without any warning, I became overcome with nausea and stumbled down the hall to the closest bathroom in the house. I was having difficulty breathing and after finishing vomiting, I had to crawl back to the living room and pull myself up on the couch where I tilted my head backwards as far as I could to open my airway. Thank goodness I wasn't home alone! My wife Donna called 911. When the EMT's on the ambulance crew arrived, they assessed my respiratory distress, unequal pupils, and loss of balance. They immediately inserted an IV and began to administer drugs to open my airway. They then transported me to the Vail Valley Emergency Room. Dr. Knerl examined me closely and ordered a CAT scan. The medical finding from the CAT scan was that **both vertebral arteries** in the back of my head were dissected! Dr. Knerl wasted no time putting me into an ambulance for the two hour drive from Vail to Swedish Hospital in Denver. Another of many miracles occurred; Vail Pass had reopened which had been closed all day by a blizzard.

"Do you know just how lucky you are?" Dr. Lampe's words didn't really sink in at first. I was in total denial. Just a couple of days before, I was chasing my son Brian who grew up on skis in Vail and a former Ski Club Vail racer down through the steep bumps on Peregrine, a run in the Birds of Prey on Beaver Creek Mountain. Brian was waiting for me down at the bottom of the long run as I skied up to him. "Gee dad you're skiing great!" I answered Brian out of breath, "Not bad for a former Vail Ski Patrolman long past his days skiing fast in steep bumps!" Forty eight hours later I was not feeling so cocky. Unlike most classic strokes, which occur in the frontal carotid arteries, my strokes were in the back of my head occluding both vertebral arteries at the same time. Dr. Lampe, the Neurologist who met my ambulance, later told me that she had never before seen both vertebral arteries dissected! The latter thinking by Dr. Claire Creutzfeldt, a professor of neurology at the University of Washington and attending neurologist at Harbor View Hospital in Seattle, Washington was that I suffered a mechanical type of dissection from the sudden deceleration skiing fast on the World Cup downhill course and then my head snapping violently forward when hitting the moguls down lower- even though I didn't fall. She noted that it was not a typical stroke and not easy to make an initial diagnosis. Thanks go out to Dr. Drew Knerl at the Vail Valley Medical Center who likely saved my life.

After one week in ICU, another one on the "Stroke floor," and another in a therapy ward, it sunk in that I was lucky to be alive and dodged an internal bullet, the dissection of both the major arteries supplying blood to the back of my brain. While in the ICU there were the daily early morning rounds of neurologists, cardiologists, internists, nurses, all concerned specialists, sometimes from other Denver Hospitals, coming by early every morning to check me out in my room in the ICU and check out my CAT scan for themselves. I knew the answer to Dr. Lampe's question, "Do you know just how lucky you are?" I could daily hear a doctor in the adjoining room loudly saying, "Betty, Betty" and never getting a reply.

At the time, it did not seem to me that all the therapy and encouragement in the world would ever get me back to anywhere near my pre-stroke life. Walking, eating, swallowing, drinking and speech were all things I would need therapy to do again. In the meantime, when I was allowed to try walking, it was with a walker and a therapist right beside me. Food was "served" via a feeding tube and "swallowing" was accomplished by a suction tube. I was so dizzy even sitting up straight in a chair next to my hospital bed I had to have a special seat belt holding me in place. If I tried standing up an alarm would go off playing, "She'll be coming 'round the mountain when she comes ...." and a nurse would come running when hearing it to help me. There is no quick fix for stroke patients. I stood a good chance of regaining independent mobility, swallowing, solid speech, and the ability to live a normal life, complete with drinking water, eating regular food that did not have to be pureed or liquid nutrition and hydration inserted via a feeding tube.

Three weeks later I was finally discharged from Swedish Hospital in Denver. Donna, the love of my life, accepted the discharge papers and the challenge of taking me home and providing the homecare and support I would need for months to come. Donna daily gave me water and hydration through a stomach tube which I lived with for months. What had really kept me going during this whole ordeal was the love and support I received from my family and friends. Even though their own lives are full and busy, all three of my children were there for me. Son John, an English professor at a Buddhist university in Daegu, S. Korea flew home. My loving daughter Amanda came down from Coeur d' Alene, Idaho and oldest son Brian who lives in Denver provided accommodations for all.

"Why me?" wondering why did this bad thing happen! The stroke was really the impetus for writing and sharing the stories of my early pioneer family in Colorado; and in my own version of being a pioneer, I served two years in Micronesia in the Peace Corps and relate what it was like being a Peace Corps Volunteer. Thirteen years after returning home from the Peace Corps and starting a family, my wife Donna and I took our 3 small children back to a remote Caroline Island for an incredible adventure and a lifetime of memories and stories. Some of the stories settings are in an historical backdrop directly impacting the main characters in the stories. Some have made me laugh, and some cry, and some have cost me dearly, and some I can only say are miraculous, including surviving a dissection of the vertebral arteries. And some of the stories will hopefully make you, as well as me, **uncomfortable**! But especially I wanted to record for you and my family these stories before they are forgotten and lost.

Don't Get Too Comfortable reflects my quiet prayer of one who was alone in an ICU hospital bed late at night and couldn't walk, swallow, or talk, and having earlier in the day been anointed with the Last Rites of the Catholic Church by my friend Fr. Ed Poehlmann. My book is ultimately about my trust in God who is always with us and answered my prayer to live and not to be, "_Done Too Soon_" (Neil Diamond).

"Be on your guard, stay awake, because you never know when the time will come. It is like a man travelling abroad: he has gone from his home, and left his servants in charge, each with his own work to do; and he has told the doorkeeper to stay awake. So stay awake, because you do not know when the master of the house is coming, evening, midnight, cockcrow or dawn; if he comes unexpectedly, he must not find you asleep. And what I am saying to you I say to all: Stay awake" (_Mark 13:33-37_). Or it could be said another way, "_Don't Get Too Comfortable_"!

Come and read stories from my Colorado family pioneers, Native Colorado Americans being pushed out of Colorado at the point of a gun, to a young Peace Corps Volunteer in the South Pacific, and Donna and I returning 13 years later with our three young children, Brian 10, John 7, and Amanda 6 years old to experience our own Swiss Family Robinson type stories.

In our case, it was a **Colorado Family Buckley** adventure along with many surprises.

"Come now, you say, "Today or tomorrow we shall go into such and such a town, spend a year there doing business, and make a profit--you have no idea what your life will be like tomorrow. You are a puff of smoke that appears briefly and then disappears. Instead you should say, "If the Lord wills it, we shall live to do this or that." (James 4:13-15)

Don't Get Too Comfortable

BOOK ONE: COLORADO PIONEER FAMILY

GEORGETOWN LOOP BELOW SILVER PLUME, COLORADO

CHAPTER 1
Coming to America

Ellen Short came in with Halley's Comet and was born in 1835 in Belfast, Ireland, County Tyrone. Ellen was known to our family as "Grandma Hickey" of Silver Plume, Colorado where, in her day and with a thick Irish brogue, spun wild yarns of her native Ireland and the danger filled wagon train journey to the Colorado Territory and her encounter with a Ute Chief. Her young audience sitting around the warm coal stove on many a high mountain, cold winter night was her 17 grandchildren listening in rapt attention. But first young grandson, Dave Collins, would have to fetch a bottle of Red Eye Whiskey from uptown at the saloon while she lit up her corncob pipe. "Don't let your ma catch you," he was admonished.

My father, Robert Emmet Buckley Sr. was one of the youngest sitting among his 13 brothers and sisters and four Collins cousins. Dad was known as Blackie or Black Bob because of his coal black hair. If you had talked to Dave Collins, the object of many of his outlandish shenanigans and practical jokes, his nickname referred to his pranks and devilish sneak attacks. But everybody loved him, until they were ambushed and hit by a snowball, over ripened tomato, or even a rotten egg, or pushed over in an outdoor privy.

Grandma Hickey told many stories on cold winter nights in Silver Plume where families didn't sit around watching television. So I was now interested in my family history and had the time to listen to my father while sitting on the front porch of the historic (and haunted) Belford House in Central City, Colorado where my newly retired father and I were spending lots of free time together. When I first returned from 2 years overseas service in the Peace Corps, I was broke, so when the occasional tourist would wander up from downtown, I would give them a tour of my parents' Belford House for a reasonable price. My father had recently sold his business in Denver and I had just returned from the outer islands of Micronesia. Both of us enjoyed the time together sharing stories as we hadn't seen or talked to each other for two years and there was much to catch up on and many experiences to share. My communications back home from the islands with my family was by ship's mail or as my folks would say "a slow boat from China." Just like my dad years earlier listening to Grandma Hickey, I listened with rapt attention to him and I wasn't sent to fetch Red Eye Whiskey.

He was a member of a very large Irish-Catholic American family of thirteen Buckley children. Today cars and trucks zoom past Silver Plume on I-70, most exceeding the posted speed limit, rushing to or returning from their favorite ski resort, or bound to destinations anywhere a major cross country Interstate might be taking them. Most drivers, whether in a semi or a Subaru, don't know what they're missing as they hurry by. If they only knew the stories this little town could tell. To truly appreciate Ellen's (*Grandma Hickey's*) story it is important to first go back to her early years in Ireland.

Far from being the idyllic Emerald Isle we see in travel brochures, Ireland in the 1800's was notable for extreme hunger, famine, poverty, disease, violence, panic, and unnatural death everywhere. John and Alice Short, her father and mother, were desperately coping with the challenge of keeping their 10 young children fed and alive. Originally John and Alice had 15 children but five boys had died, with four boys and six girls still surviving.

The potato blight of 1845 through 1849 in Ireland killed over one million people in the small country from starvation and disease. The potato crop, the basic staple in the Irish diet, was devastated. Famine fever- better known as **cholera**, dysentery, and typhus was rampantly spreading throughout Ireland. The Irish were dying so fast, like **The "Black" Death**, that at times there wasn't anyone left to bury the bodies of the dead and were left to lay where they fell. Despite terrible hunger and rampant disease people were also caught in the crossfire of English soldiers and Irish revolutionaries. Ireland was a nightmarish place to live during Grandma Hickey's childhood. (*Atlas of Irish History,* by Sean Duffy)

Cholera was also rampant in the United States claiming the lives of Presidents James K. Polk and his successor, President Zachary Taylor. The California Forty-Niner gold camps were rampant with young gold seekers being killed by the dreadful and painful quick killing disease.

Religious and racial hatred and warfare were always just around a corner in Belfast. The desperate hunger, fearful diseases, and the bitter fighting between the Protestants and Catholics left as its legacy deep and lasting feelings of bitterness, distrust, and hatred toward the British! And like DNA, anti-British attitudes were passed down through the generations in Ireland to the modern generations, even in Silver Plume, Colorado.

Alice Short (Grandma Hickey) was very lucky to be alive and able to escape to America and survive to tell her stories. It was during these times that emigration reached a peak from Ireland to America filling ships with virulent and contagious diseases killing many of the desperate immigrants.

Many ships arriving in America had more dead than alive when arriving in North American ports and some of the fortunate survivors carried cholera, smallpox, and diphtheria, and typhus. It was no wonder that the Irish were not looked upon as a blessing but were looked down upon in American port cities like Boston and New York where the destitute Irish congregated in ethnic slums.

Understandably panic set in among the cities citizens fearful of having their families dying in widespread epidemics brought from Ireland. It was common to see signs in New York City saying, "Irish or Catholics not welcome, or Irish need not apply. Irish not allowed." The mass panic and desperate conditions and contagious fatal diseases in the United States, were not only brought to New York City by the Irish but some also brought their anti-Protestant prejudice and may have infected the ancestors of an Irish-American Jesuit priest on Punlap Island in the South Pacific. Padre was from the New York Jesuit Province-an older man hard of listening.

Most surnames are easily recognizable as Polish, German, French, English, Arabic, and, of course, **Irish.** No one would ever confuse **Buckley** or **Collins** as Polish names. My name, Robert Emmet Buckley Jr. sure drew the attention of English Customs when I travelled to London on business in the spring of 1982; perhaps because "Robert Emmet" was an Irish patriot executed by the British in 1803.

After handing over my passport to the agent, I was quickly notified that I would need to step aside and was escorted by a tough looking agent to step into what was an interrogation room. He and another agent brusquely searched me as though I might be entering England as a member of the IRA, and after strip searching me and carefully examining the contents of my briefcase, I was reluctantly allowed to pass through customs and join my other two Vail Associates, Inc. companions who were wondering what I did to create the big delay. "It was just my name and blue eyes inherited from my IRA ancestors!"

But sadly just a few short months later, the IRA detonated two bombs during British military ceremonies in Hyde Park and Regent's Park, in central London, killing eleven, four soldiers of the Blues & Royals at Hyde Park and seven bandsmen of the Royal Green Jackets. Seven of the Blues & Royals' horses also died in the attack. Just months earlier, I enjoyed the impressive tourist spectacle of the Blues & Royals in colorful uniforms riding by on their sleek horses. As an American, who lives in the Rocky Mountains, I had never witnessed such Royal pageantry. The Fourth of July parade in Vail, Colorado featured the folding lawn chair brigade dressed in Hawaiian shirts and the Town Council precariously riding by on horseback and the Jo Jo Lyle and Packy Walker kazoo marching band.

A footnote to the suffering in Ireland, and not widely known in the United States, was the Choctaw tribe's gift in 1847 to Irish Famine Relief.

The Choctaws were driven from their land in the 1830s in the States of Mississippi, Alabama, and Louisiana and forced to march 500 miles to Indian Territory located in the future State of Oklahoma. *The Long March* is one of too many of a series of tragic death marches made by Native Americans being dispossessed of their lands by white Americans and their notion of entitlement- *Manifest Destiny*. Or Native Americans might think the notion was **The "White" Death**. The gift of $170.00, equivalent to $5000.00 today, was generously donated to starving "white Europeans" by the Choctaws while still in the grip of their own tragic and destitute circumstances.(*The Long March by, Marie-Louise Fitzpatrick)*

Ellen Short, Grandma Hickey, didn't have the option to pick when and where she was born, but if she did Belfast, Northern Ireland in 1835 would not have been on the list. Today, if she were alive, it could rank near the top thanks in large part to the heroic and courageous efforts to bring peace to Belfast by two Irish-Catholic women. Betty Williams was born in Belfast and was thirteen when her mother suffered a severe stroke. Betty had joined the IRA after Protestants had killed one of her cousins.

However, later she witnessed the wounding of a British soldier, knelt and personally comforted him much to the vocal criticism of the Catholic neighborhood. She became an activist for peace when she witnessed a car accident killing three children and severely injuring their mother. The accident was caused by a wounded member of the IRA losing control of his car after first shooting at a British patrol. These dead children were the nephews of Mairead Maguire. Williams, a passer-by, stopped and attended to the victims. Without this tragedy these two women likely would never have met. After the accident she collected over 6000 signatures in support of a petition for peace in Northern Ireland; furthermore, she succeeded in attracting the media to her petition.

Mairead Maguire, hearing about her efforts, asked Betty to attend her nephews' funeral. Soon they managed to organize over 10,000 Catholic and Protestant women to join in a march demanding peace. The next march organized by Williams and Maguire brought together 35,000 Christian women. Northern Ireland has not been the same since all these women stood up to their respective husbands, brothers, sisters, and sons and daughters waging this war in the name of God and who will control Northern Ireland.

The **Women for Peace** started the nonviolent movement in 1975 to make a better life for their children and at a time considered the most brutal in Northern Irelands' history. The momentum finally brought forth The Belfast Agreement of Easter of 1998 *(Irish Times, 11ᵗʰ April, 1998)*. The net effect of this agreement was that the Protestant Unionists Party and the Catholic Nationalist Party agreed to a power-sharing arrangement together for the most of Northern Ireland. "Thanks be to God" (a phrase I heard my Aunts Alice and Bernadette say many times), Belfast is today one of the safest cities in the United Kingdom. Tourists there can enjoy the energy and youthful vibrancy of a city brought back from the edge. Belfast is a living example of what God's plan living within us can accomplish when we choose to live in peace, love, faith, and courage. It is also a strong example of the "power of women."

Records show that John and Alice Short and their family immigrated to Dundee, Scotland and John attended to Alice in the birth of son Michael born there on November 1, 1855. The 42 year old flax weaver moved his family there to take a job in a linen factory. At that time, Dundee- Angus Scotland was the hub for the linen industry employing 50,000 workers, many from Ireland. The Scottish and English people responded to the Irish humanitarian crisis by welcoming thousands of Irish refugees.

In the 1900 U.S. Census, Ellen recorded she immigrated to the U.S. in 1850, but in the 1920 U.S. Census she recorded that she had immigrated in 1860. Many young Irish girls were illiterate due to the circumstances of poverty, religious, and racial discrimination, as well as the necessity to help their parents take care of younger brothers and sisters.

We know that Ellen Short was deprived of a formal education and was illiterate, and would have had difficulty with the government forms but an unshakeable faith in God gave her the strength to overcome this and the many other challenges which faced her life's journey.

CHAPTER 2
Hitch' Em Up – Wagons Ho!

While there is a question whether Ellen (*Grandma Hickey*) arrived in 1850 or 1860 in America, there is no doubt when she married the first of three husbands in her life. On April 22, 1861, Ellen Short and Daniel Griffin hitched their lives and married in St. Joseph, Missouri in a celebration officiated by Rev. John Hennessy. From the oral history description of Ellen by our family, she was very beautiful with red streaked long auburn hair. Only a few days earlier the church bells tolled signaling the start of the Civil War, and now they were ringing for the newly married couple. Daniel Griffin, the church records show, was the son of Michael and Catherine Griffin, who also hailed from County Tyrone, Ireland. I'm sure John and Alice Short would have been very happy for their beautiful daughter who married another kindred adventurous spirit, and an Irishman. No parents were present at the wedding, but Dan and Ellen did have a couple of friends witness this special day and share in their happiness.

As with any move, there had to be much planning and organization, things that take time. They couldn't just throw a few things in a wagon and leave. McDonalds hadn't peppered the route west at this time. St. Joseph Mo. was the starting point on the Oregon Trail for the wagon train. The young newlywed immigrants had many expenses to join a wagon train and at the top of the list was the purchase of a covered wagon which was like buying a car or truck today, oxen to pull the wagon, and a milk cow. The covered wagon for just two people didn't need to be as big as one for a large group or family and was primarily used to transport the supplies while the pioneers would usually walk beside the team of oxen. The wagon had been stuffed with all the necessary self- sustaining supplies that the arduous journey would require. And all necessities could be purchased in St. Joseph which catered to the wagon trains. Essential basics for Dan and Ellen consisted of many the same items that Donna and *I loaded up with on our family's journey to a remote Pacific Island. Donna thought we could never eat in our lifetime fifty pound bags of flour and rice. Was she ever surprised*! But we didn't have to pack a barrel of gun powder, lead shot, and rifles.

They would need cooking utensils, cast iron kettle and cover, skillet, tableware, a Dutch oven, coffee grinder, teapot, coffeepot, butcher block and knife, and wooden buckets for watering the animals and carrying water for personal use. Clothing was a big item packed in steamer trunks, including but not limited to boots, long cotton and woolen dresses, long underwear, buckskin pants, cotton trousers and shirts, and flannel shirts, wool coats, rubber rain coats, broad brim hats, sun bonnets, and rags used for sanitary purposes and a bucket for washing the rags (*Costco's extra sized toilet paper wasn't yet invented*), wash bowl, and chamber bucket or pot. So much easier and comfortable today to just pull into a Best Western!

Many types of tools and equipment were necessary for the wagon trail and Dan, being a trade mason, brought along his tools for his craft. They didn't worry like Donna did when she travelled west about a good spare tire, but they did bring along spare wagon wheel and wheel parts, extra oxen shoes, heavy ropes, spare reins, and two wooden stools which amazingly my cousin, Sharon Kennedy, still has in her possession. And like Donna, who stopped driving her Chevrolet Corvair before nightfall, brought along a bottle of Scotch for just "one scotch and water evening relaxer." Dan and Ellen enjoyed the same with a bottle of Red Eye Whiskey. The wagon was packed to the gills!

The American dream burned in Dan and Ellen's hearts but not totally displacing the homesick feeling of moving farther away from their loved ones, especially mothers, left behind. The time came in early May to start their new and exciting journey of a lifetime. At dawn the wagons were assembled on the eastern bank of the wide Missouri River awaiting their turn loading onto the assembled large flat boats to ferry the loaded wagons, animals, and pioneers across to the other side. After everyone was ashore and the wagons were placed for the first time in a circle, the nervous animals were fed and bedded down; the excited pioneers assembled to hear the final instructions for the early morning departure from the wagon master and his scouts.

At dawn everyone was awake and fixing their first of many breakfasts on the trail and going about the tasks to start on the new and exciting journey west. Imagine the start of the Indy 500 race with rows of cars all lined up and ready for the dropping of the flag and you have an idea of what this scene of nervous anticipation looked like. Just like the excitement of racing in the Indy 500, there was the ever present knowledge of the risk of danger and death during the long race. At the wagon masters' signal and shout of '*Wagons Ho*' the heavily packed wagons slowly moved out onto the Oregon Trail.

There were no convenient I-70 roadside rest areas with clean toilets and toilet paper, not even a tree or bush to hide behind while you performed your bodily functions, and it wasn't safe to wander even a short distance from the safety of the wagon train. When nature called for a woman her ankle length dress allowed her to squat down. You might ask what was used besides toilet paper because that hadn't been invented yet. A wash rag worked just fine, and would be rinsed in a river or a bucket of water used just for this purpose. (*On the islands of the South Pacific one would wade out waste deep in the lagoon and let the bowel and bladder movements float away in the strong current. A smooth coral rock under foot was perfectly comfortable to finish the job.*)

The wagon trains' route followed the Missouri River up North to the confluence with the Platte River in Nebraska, the milestone where you left the Missouri and headed west following the Platte west to the Rocky

Mountains; this portion of the Oregon Trail is referred to as the Platte Road. It was important to follow the river valleys because water and grass were vital for man and oxen in the hot and arid plains. I have fond memories fly fishing in the clear and clean mountain stream of the upper South Platte near Deckers, Colorado. But what the Oregon Trail followed now was anything but the mountain stream in Colorado. It was very wide, shallow, and muddy slowly meandering its way across the flat prairie. But unlike the Missouri the Platte was too shallow to navigate by steamboat, but it did provide essential water for man and beast alike to drink and provided easy navigation for this leg of the trip. (The covered wagons, *prairie schooners*, riding through the waves of tall grass appeared every much akin to the outrigger sailing canoes of Micronesia in the Western Islands of Truk with sails bobbing on the waves of the South Pacific.)

It was profoundly sobering for the pioneers seeing hundreds of wooden grave markers on the side of the trail which resembled in stretches a long and narrow cemetery. You would mistakenly think that most of these marked the deaths of people killed by the fierce and marauding Cheyenne, Sioux, and Pawnee Indians. But the vast majority of deaths on the trail were caused by **cholera**. Poor sanitation along the trails' watering holes and preferred camping spots used by thousands of people killed the vast majority and not arrows. Literally hundreds of pioneers died from fecal contaminated drinking water causing the spread of the cholera bacteria. The symptoms of cholera are nonstop diarrhea and vomiting, leading to dehydration, weakness, and many times a quick death.

A person could be healthy in the morning and dead that night. *Cholera, sadly, is one of those threads which bound Dan and Ellen's Ireland, the Oregon Trail, the Native Americans, and the outer islands of Micronesia where I served in the Peace Corps.*

The wagon train was painfully slow and dusty averaging ten miles per day and after a little less than one month on the trail, reached Fort Kearny about a 300 mile journey. By this time everyone could use a bath, rest, and a chance to resupply. It was built by the government on the Oregon Trail to aid western expansion and to provide an army presence protecting the pioneers from Indian attacks. The stores at the fort carried all food and clothing essentials and wagon repair parts and service.

It was an earlier version of *Little America* on Interstate 80. Probably at this time Dan and Ellen and three other wagons made the decision to leave the wagon train when it reached the South Platte branch of the Platte River and travel down and jump in the exciting Colorado Gold Rush to the Rocky Mountains in the newly formed Colorado Territory. The South Platte would lead them to the heart of what is now known as Denver at the confluence of the South Platte River and the Cherry Creek Rivers. This decision, for whatever reason, was not without potential serious danger, especially leaving the larger wagon train and venturing into even more dangerous Indian territory. But their final destination would be much closer at hand than travelling all the way to the Oregon country.

The United States Government promised the Cheyenne and Arapahoe Indian Tribes, in the *Fort Laramie Treaty of 1851*, control over the Colorado area of the Eastern Plains between the North Platte River and the Arkansas River in Southern Colorado and eastward from the Rocky Mountains. The Colorado gold rush and the flood of homesteaders resulted in rapidly deteriorating relations with the Indians. The Government's solution was to write a new treaty with the Cheyenne and Arapaho tribes.

The Treaty of Fort Wise, February 18, 1861, was signed by several chiefs resulting in further reducing Indian lands and keeping only a tiny fragment of the original reserve. Most of the other Cheyenne and Arapahoe chiefs repudiated the treaty which Chief Black Kettle and Chief White Antelope of the Cheyenne tribe signed, and took the opposite path. 'Cheyenne Dog Soldiers' (Warrior Clan) began attacking 'Whites' encroaching on their best bison hunting grounds. This is the very land that Dan and Ellen Short and their four lonely covered wagons were travelling, easy pickings. The Cheyenne Dog Soldiers and Chief Roman Nose were now looking for whites' blood. Murderous revenge and vengeance always means innocent blood will be shed and an opposite reaction to avenge innocent blood results with more blood sought and round and round again.

A splinter group of the IRA, like the Cheyenne Dog Soldiers, didn't agree with their chiefs who signed the Easter Agreement of 1998, and on August 15 carried out a car bombing in Omagh, County Tyrone. Twenty-nine people were killed, mostly children, including 18 month old Maura Monaghan, and 220 were injured.

*It took experienced and battle hardened Protestants and Catholics who knew the challenge facing them! Both sides rose to the challenge and laid down their arms and became statesmen, **finally!** Thanks to the brave women of Northern Ireland who were tired burying their dead children.*

The main wagon train continued on past the South Fork of the Platte River, following the North Platte Fork on its still long journey to the Oregon Country. The four wagons left behind seemed quite alone and vulnerable to the dangers facing them on the journey down the South Fork. Obviously, four wagons on the prairie did not enjoy the safety of numbers afforded by the larger organized wagon train. Why leave? As there is no written journal from them to answer this question, I am going with a reason that had my wife make a similar journey from upstate New York over a hundred years later, sunshine and blue skies! Donna left Rochester and came west alone in a Chevy Corvair. Certainly as dangerous as a covered wagon, but the motivation was the same. Get away from the grey skies and damp, dreary weather to sun, blue skies AND... OPPORTUNITY.

Ellen and Dan grew up under the *grey* and *rain laden skies* of Northern Ireland and were just so happy seeing blue skies and sun, almost day after day! Hearing from the wagon train master how depressing the winter weather could be in the Oregon Territory, they simply wanted to live in a warmer sunnier climate. "Blue skies up above, everyone's in love," as the song goes. Of course, it didn't hurt that the Colorado Gold Rush was on and great opportunities were available to strike it rich for the young stone mason building homes in the new towns for the miners, and who knows, finding gold himself. They weren't the first to be bitten by gold fever, or the last, but the dreary prospect of the Northwest's weather was as good a reason as any to make a left turn and *"go for the gold"* whether it be the real kind you hold in your hand, or the kind you see in the sky.

Former Governor of Colorado, William Lee Knous, who as a young lawyer accepted a lucrative position in Rochester N.Y. returned to Colorado within a year when he learned, "I'd rather be poor and live in Colorado than get rich and stay in New York." (grandson, Bob, was the President of the Vail Valley Foundation which hosted the 1989 World Ski Championships) This route along the South Platte River would lead them alone through Indian danger and unexpected new Indian friendships. With their faith in God as strong as ever, they knew that they were not venturing forth alone! They would need God's help rolling warily into Indian danger.

Cheyenne Chiefs Black Kettle and White Antelope were noted warriors in their youth, but now older and wiser, they wanted to peacefully limit more encroachment on their lands by the whites who kept moving the goal posts from the Fort Laramie Treaty of 1851, which guaranteed to them vast territory in the southern plains. By the 1861 Treaty of Fort Wise, Black Kettle and White Antelope hoped to retain a peaceful compromise that would satisfy the seemingly insatiable appetite for their lands and stem the flood of blood from the arteries of their people.

The Cheyenne Chiefs were not absolute monarchs of a European country in the 19th century. The American Government treaty representatives knew that the signatures of the peace seeking men didn't bind the other chiefs of the Cheyenne or Arapahoe or even all the young warriors in their own villages. The Indians had a different culture, language, and system of managing their lives. Truth is the American Government didn't really care. These treaties were only a tangible exercise to rationalize reducing the land size of the previous treaty, and knowing the new treaty would likely be again broken by both parties. The challenge was the nomadic lifestyle of the plains Indians required so much land following the buffalo herds and the flood of immigrants, miners, and settlers to the region was an unstoppable tidal wave.

The Cheyenne Dog Soldiers' warrior society didn't accept the terms of the new treaty the chiefs signed and were looking to violently frighten away and kill encroaching whites! The four covered wagons were travelling through the best Cheyenne bison hunting grounds and into a hornets nest of a terrifying warrior clan who were every bit as terrifying and dangerous as the Irish Republican Army. (*In Northern Ireland in 1940 actually violently collaborated with Nazis Germany*)

At night when the coyotes began to howl the immigrants feared the eerie sound could be made by warriors signaling to each other and sneaking up on them in the dark! It made for sleepless nights and a frightening honeymoon!

This time of year the bison were plentiful in the South Platte River Basin and it wasn't long before the small group of wagons caught sight of huge herds of buffalo. Soon contact was made with a very special Native American. A very large Native American man wearing his favored frightening yellow paint on his face approached Dan's lead wagon on a magnificent horse and gestured he was peaceful and wanted to speak. We know that the small wagon train met Chief Colorow and his Ute hunting party early on its journey down the South Platte.

The large Indian wearing yellow paint on his face (protection from the burning sun and drying wind) gracefully dismounted his magnificent horse and sat down and pulled out an empty pouch of tobacco and asked in broken English, did Dan have any tobacco? I can envision that Ellen nervously fetched some from inside the covered wagon. All the members of the four covered wagons would have gathered around in a circle and passed around and shared with the big Indian Dan's peace corncob pipe, lit from Ellen's match. (*This same scene minus the horse played out many times on the remote Islands where I was in the Peace Corps. The men wore their customary loin cloths and the topless women wore colorful wrap around skirts. Tobacco would be rolled in a dried banana leaf or, if anyone had a cigarette, it would be shared and when it was nearly burned down it would be rolled in a dried leaf so you could smoke the entire cigarette. It would be offered to everyone sitting around the fire. In the evening I shared the fermented falluba or ari, the coconut palm wine gathered from cutting the stem flower at the top of the tree and collecting the dripping sap into a coconut cup and harvested in the morning and evening. And while relaxing at night enjoying a cup or two, I heard some amazing stories of the islands' heroes.)*

It was obvious the wild looking yellow painted Native American admired the beautiful young white woman with the red streaked auburn hair. He spoke some English and gestured to the west that he had come from the Shining Mountains to hunt buffalo with other hunters from his tribe. After sharing Dan's pipe, the big man offered to return with his hunting party in the evening with fresh buffalo. "You cook biscuits!" He remounted and rode off to a collective sigh of relief from the nervous pioneers. But as promised he did return with fresh buffalo meat.

In the evenings around the campfires the Irish immigrants and the Utes shared buffalo and Irish biscuits, smoking Dan's tobacco, and recounting stories of the Shining Mountains and Ireland. (*I was privileged to share in the same way with my island hosts in the outer islands of the South Pacific.*) It must have taken many such exchanges for the chief to understand the strange sounding Irish accent spoken by these young white people. While I am sure there were many exciting stories told by Chief Colorow to these young Irish immigrants, the family tradition is that he saved Ellen's beautiful auburn hair from hanging in a Cheyenne Dog Soldier's lodge. Such an easy target wouldn't have made it to Denver without his protection.

He later offered Dan "**16 ponies for Ellen** because he liked the red colors in her hair and her biscuits and syrup." Obviously, I wouldn't be here to write this family story if Dan had taken him up on the trade! I can only imagine there might have been some serious thought to taking the offer from such a big and intimidating man; I doubt Ellen thought this trade was a great idea and prevailed in pushing the no vote.

In September of 2004 my two sons Brian and John and myself plus two of my cousins were digging a grave next to my father's in the Buckley Family plot in the Silver Plume Cemetery for my mother who had just died. Stories of Grandma Hickey were helping to pass the time as we struggled to break through the rocky soil to provide a final resting place for her. It was quite an unusual experience for my two boys to be doing this. *Gravedigger* was not a job experience they had on their resume but the stories fascinated them and definitely made the task easier. John, who has done some writing, put pen to paper, and wrote the following anecdotal account of the day which was published in Vail, Colorado's local paper.

The Vail Trail
"DIGGING UP THE PAST"
Buckley funeral brings memories of one of Colorado's oldest families
By **John Buckley**

Editor's note*:* A few weeks ago, the Vail Trail learned of the death of Donna Buckley, an early pioneer in this part of Colorado. When we looked into the story behind the obituary, we learned that Donna and her family have deep roots in Colorado (and an interesting family history). We asked Donna's grandson and lifelong Vail local John Buckley to tell us about his storied family- and what it was like to take part in one of their oldest traditions. **VT:**

"Deep in the woods, on a hill above the historic train tracks in Silver Plume, sits a cemetery. On a quiet hillside within this cemetery, closed in by cement walls and up a flight of cement stairs, sits the Buckley family plot. It is beautiful, remote and simply impossible to access with heavy digging equipment. For generations the Buckleys have been put to rest in this spot next to their kin the Haskins' and the Collins'. And for generations, surviving family members from both sides of the lineage have been digging the graves.

And so it came to pass on warm autumn day in September, I joined my father Bob, Brother Brian, and father's cousins Ed and Gerry Haskins in digging a grave for my departed grandmother, Donna Buckley, right next to my grandfather Robert Buckley Sr.

There are certain unwritten rules involved in digging a grave, the first being that 'what's said while digging the grave, remains in that grave.' I'm breaking it right now, I suppose, but only with the blessing of the family.

Despite what people may think, digging a grave is not a solemn occasion. There's plenty of time for tears during the funeral. Mainly digging a grave is about old men getting a job done, telling jokes and spinning tales from memories past. The one-liners were of old Irish wit and born out of generations of making the best out of difficult situations.

Standing 5'9" and waist deep in the hole, for example, my brother Brian asked how we'll know when we're six feet deep, to which cousin Ed replied dryly, "When you can't see anymore, stop digging."

There are also certain things one learns about himself, his family and his history while digging the grave of a loved one that frankly does not come to pass under ordinary circumstances. Back in the 60's and 70's dad and Gerry were on Vail's ski patrol, and on this day I was treated to an earful of stories about men in their 20's, living in Vail in its early heyday. Stories, for example, like the one involving some trouble nearly caused when strippers were brought in to entertain a delighted group of ski patrolman at my father's bachelor party. And of my dad recalling the play-by-play given over the radio, as Gerry was swept away in one of the largest avalanches ever witnessed by the patrol on Vail Mountain down present-day Genghis Kahn.

The talk didn't stop at the early history of Vail and old triumphs and travails of the ski patrol. I also heard about the history of my family when mining, not skiing, was the big industry in the Rockies. All of us digging the grave that day are linked into the same family history through my grandfather's grandmother, Grandma Hickey. She had three husbands, all who died young- and gave birth to two daughters(my great-grandmother Alice Buckley and Mary Collins, Gerry and Ed's grandmother).

I have long been aware that my family has been in Colorado for quite some time. My great-grandmother Alice, or Ma Buckley, was the first registered white child born in the Colorado Territory. But it wasn't until my grandmother passed away and the stories started flowing that I really began to get a sense of who my relatives really were.

Born in Belfast, Ireland, Grandma Hickey came out to Colorado on a wagon train just about the time that the Civil War was breaking out in the East. Newly married Ellen Short had just "hitched her wagon" to Daniel Griffin. They travelled through the new territories and eventually after many hard days arrived in a new bustling town on the side of the Platte River, called Denver. Along the way, it is told that a Ute Indian chief became mesmerized by her red hair and beauty, and offered to trade 16 ponies for her. The trade never took place, but the story has it that the Ute band escorted her wagon train all the way to Denver for protection. Ed couldn't resist commenting: "I wish somebody would offer me that deal for my Alice!" When Ellen and Daniel arrived in Denver the echo coming out of the foothills and lower mountain valleys was the resounding call for gold. The rush was on, and everything seemed to be happening around the areas of Nevadaville, Central City, and Black Hawk. Dan and Ellen soon found themselves caught up in the excitement, living in Nevadaville and proud parents of a daughter named Alice.

One day while Alice was a small child, Dan heard that one of his good friends was being harassed and assaulted by a provost marshal conscripting for the Union Army. Daniel, in coming to the aid of his friend, somehow became embroiled in the scuffling and pushing. A shot rang out and the young family man lay mortally wounded. Daniel was buried next to the Catholic Church in Central City. This church later burned down and was rebuilt next door and over the cemetery. History now shows that Daniel Griffin is still buried underneath that Catholic Church. Ellen went on to marry two more times and lived out the rest of her life in Colorado. She eventually died in Silver Plume while living with her second daughter Mary, and across the street from her first daughter, Alice.

Ellen was quite a character, noted for her corncob pipe, occasional taste for hard liquor and the many adventures of her plains crossing. Her daughter

Alice had met and married Jerimiah Buckley and was busy bringing up her own family that would eventually total 13 children, my grandfather being number eleven. She was widowed at a very young age as well, leaving her to raise her children on her own. Facing the future with courage, she formed a family corporation and employed her children in a variety of occupations including trucking, fuel, garage and repair, grocery and butchering. The Buckley Bros. sign still stands on the side of I-70 in Silver Plume in between Vail and Denver.

Though it was with sadness that we buried my grandmother, I was honored to have the opportunity to join in a family tradition of carving her final resting place with the Buckleys', Haskins', Collins', and with Grandma Hickey. The day was tough, dirty, and exhausting, but as Gerry aptly put it, "I wouldn't have it any other way." Neither would I. VT

Photos are by John Buckley

Bob, Brian, and John Buckley set headstone for R. Gary Buckley. John wrote the article above for the Vail Trail when burying his grandmother.

Accompanying the buffalo were huge flies which refused to fly away, camping on your arms and neck or any other exposed skin until they got their fill of your blood. Around the end of June the weary travelers saw what seemed to be faraway low laying clouds on the horizon. Slowly the faraway clouds revealed themselves to be snowcapped mountain tops. Thrilled would not adequately express the joy in their hearts. Irish biscuits all around! The Mountains kept getting closer and taller.

What a mind blowing experience it was for those who experience for the first time the view of the Rocky Mountains from the prairie below. The early dawn sun sparkled on the snowcapped mountain peaks inspiring the souls of the men and women who knew how lucky they were to witness the joy of seeing for the first time the *Colorado Rocky Mountains.* It's no wonder that the Utes called these mountains the Shining Mountains. The four covered wagons and the excited young Griffins couldn't move fast enough to their new future so close in sight, and a hot steaming bath! The grasshopper sparrows' trill was sung just for them, Dan and Ellen were happy in this memorable moment of their journey from Ireland and across the prairie. The two newlyweds' hopes and dreams and a journey's end are close, and they were like small children enjoying this special day. Gratitude to God was in their hearts. "Thank you and goodbye Chief Colorow for guiding us on our journey."

Dan and Ellen stayed in the new settlement along the South Platte and the Cherry Creek long enough for Dan to build a small stone house putting some most needed gold in his pocket. The stone house was located where the iconic Denver Dry Goods Store was built some few years later. Its address today is between 15th and 16th and California St. in the heart of today's downtown Denver. I remember as a young boy going to the top of the Denver Dry Goods with my cousin Raymond Buckley and sailing square post card size advertisements off the roof down to California Street six stories below. That was very memorable to me since we were quickly apprehended and escorted downstairs where Raymond's mother was shopping. The Historic Denver Dry Goods Store was built in 1877 and was advertised in 1916 as the largest dry goods store west of Chicago. It was converted to apartments in 1994. But I remember it for the day Raymond and I were sailing pamphlets off its roof.

Dan and his young wife Ellen (Grandma Hickey), still living out of their covered wagon and tent, moved up into the mountains and built a small stone and log home in the small town called Nevada City (later Nevadaville), just above Central City and Black Hawk. Happy news soon followed when Ellen gave birth on November 8th, 1862 to their daughter Alice Griffin, named after Ellen's mother. Baby Alice was the first registered birth in Gilpin County, Colorado Territory. Dan and his construction partner and fellow Irishman from the wagon train started a building career in the booming gold camp. There was more ways than digging for gold to strike it rich in Central City, but I am sure in their spare time the gold fever had them gold panning in the surrounding creeks.

The Civil War Military Draft Act was enacted March 3, 1863 and enforcement of the act sparked draft riots among Irish Immigrants in New York City, Boston, and Philadelphia where draftees who didn't have the $300 commutation fee were being dragged off the streets and out of the saloons and immediately impressed into the Union Army. Dan heard that his partner was being severely beaten by a Colorado Provost Marshall down on the main street of Central City. The official was dragging the severely beaten and bleeding young man into custody to shanghai him into the Union Army and Dan came to his partner's rescue and **was shot and killed** by the Provost Marshall.

> "*Oh Danny Boy*, the pipes, the pipes are calling,
> From glen to glen, and down the mountain side.
> The summer's gone and all the roses falling
> Tis you, tis you must go and I must bide."

"Danny Boy" Griffin was buried next to the Catholic Church, then a wooden structure, back in May of 1863. In 1874 most of Central City burned to the ground, including St. Mary of the Assumption. The church and the town were eventually rebuilt, this time of brick and stone. A portion of the new church was built over the cemetery and consequently over my great-grandfather.

In 1967 my parents bought a historical house in Central City that had originally been owned by a Colorado Territorial Judge named Judge James B. Belford. This house had replaced Judge Belford's original wooden home which also been burned down in the fire of 1874 and later rebuilt, becoming the first residential home to be constructed of brick. When my mom and dad were living in the home a century later, some very inexplicable and unexplainable strange and spooky things occurred in the house leading them to conclude that the home was inhabited by a friendly, if not a pesky, ghost.

Squeaking doors opening and closing, sounds of footsteps walking across the wooden floors, creaking stairs to bedrooms on the second floor would startle and frighten them, especially in the middle of the night. One time my dad was using a reading light when it would go off and on while none of the other lights were affected, and my dad got tired of the game and said "dammit ghost leave the light on until I'm finished and you can play with it all you want." It came on and stayed on!

My mother had lost her partial dental plate on a vacation in Arizona and one morning it just happened to magically be smiling at her on her dresser. Books would be moved around from place to place in the house as money would disappear and magically appear in coffee cups, socks in a drawer, and sugar bowl. Many like incidences convinced them that they weren't alone. Right! Skeptically I would nod and yawn when I returned to Central City after working two years overseas in the Peace Corps.

My folks also purchased another historical home in Central City, The McFarland House, built by the owner of the Historic Opera House. My mom was an antique home collector as well as a collector of the original estate of the Belford family. She moved her furniture over to the McFarland House and decorated the Belford House with the recently acquired antique furnishings from Judge Belford's original estate which Judge Belford's grandson thought was "just old junk gathering dust." Amazingly after finding old photographs of the interior of the house in the collection, she had placed the rugs, wall hangings, furniture, and a beautiful painting of a daughter in a long flowing dress on the living room parlor wall- all in the same locations as in the old photographs. The home was like walking through a Victorian era museum.

Practically broke after 2 years in the Peace Corp, I talked my folks into letting me run tours through the historic house when I first got home. We placed plastic runners down to protect the hardwood floors and oriental rugs. Though I was skeptical of my parents thinking the house was haunted, I would play that up in my tour. Until one day I had a woman looking past me in the red papered dining room and not paying attention to my rehearsed spiel. I thought she might be looking at the glass shades on the ceiling chandelier which had been etched with the State of Colorado official seal.

No! She wasn't looking up at the chandelier.

She asked me, "What was stirring the glass serving ladle in the cut glass punch bowl sitting atop of the tall dark brown dining room hutch?"

"What!" I looked behind me up to the punch bowl and, sure enough, the glass ladle was stirring round and round in the punchbowl. I couldn't believe my eyes!

The Belford House must be haunted! But who is stirring the ladle in the punch bowl? Maybe the young beautiful girl in the living room painting or maybe it's the Red Headed Rooster, Judge Belford, stirring the ladle in order to scare away the tourists!

Or maybe it was the good spirit of Dan Griffin welcoming his great-grandson safely back from his 2 years in the Peace Corps in Micronesia where superstition, ghosts, and curses were frightful and very powerful realities of life, especially as witnessed later by me and my family when we lived on Punlap Island.

Colorado Territorial Judge James B. Belford's living room in Central City, Colorado

CHAPTER 3
Shafted

In Ireland Ellen witnessed violence, survived famine, racial and religious bigotry. She emigrated from Ireland to the United States and travelled by wagon train with her new husband, Dan Griffin, to Colorado walking most of the way from St. Joseph to her Colorado mountain home. Two years later she buried Dan who was shot and killed by a Colorado provost marshal raising troops for the Civil War. Alone and grieving over the loss of Dan, she depended totally on her unshakeable faith and trust that God would provide for her and her five month old baby- Alice.

She not only survived the rest of 1863 but met a handsome young Irish immigrant miner, Eugene (Owen) Feenan. The two married in Central City's St. Mary of the Assumption Catholic Church on September 22, 1864. Buried in the adjacent cemetery, Dan Griffin would have approved knowing Ellen and baby Alice were entirely alone in a strange and wild country with no substantial means for procuring food and protection. God provided a husband for Ellen and a father for baby Alice and additional treasured family members.

The Western Frontier that Ellen, Owen and their family were living in was a place where unrest, violence, disease, and broken promises were common for the immigrant pioneers in Central City and also for the Native Americans under the same blue skies of the Colorado Territory.

A cold wind was blowing in Colorado and was about to change forever the life of Native Americans in ways never imagined. Chiefs Black Kettle and White Antelope of the Southern Cheyenne Tribe, who signed the *Fort Wise Treaty of 1861*, will once again find that written treaty promises did not match the actions of the whites.

In September of 1864, Chief Black Kettle met with Major Edward Wynkoop, the commanding officer of Fort Lyon, and Captain Silas Soule and turned over white hostages that were captured by Cheyenne Dog Soldiers. This meeting was held at Black Kettle's camp and was later called the *Smokey Hill Council*; Major Wynkoop, wanting to secure the hostages as soon as possible, didn't bother with going through the lengthy process of leaving his remote fort on the eastern plains of Colorado to travel to the Kansas military headquarters and gain permission to meet with Black Kettle. He seized the opportunity to save the hostages! At this meeting Black Kettle wanted to discuss a peace treaty which would protect his band of Southern Cheyenne from getting caught up in the murderous violence between the Cheyenne Dog Soldiers and the American Army. *(Peace Chiefs of the Cheyennes,* By Stan Hoig)

Major Wynkoop who was known as a skilled negotiator prevailed upon Territorial Governor John Evans to meet with the peace seeking Cheyenne. The Governor was reluctant to meet with them as he had his own military plans already in motion and every Indian killed was met with public approval and enthusiastic support and meeting with the Cheyenne chiefs would only be met with public scorn. But the articulate and passionate Major Wynkoop argued that the Governor should at least meet with the chiefs and attempt to work out a peaceful solution to the existing war being waged east of Denver. Major Edward Wynkoop did his part and could only hope that the Territorial Governor was just as skilled a negotiator as he was a successful doctor and businessman.

At Camp Weld, near Denver on September 28, 1864 Cheyenne Chiefs Black Kettle, White Antelope, Bull Bear, and Arapaho Chiefs Heap of Buffalo, and Neva assembled for peace talks with the Territorial Governor Evans and Colonel Chivington. John Evans was a railroad tycoon from

Illinois who was **appointed** to his position in the Colorado Territory by President Lincoln in 1862, and Colonel John Chivington was the commander of the First Regiment of Colorado Volunteers.

Both Governor Evans and Colonel Chivington had political and financial ambitions when the Colorado Territory would soon become a state. Aside from his national political ambition, Governor Evans was most interested in the creation of a transcontinental rail hub in Denver; and Colonel Chivington wanted to represent Colorado in the U.S. Congress when it entered the Union. Colonel Chivington was a Methodist pastor in Ohio, Illinois, Kansas, and Nebraska and in May of 1860 moved his family to the Colorado Territory where he began missionary work in the South Park mining camps. He joined the Colorado Volunteers to fight in the Civil War and became a celebrated Colorado war hero at the Battle of Glorieta Pass in New Mexico. Like most all white people living in the Colorado Territory, these men were newcomers to the Colorado region. Also present at these talks was **Captain Silas Soule**, assigned the command of Company D, 1st Colorado Cavalry. Captain Soule was with Major Wynkoop at the Smokey Hill Council and an officer in the Colorado Cavalry during the Civil War and had also fought at Glorieta Pass with both Colonel Chivington and Major Wynkoop. Captain Soule, before moving to Colorado during the gold rush, was an ardent anti-slavery abolitionist in the Kansas Territory before the Civil War.

The Cheyenne and the Arapaho tribes were relative newcomers to the area arriving in the early 1700's and migrating from the Dakotas. Although the Utes living in the Shining Mountains can trace their ancestors in Colorado back 13,000 years to the Folsom archeological site found in Larimer County, Colorado. These Cheyenne and Arapaho **Native American** chiefs, recognizing the futility of war with the new white immigrants to Colorado and wanting to stop the senseless killing and salvage what they could for their children and grandchildren met in good faith with Governor Evans and Colonel Chivington. Chief Bull Bear, leader of the Cheyenne Dog Soldiers and brother of Lean Bear who had been gunned down earlier by the First Colorado Regiment, intended to end the fight with the whites and even die like his brother- if it meant peace.

This was an opportunity for Governor Evans and Colonel Chivington to end the hostilities with the Cheyenne Dog Soldiers and to put an end to the merry- go- round of bloody violence! Instead both whites were hard of listening and didn't take Bull Bear up on his offer, sadly choosing another pathway. (*The Peace Chiefs of the Cheyennes,* by Stan Hoig p. 86) Starting in April of 1864 the First Regiment of Colorado Volunteers commanded by Colonel Chivington had started a campaign of retribution against the plains Indians for attacks on wagon trains and new immigrant farmers. Just like all the other acts of violence between men, revenge and retribution are a **vicious cycle** which each act of killing begins another horrible cycle of revenge. On May 16, 1864 a contingent of the First Colorado Regiment under Lieutenant George Eayre encountered a Cheyenne buffalo hunting camp at Big Bushes near the Smokey Hill River. Chiefs Lean Bear and Star signaled the soldiers their peaceful intentions, and were shot down and killed by the Lieutenant's troops.

The incidents of violence of the First Regiment were in response to the incidences of violence against the new homesteaders and wagon trains headed into Colorado. Another round of retribution was set off spiraling out of control with both sides committing vicious atrocities. Something needed to be worked out soon. The Cheyenne Dog soldiers were reeking vengeance with despicable atrocities committed against innocent whites like the attack just outside of Denver on rancher Nathan Hungate's family whose desecrated bodies were displayed in Denver which was becoming isolated and unable to receive provisions and the fear stricken citizens were hungry and thirsting for blood. "*Who killed who,*" a definition of history described by Franciscan Father Richard Rohr, inspired the many marble memorials to long fallen warriors.

At the *Camp Weld Council* in September of 1864, Black Kettle and the other peace seeking Cheyenne chiefs and their bands thinking they were directed by Governor Evans to put themselves under army protection; and they would be regarded as friendly and to report to Fort Lyon or be considered hostiles. Chiefs Black Kettle and White Antelope and the other chiefs set out with a group of some eight hundred Southern Cheyenne, without the Dog Soldiers, and reported to Fort Lyon to surrender their band, along with some Arapaho under Chief Niwot. They were ordered by the army to camp on the nearby Big Sandy Creek and assured that by doing so would be considered friendly and not hostile by the army.

Chief Black Kettle sent most of his remaining young men out to hunt leaving only 60 men in the village who were either too old or too young to hunt. Chief Black Kettle was told to fly his American flag over his tipi and his people would be safe from any passing U.S. soldiers. Black Kettle had visited Washington with other Cheyenne chiefs and met personally with President Lincoln. He knew from this trip that the Cheyenne didn't stand a chance opposing such a formidable foe with so many people and machines. Black Kettle was a peacemaker! *(The Peace Chiefs of the Cheyennes,* By Stan Hoig)

After completing his peacekeeping duties, Major Wynkoop was relieved of his duties at Fort Lyon by a rankled General Samuel Curtis at the Kansas District Army Headquarters. Major Scott Anthony, an ally of both Governor Evans and Colonel Chivington, took command of Fort Lyon which was Anthony's command before Wynkoop. General Curtis had relieved Major Wynkook at Fort Lyon after he had heard a false rumor that Major Wynkoop was feeding the Cheyenne at Fort Lyon. Major Wynkoop travelled to Kansas to meet with General Curtis with the hope of persuading him to accept the Camp Weld Agreement and argue the false nature of the accusation. Therefore the young Major wasn't at Fort Lyon to help Captain Soule dissuade Colonel Chivington and Major Anthony from attacking the village that Major Anthony personally placed on Big Sandy Creek.

November 28, 1864 the Fighting Pastor was eager to teach the Cheyenne a catechism lesson, and it wasn't the Sermon on the Mount's, "Blessed are the Peacemakers!" About eight hundred troops made up of mostly the 100- day- short term recruits of the Colorado Militia, which Governor Evans authorized to be recruited from Denver and the nearby mining towns, along with regulars from Fort Lyon with four howitzer cannons slowly moved out from the fort. It had been snowing heavily and two feet of snow impeded their progress toward the trusting Cheyenne and Arapaho encampment 40 miles away on the Big Sandy Creek. After camping for the night, the Colorado militia drank heavily anticipating the upcoming fight. In the predawn of **November 29, 1864,** Col. Chivington and his 100- day recruits and Major Anthony's Fort Lyon troopers ordered the attack on the village full of old men, women, and children. But Captain Soule ordered his Company D, Colorado Cavalry, not to fire on the betrayed, defenseless village. Colonel Chivington was quoted by some as saying, "I have come to kill Indians, and believe it is right and honorable to use any means under God's heaven to kill Indians. Kill and scalp all, big and little, nits make lice." The *Denver Ubermensch* opted for the exterminating of the "lice and nits" with "**White Death**"!

The Battle of Sand Creek, also known as *The Sand Creek Massacre,* killed 14 troopers wounding 40; and killing approximately 150-200 Cheyenne and Arapaho, mostly unarmed women and children and elderly. Unknown is the number of wounded Cheyenne and Arapahoe who escaped or were carried away by the survivors. Chief White Antelope's death song could be heard as he was being killed in the nearby creek bed. Besides scalping him the soldiers cut off his nose, ears, and testicles. Before Colonel Chivington and his men left the village the second day, they plundered the tipis, scalped many of the dead women, children, and infants cutting off body parts, including male and female genitalia which they proudly displayed as trophies when returning to Denver. "I saw the bodies of those lying there cut all to pieces, worse mutilated than any I ever saw before; the women cut all to pieces with knives, scalped; their brains knocked out; children two or three months old; all ages lying there, from sucking infants up to warriors. By whom were they mutilated? By United States troops," *(John S. Smith, Congressional Testimony, 1865).*

"I refused to fire, and swore that none but a coward would, for by this time hundreds of women and children were coming towards us, and getting on their knees for mercy. I tell you Ned it was hard to see little children on their knees, having their brains beat out by men professing to be civilized," (*Captain Silas Soule, letter to Major Edward W. Wynkoop, 14 December 1864*). Captain Soule, despite death threats from some of the Colorado militia who participated at the Sand Creek Massacre testified to the *Court of Inquiry of the Joint Committee on the Conduct of the War.*

The newly married Silas Soule was assassinated five weeks later as he was walking with his wife down 15th street in Denver, probably passed by the stone home Dan Griffin built just two years earlier. In 2012, a memorial plaque was placed on a building at the northwest corner of 15th and Arapaho Streets in downtown Denver.

Captain Silas Soule (July 26, 1838-April 23, 1865) was buried with full military honors in Denver's Riverside Cemetery. Cheyenne still honor his memory by placing small rocks on his grave. Among the chiefs killed at Sand Creek were White Antelope, One Eye, Yellow Wolf, Big Man, Bear Man, War Bonnet, Spotted Crow, and Bear Robe. These were the traditional council chiefs, mature men who sought a peaceful future for their people (*The Peace Chiefs of The Cheyennes,* By Stan Hoig).

Some modern day historians dispute the three governmental hearings and their witnesses following the Sand Creek Massacre saying that they had conflicts of interest. Just like some, including a Catholic priest on Punlap Island, say the Jewish Holocaust of World War Two, was a hoax! But the modern day Cheyenne and Arapaho descendants know their side of truth which has been passed down to them through the oral stories of their ancestors who escaped alive.

And Philip Bialowitz shared his story in Vail when he escaped from the Sobibor Nazi death-camp in Poland. The survivors of the Jewish Genocide, called a Holocaust because there were so many victims(6 million) knew the truth and their stories will be passed down by their descendants just like the palu (navigators of The Western Islands of Micronesia) passed their navigational information orally down a thousand years through each generation to the next.

Whether Sand Creek was called a Massacre or a Battle, I will leave to the historians to fight that battle. But there is no argument that ultimately the tragedy occurred because of the broken written promises to Indians in treaties, overwhelming white migration called *Manifest Destiny,* and mismanagement by government officials in the Colorado Territory who resorted to bloody violence instead of honest negotiations and compensation to solve the Indian troubles.

Chief Black Kettle survived the Sand Creek Massacre, even when he returned to rescue one of his wives who had been shot nine times! Stubbornly he continued to seek peace, while Bull Bear and Roman Nose and the Cheyenne Dog soldiers sought their cruel revenge on settlers and wagon trains throughout the Platte River Valley. Many whites were tortured and killed including women and children and the bulk of the warring Indians moved north into the Powder River Country of Chief Sitting Bull and the Sioux. In October of 1865 Black Kettle accepted the Little Arkansas Treaty for land in southwestern Kansas. Once again Native American treaty land was desired by the whites, Black Kettle agreed in the Medicine Lodge Treaty of 1867 to move his surviving people to the Indian Territory of Oklahoma and camp on the Washita River. The American government didn't honor the terms of the agreement and deliver the promised food supplies to the camp. Many young children were starving, like in the *Irish Famine,* and some fathers took matters into their own hands and began raiding local farms and ranches. General Philip Sheridan, famous for saying "The only good Indian is a dead Indian," ordered Gen. George Armstrong Custer and the Seventh Cavalry to undertake a campaign against the Indians winter camps.

On November 27, 1868, nearly four years to the day of the Sand Creek Massacre, United States troopers charged another Cheyenne village clearly on the mandated Indian Territorial Reservation. The display of a white flag flying above Chief Black Kettle's lodge proved useless once again. Both Black Kettle and his wife, Woman to be Hereafter, were riddled with bullets shot in the back and scalped... Gen. Sheridan could say Chief Black Kettle was a, "Good Indian!" Black Kettle rests in peace but surely the "Good Indian" will not suffer any more from the **White Death** and will not be forgotten!

Colonel Chivington was not forgotten by *The Congressional Committee* which, "Can hardly find fitting terms to describe his conduct. Wearing the uniform of the United States, which should be the emblem of justice and humanity; holding the important position of commander of a military district, and therefore having the honor of the government to that extent in his keeping, he deliberately planned and executed a foul and dastardly massacre which would have disgraced the verist savage among those who were the victims of his cruelty. Having full knowledge of their friendly character, having himself been instrumental to some extent in placing them in their position of fancied security, he took advantage of their inapprehension and defenseless condition to gratify the worst passions that ever cursed the heart of man. Whatever influence this may have had upon Colonel Chivington, the truth is that he surprised and murdered in cold blood, the unsuspecting men, women, and children on Sand Creek, who had every reason to believe they were under the protection of the United States authorities, and returned to Denver and boasted of the brave deed he and the men under his command had performed. In conclusion, your committee are of the opinion that for the purpose of vindicating the cause of justice and upholding the honor of the nation, prompt and energetic measures should be at once taken to remove from office those who have disgraced the government by whom they are employed, and to punish, as their crimes deserve, those who have been guilty of these brutal and cowardly acts," *(Report of the Joint Special Committee on the Conduct of the War. United States Senate 1868, Massacre of the Cheyenne).*

Dr. John Evans, the renowned physician, missed an, "Ah, Ha!" medical like breakthrough moment to **save lives** after Camp Weld. Instead of writing a prescription for health and life, he fell back on the ancient poisonous potions of greed, war, racism, violence, and death. The decision to pursue the Indians that surrendered at Fort Lyon, instead of the Dog Soldiers, spoke volumes as to his lack of knowledge, empathy, wisdom, and political skill as a Territorial Governor. John Evans was dumped from his federal appointment as Governor of the Colorado Territory. Colorado's statehood was delayed for 12 years as a direct result of the Sand Creek

Massacre and a whirlwind of violence and death on the eastern plains of Colorado was suffered by the white settlers and wagon trains. John Evans lost a Colorado *golden* opportunity for peace but will not be forgotten! The Colorado Legislature in 1895 honored John Evans, the disgraced 2nd Territorial Governor of Colorado, by renaming Mt. Rosalie the 14,265' peak, *"Mt. Evans"* which dominates the western skyline of Denver and can be seen on a clear day 100 miles away on the prairie. How many people when looking on Mt. Evans today will see only a beautiful tall mountain which the Cheyenne and Arapaho Native Americans see through their tears?

John Evans had been one of Illinois most accomplished men before coming to Colorado where in Chicago he was one of the founders of Mercy Hospital, edited the Medical and Surgical Journal, a professor at Rush Medical College, and founded the Illinois Medical Society. Doctor Evans was a pioneer in cholera research and was responsible in developing quarantine laws for the prevention of the scourge. John Evans was also a founder of Northwestern University where he was the Chairman of the Board of Trustees. Making a fortune in his investments in the Chicago and Fort Wayne Railroad and the Chicago and Evanston Railroad he helped to found the Illinois Republican Party and ran for Congress and became a backer and a friend of Abraham Lincoln. He turned down an offer from President Lincoln in 1861 for the governorship of the Washington Territory. In our system of government sometimes what counts is not what you know, but who you know!" What did Evans know about Colorado? He was like most the other whites who had just recently arrived in Colorado. What did he know about fighting a war? He was a doctor and a successful business man. What did he really know about the different tribes of Indians, or more importantly what did he know about the Cheyenne Dog Soldiers and the opportunity he had blown to make peace with Bull Bear instead of lecturing him like a medical professor? If he really knew anything about the most feared and ruthless warriors on the plains, and easily the best horsemen, he sure as heck wouldn't send a former Methodist Pastor and a 100-day, undisciplined, untrained, inexperienced, rabble army to chase them down some of the best warriors in Colorado, which of course they couldn't. But he knew where the peaceful Indians would be camped and a good business opportunity when he saw one and making another railroad fortune, this time in Colorado. At this time a Civil War was being fought over the premise that Black Slaves were not equal human beings, just chattel to be done with as the slaveholder pleased, and Native Americans were exterminated as, "Nits and Lice" in an American Holocaust.

Who was Governor Evans kidding? The only Cheyenne and Arapahoe this army could catch were those peace seeking Indians that signed the Treaty of Fort Wise (1861) and who had just attended the Council at Fort Weld and reported to Fort Lyon showing Governor Evans that they were not hostiles. The Sand Creek Massacre was carried out by his 100-day Colorado Volunteers, raised to kill Indians, including women, children, and the elderly and break the siege of Denver brought on by the cycle of violence, and broken promises. "Blessed are the **peacemakers** for they shall be called the Children of God (Matthew 5:9)." *The Peace Chiefs of the Cheyennes* could be called "**Children of God.**" What would Governor Evans and Colonel Chivington be called?

Mountain man and soldier, Kit Carson said at the time, **"Jis to think of that dog Chivington and his dirty hounds, up thar at Sand Creek. His men shot down squaws, and blew the brains out of little innocent children. You call sich soldiers Christians, do ye? And Indians savages? What der yer 'spose our Heavenly Father, who made both them and us, thinks of these things? I tell you what; I don't like a hostile red skin any more than you do. And when they are hostile, I've fought 'em, hard as any man. But I never yet drew a bead on a squaw or papoose, and I despise the man who would. I've seen as much of 'em as any man livin,'and I can't help but pity'em, right or wrong. They once owned all this country yes, Plains and Mountains, buffalo and everything. But now they own next door to nuthin, and will soon be gone."** (*Blood and Thunder, An Epic of the American West*, By Hampton Sides)

After his son, Thomas, drowned in 1865, John Chivington returned to Nebraska to take care of his son's estate and married his son's widow, his daughter-in-law, Sarah. She divorced him in 1871 for non-support after his freight business failed and he skipped town without repaying money he borrowed from her shafted relatives. He returned to Denver where he worked as a deputy sheriff and coroner until his death from cancer in 1894.

The Battle of the Little Big Horn in Montana, or better known as *Custer's Last Stand*, June 25th and 26th of 1876 - the same year as Colorado Statehood - five of the 7th Cavalry's companies were annihilated by Lakota(Sioux), Northern Cheyenne, and Arapaho Native Americans. General Armstrong Custer led his last surprise charge of an Indian village and was killed as were two of his brothers, a nephew, and a brother-in-law. The 7th Cavalry causality count, including scouts, was 268 dead. After the battle, two Southern Cheyenne women recognized the body of General Custer. Related to Custer's Cheyenne mistress, they didn't mutilate his face out of respect for their Cheyenne relative, but they did take an awl and pierce both of his eardrums so that he might hear better in the afterlife. As a final display of their hatred for the man, they **shoved an arrow up his penis!** (*The Last Stand,* By Nathaniel Philbrick)

Working for the Arapaho National Forest as a Trail Construction crew boss, Hank Aldefer worked alongside me as the Trail Maintenance crew boss. In the summer of 1967, our combined crews rebuilt the Mount Evans Trail from the Rest House Cabin up to the top of the 14,264 foot Colorado peak. During a lunch break, we picked a rocky precipice overlooking the Bear Tracks Lakes about 1000 feet below our perch to rest and enjoy the view and our lunch. While the crew was sitting and eating lunch, I stretched my arms out and one of my hands came upon a flat oval stone. Picking it up for a casual look, I was surprised to see it was an Indian metate used to grind corn and berries. This artifact may have belonged to an elk or deer hunter resting and having lunch on the same meadow and enjoying the high mountain view above Bear Tracks Lakes. Just possibly this artifact belonged to a Sand Creek victim!

Hank's cherished friend and neighboring rancher, Tom Hayden, the great- great grandson of Territorial Governor John Evans, worked and lived on the Evans Ranch with his family in the evening shadow of Mount Evans. *KGNU NEWS* reported, "Tom Hayden sat on a panel with his daughter, Laurel Hayden, and his sister, Anne Hayden, along with Cheyenne and Arapaho descendants of the Sand Creek Massacre- Henry Little Bird Sr. and Gail Ridgely Two Eagles. Tom said, 'This knowledge of the Sand Creek Massacre was something I didn't think I could ever be at peace with knowing my great-great grandfather was so involved. He set the stage. He choreographed it. He did everything he could but pull the trigger, and he might have well done that, which is why I am so grateful for *The John Evans DU Report*. It's nasty and it hurts. And It's time for the Cheyenne and Arapaho to tell us what it is that we can do 150 years later for them. An apology is not enough without some actions. Some of the Native American Community have suggested that a renaming of Mount Evans and Evans Avenue in Denver would be a beginning point of the healing process.' Tom Hayden said that his family would approve of the renaming of the two areas of namesake to the former governor."

Tom Hayden (1956-2016) and his Evans Family, along with Henry Little Bird Sr. and Gail Ridgely Two Eagles, possible blood brothers of the original owners of the lost grinding stone and Evans Ranch, reached historically across generations of hatred, anger, and sorrow for a beginning point of the healing process of the Sand Creek Massacre. A brave generational agreement was reached to rename Mount Evans and Evans Avenue to move positively into a shared American future.

The Arapaho and Cheyenne Tribes should have the honor of renaming Mount Evans and Evans Avenue. But I would suggest that Mount Black Kettle or Mount White Antelope or Silas Soule Avenue would make us all proud honoring these three brave American heroes.

Located at 15th and Arapahoe Street in downtown Denver, Colorado

CHAPTER 4
Light in a wind

The range of snowcapped mountains in high Colorado where Ellen, Owen, and baby Alice lived were drained by streams and rivers cascading into winding steep rock canyons whose roads were not much more than jack mule trails. The early mining roads in the canyons were subject to frequent rock slides and flash floods and wooden bridges that would be washed out or just collapse from heavy ore loads. In the first years of prospecting most of the miners lived at the base of the canyons. Owen was working a mine in Central City, but was always on the lookout, as were all prospectors, for another gold strike. In 1869, on one of his prospecting trips to Republican Mountain, above where the town of Silver Plume now sits, he discovered a promising outcrop of lead and silver. This could be fantastic! He was very excited when he returned to his work at the mine in Central City. Unfortunately, you just never know when God will have a Plan B to your Plan A.

From out of nowhere, a fully loaded ore bucket fell straight down the mineshaft and hit him full force when the heavy bucket detached from the wench cable. As these ore buckets weighed hundreds of pounds fully loaded, he was seriously injured. In the sure belief he was dying, and thinking of his family, he disclosed to Thomas McCunnife, a fellow mine worker and friend, what he had found on Republican Mountain. He extracted a verbal promise from Thomas that he would take care of Owen's wife and daughter, if the find turned out to be as good as it looked.

McCunnife checked out the silver find and filed a claim only in his name. Owen had been right! It was a great find and Thomas McCunnife developed the discovery into the famous Pelican Mine which turned out to be one of the richest silver mines in the West. Developing this mine entailed huge expenses and labor and an ability to raise the necessary capital. But the Pelican Mine involved more than just developing the mine. The neighboring Dives mine shaft, following its high grade surface outcrop, intersected the underground silver vein of the Pelican Mine spawning both violence and legal battles. These two mines were the largest in the Silver Plume area. Armed guards were hired by both mines and tensions ran high, resulting in the shooting and killing of Jacob Snider, a Pelican investor/owner. Although one newspaper reported the name of the dead man was J.H. McMurdy. Judge James Belford, known as the Red Headed Rooster of the Rockies and a Federal Territorial Judge appointed by Abraham Lincoln, while reading the verdict on the Pelican and Dives dispute, had a loaded shotgun on his lap, just in the very real prospect of a gun battle breaking out between the disputants in the courtroom. The Pelican owners won the legal dispute, but later sold out to William A. Hamill.

My mom and dad lived in the Belford House in Central City a century later. On a very dark night I was walking by myself up a dirt path leading back up to a barn which was being used by my family as a garage. My parents were out of town and I was alone when I suddenly fell straight down a freshly dug narrow six foot shaft hitting the bottom which was full of glass whiskey bottles. Being a mountain climber I was able to extricate myself and went immediately downtown to tell the sheriff.

He and I returned to the back of the house now with the back porch light on and the sheriff's flashlight. He shined his light down into the deep narrow hole where now the bottles had disappeared. He knew the shop owner who had an antique store on the main street who sold old buried bottles from old dump sites and outdoor latrines which had turned blue and green over time. He had waited until he knew my folks were out of town. For years this man was known to dig for bottles in backyards around Central City where the outdoor privies were located. Judge Belford's whiskey bottles were discarded a century ago while he drank in his outdoor privy. Good thing Black Bob hadn't been alive back then to push him over! Dad most likely would have been blasted with a shotgun. I was lucky I didn't break my neck or any of Judge Belford's discarded whiskey bottles!

Owen and Ellen had four children, Alice (Griffin) was eight, John (Feenan) was four, and Teresa (Feenan) was two. Mary (Feenan) was born the 21st of January, 1870. Owen's serious injuries would have benefitted from a well-placed orthopedic pin or two, but at that time this technology was not available and he healed slowly and not very well. He was unable to go back to dangerous mine work, but Tom McCunnife cared for the family by making Ellen manager of the miner's boarding place, the Pelican House, in Silver Plume and giving Owen a much appreciated job driving a Pelican Mine ore wagon. There was no workman's compensation back then.

The family moved into the boarding house in 1870 where Ellen cared for her husband and four children, including newly born Mary, and managed the boarding house. Thomas McCunnife also honored his **handshake promise** made to Owen and Ellen by giving them the money to buy a boarding house of their own in Silver Plume. This wasn't exactly striking it rich, but owning a home and a business was a good start, especially since they had a roof over their heads and a business and could care for and feed their children. I know some in my family, including my dad and myself, felt that they had been "shafted!" But Owen could have easily been killed in the Central City mine accident and he likely didn't have the connections or know how to finance the promising outcrop. God sees the big picture and knows what's best for us. All that glitters is not gold, and in that day and age and circumstance it was a blessing owning a miners boarding house, having food on the table, and a roof over your head-same is true today!

A few years later, William Hamill sold the combined Pelican and Dives mines for $5,000,000 dollars which was an enormous sum in that day, especially without any taxes! Hamill also owned the granite quarry on the west side of Silver Plume from which was mined the granite for the Denver City and County Building. He built an impressive home for himself below in Georgetown which is open for tour in the summers and hosting weddings. Ellen and Owen came a long way from their humble Irish roots but likely could have really struck it rich.

Young daughter Alice had many special memories of growing up in the boarding house. How could she forget the grizzly and black bears that in the springtime would wander the streets of Silver Plume looking for food and send her and everyone else scurrying inside for safety; or the sight and sound of the thundering avalanches pounding down the steep mountains ripping out trees and everything and anything in their path to the valley below? She remembered Father Joseph Machebeuf, the first Bishop of Denver, offering mass on the dining table in the boarding house. She also remembered helping her mother make Cornish pasties for the miners. For the uninitiated, a pasty is a sealed meat pie baked in a heavy rich suet crust that the miners would wrap in a tea towel hot from the oven and stick under their shirts for the dual purpose of keeping them and the pasty warm down in the cold mine.

A special memory was Chief Colorow and his hunting party travelling through Silver Plume on their way down to the plains to hunt buffalo. Likely he still had a healthy appetite for Ellen's biscuits and could have discovered new family favorites –Cornish pasties and rhubarb and apple pie for dessert. My cousin Gerry Haskins told me that the Utes camped just below the Ashby Tunnel dump in Silver Plume and were the most peaceful Indians in Colorado. They chose negotiation with the whites rather than violence. They chose to abide by the written Treaty of 1868 defining the territory for the seven bands of Utes in the *Shining Mountains'* homeland which left them with territory to hunt and roam freely. Under this treaty the Utes had the right to stop any whites from entering the Western Slope. But white miners and homesteaders, in violation of the treaty, kept filling up the treaty lands of the Utes. Chief Ouray of the Uncompaghre or also known as the Mountain Utes sadly reflected to reporters in Washington after he and five other chiefs courageously signed the treaty: "Agreements the Indian makes with the government are like the agreements a buffalo makes with the hunter after it has been pierced by many arrows. All it can do is lie down and give in."(Robert Emmitt, *The Last WarTrail*)

The only reason Chief Ouray signed the treaty which was very unpopular among the Utes was that he was promised that the army would remove the encroaching whites. Chief Ouray was facing a *Catch 22* decision whereby there was not a right answer as Yosarian faced in the classic book by Joseph Heller which I read in the Peace Corps. The Utes showed incredible tolerance with the encroaching whites who refused to live within the stipulations of the Treaty of 1868, and as Ouray suspected, the government didn't attempt to enforce the written provisions. You have to wonder why the government had any treaties at all with Native Americans, or for that matter anyone else, if your word isn't worth the paper it is written on.

The White River Utes of Chief Colorow, Chief Douglas, and Chief Nicaagat (Captain Jack) were located on the White River Reservation close to the spectacular Flattop Mountains of Northwestern Colorado 15 miles above where the town of Meeker is today. One of the most contentious initial orders of Agent Meeker was to move the existing reservation downstream to the better farm land located near the present day Town of Meeker. This was the Utes traditional winter camp and horse pasture and horse racing track.

Donna and I took a drive over the Flattops Wilderness Area on the Dunkley Pass road on our way to Meeker from Yampa and were in awe of the majestic and serene beauty of the drive. We enjoyed a picnic at the Dunkley Pass Overlook campground and were blown away by one of the most scenic views in all of Colorado. After eating our picnic we sat on the top of the picnic table enjoying the truly majestic view in silence and were both feeling a special connection to nature and God and to our earlier native ancestors. It was an unforgettable blue sky day when you could sense the tragedy of the oldest tribe of Native Americans in Colorado blown out of Colorado like a candle in the wind.

In 1870 Nathan Meeker was a newspaper journalist working for Horace Greeley, the editor at the New York Tribune. While he was out west in the Colorado Territory he was inspired to develop a utopian Unitarian farming community in the South Platte River Basin where earlier Dan and Ellen's covered wagon must have camped. With initial funding from Horace Greeley and additional money raised from 200 investors chosen by Meeker for their "high moral standards," an agricultural cooperative was founded called the Union Colony. Using the money that was raised by Meeker, he bought 2000 acres and started his farming cooperative, now the location for the Town of Greeley. It failed financially and left Nathan Meeker owing Horace Greeley his investment funding. Needing to repay Greeley back the money he owed him, Meeker campaigned for the job of Indian Agent to the Utes at the White River Reservation, despite the fact that he had absolutely no experience with Indians or the Ute Tribe.

Using his connections in the government, **"It's not what you know, but who you know"** on May 15, 1878, the broke and indebted Meeker received the appointment as Indian Agent to the White River Ute Reservation. He was purely a political appointee, like John Evans, with the stubborn arrogance to try to convert the Utes, some who spoke Spanish and English, from hunters and expert horse breeders into farmers and ranchers of fenced cattle. Not lacking in self-confidence or self-importance he talked a good game and pushed his own agenda. Previous agents worked with the Utes and would trade furs and wild game antlers and bones brought in by the hunters. The profits were shared between the agents and the Utes. (Robert Emmitt, *The Last War Trail*)

The stubborn Meeker gave little respect to the Ute treaty terms and withheld agency food from the Utes who wouldn't farm and raise cattle on the Utes most precious winter horse pasture. This was very unpopular with the Utes, especially Chief Nicaagat who preferred the existing location of the agency mandated by treaty. The Utes had lived on their lands of the Western Slope of Colorado for nearly 800 years; the lesson is "Don't Get Too Comfortable!" (*The Last War Trail, by Robert Emmitt*)

The Rocky Mountain News and Governor Fredrick Pitkin were

advocating the expulsion of the Utes from Western Colorado. Maybe the frustrated Utes could be changed from a peaceful tribe to one retaliating against the white man's new rules and provide the rationale for removing them forcibly off their desirable land. The slogan of the day was, "The only good Ute was a dead Ute." Governor Pitkin wanted the expulsion of the Utes because they "Were paralyzing the progress of a great state." As a side note, Governor Pitkin was an investor in lucrative mining operations in Chief Ouray's pristine reservation lands in Southwest Colorado. The whites wanted the rich lands of the Utes, just as they wanted the lands of all the Plains Indians. It was all about the land, and the newly arrived whites had the military might and the guns to take what they wanted by force. (*Last War Trail*, by Robert Emmitt)

After plowing the Utes horse racing track, a shoving match ensued and Meeker backing up tripped over a horse rail and ended up on the ground, but nobody was hurt. Nathan Meeker panicked and telegraphed for army help.

Major Thomas Thornburgh, commander of Fort Steele in Wyoming, arrived with 200 soldiers and was met by Chief Nicaagat and group of Utes who rode out to meet the soldiers and warned Thornburgh not to trespass onto the White River Reservation. Chief Nicaagat and Major Thornburgh agreed that the bulk of the army would camp off the Reservation, and he and five men would accompany Chief Nicaagat to the Agency to peacefully work out the dispute with Agent Meeker. The Utes legitimately feared another **Sand Creek Massacre**. The Utes also knew about the **Bear River, Idaho Massacre** when the 'blue coats' attacked a sleeping Shoshone village on their reservation and killed over 400 unsuspecting people.

Thornburgh assured the Utes that the main body of his troops would remain off the White River Reservation; but the next day, **September 29, 1879** he broke his word and crossed with his army onto the White River Reservation. The US soldiers and the Utes met at Milk Creek on the Reservation and an unknown person fired a shot starting a shootout. The Utes controlled the high ground and were able to stop the army from advancing to their village. After the battle started, Utes attacked the White River Agency and killed Meeker and ten employees capturing three women and two children (Robert Emmitt, *The Last War Trail: The Utes and the Settlement of Colorado*).

After he was killed, Nathan Meeker had a **wooden barrel stave driven through his mouth**. Chief Colorow explained at the later government investigation, "It had been necessary to stop his infernal lying on his way to the spirit world." The hostages, including Nathan Meeker's wife and daughter were later turned over to the government. After six days of fighting at the Battle of Milk Creek, the casualties included Major Thomas T. Thornburgh who was killed along with 12 other soldiers. The Utes suffered 37 fatalities between the Battle on Milk Creek and the uprising at the White River Agency. This could have been avoided if the government had appointed a qualified Indian agent or if Major Thornburgh had honored his word and the Treaty of 1868 and stayed off the Reservation with his troops. Governor Pitkin now had his rationale to expel the Utes from Colorado without paying them just compensation.

Long held traditions and culture cannot be changed overnight, nor should they. When I was in the Peace Corps, I came to appreciate this on the outer islands of the Caroline Islands, and the longer I lived with the islanders, I came to understand their language and their way of life. The Peace Corps had strict recruitment criteria and required that I had to pass written tests, have physical and psychological testing, and do three months of intense language and cultural training including total immersion in-country. With all this I only just began to learn the language and the culture. Nathan Meeker was not only a failure in Colorado with the Union Colony but his stubbornness and lies caused a very avoidable tragedy including his own death! The government that put him into this situation that was beyond his abilities and training was an inexplicable placement with a tragic outcome for the Utes and Nathan Meeker and his family.

At nearly the same time of the Meeker Massacre not too far away in Silver Plume, tragedy was visiting Ellen once again. This time it was the loss of her eleven year old daughter, Teresa, who was run over by a wagon team of horses and killed. She was buried in the Georgetown, Colorado Cemetery. Unfortunately this was a time for, not only Ellen and Owen Feenan and their children for grieving, but simultaneously their friends the Ute Indians of the Shining Mountains were singing many of their own death chants.

The White River Utes and Chief Ouray's Uncompahgre Band (who weren't even involved at the White River Agency) were forced by gunpoint to leave behind their beautiful land in the Shining Mountains of western Colorado and moved to the new Uintah Reservation in eastern Utah. Governor Pitkin ordered that, "Any Ute seen outside the reservation boundaries should be hunted down and shot like the animals that they were." Chief Colorow continued to hunt elk in Colorado until 1888 when he was hunted down and seriously wounded by a posse. He made it back to the Uintah Reservation to sing his **death** chant. The good Native Coloradoan passed on to his happy hunting grounds where there would be plenty elk, deer, buffalo, and biscuits. He guided my great-grand parents safely past the Cheyenne Dog Soldier war parties on the eastern plains of Colorado to Denver and the Utes will not be forgotten by many of their white friends.

The Maroon Bells are still ringing for the Utes who lived in Pitkin County! Is anyone listening in Aspen? And the Bowl of Tears below Mount of the Holy Cross near Vail is still filling up in the White River National Forest. Does anyone in Aspen or Vail even care today that the Utes got shafted and the whites got their land. It's all about the land, mining, and money and some sheep and cattle ranching white homesteaders and their heirs have become mega-millionaires selling off their lands in Western Colorado. **Ka Ching!** The slot machine banged loudly from pulling the trigger and the seeming endless spilling out from the machine a vomit of heavy gold, silver, and blood, as tear drops instead of cherries lined up in a row. The whites, including me, called that a **jackpot** and the Native Americans called it an endless **trail of tears!** **PITKIN County** could be fittingly renamed after any of the stunning mountains around Aspen, such as Capitol Peak, Pyramid Peak, Snowmass Peak, or Sopris Peak, or **Maroon Bells County**. We can all be awakened and reminded by the tolling bells to be a better people and hear the many death songs of our Indian predecessors who had lived there for many centuries, possibly 800 years, who it has been thought when being marched out of Colorado at the end of a gun a barrel, left behind **The Ute Curse**!

Dan and Ellen Griffin marveled at the beauty of the Shining Mountains on their journey down the South Platte River in their covered wagon. One of the most spectacular and prominent mountains in all of Colorado is the 14,259 foot tall Longs Peak which is connected to another of the most prominent peaks, Mount Meeker at 13,911 feet and its spectacular glaciated cirque. Separating the two world famous massive peaks is the heavily glaciated ridge called the *Ships Prow*. These two spectacular peaks are in Rocky Mountain National Park and overlooking the northern plains of Colorado. Chief Colorow, who safely guided Dan and Ellen Griffin past the Cheyenne Dog Soldiers, would have whole heartedly agreed to change the name of Mount Meeker from the name of one of Colorado's most notorious and ill-suited failures! I think it would be fitting to rename this **Mount Nicaagat** after the Ute chief who rode to Denver and tried to have Governor Pitkin remove Nathan Meeker as agent to the Utes on the White River Reservation. As Ute Chief Nicaagat (Captain Jack) said to Pitkin, "Diss agent iss no good, we want new agent"*(Last War Trail, by* Robert Emmitt). Problem was that Pitkin just laughed at Captain Jack. Chief Nicaagat also thought he had convinced Major Thornburgh not to invade the White River Ute Reservation. Chief Nicaagat (Captain Jack) was a Colorado hero- not Meeker!

While it might seem as if all men in authority were out to rid the West of Native Americans and feather their nests in the process, there was a brave man that sympathized with the Utes and tried to get to know and understand them. In 1868, **Major John Wesley Powell**, a Civil War veteran who lost his right arm in battle, camped on the same meadow that Nathan

Meeker later plowed under. While I worked for Vail Associates, Inc. on Vail Mountain I could see **Mount Powell** in the Gore Range and, like most mountain lovers in Colorado, enjoyed the truly stunning view of this mountain from the front side of the Vail Ski Mountain. Major Powell learned the Ute language and became a special friend to them. Although he did upset them when surveying his campsite, he quickly pulled his survey stakes from the ground. Major Powell travelled unarmed for twenty years throughout the entire Ute territories and never had any confrontations with them.

Black Elk (*Black Elk Speaks,* as told to John Neihardt pg. 242) had a vision of Heaven where he could see, "A beautiful land where many, many people were camping in a great circle. I could see that they were happy and had plenty. Everywhere there were drying racks full of meat. The air was clean and beautiful with a living light that was everywhere.....Then they led me to the center of the circle where once more I saw the holy tree all full of leaves and blooming..... Against the tree there was a man standing with arms held wide in front of him... He was not a Wasichu (white man) and he was not an Indian.... He was a very fine-looking man. While I was staring at him, his body began to change and became very beautiful with all colors of light, and around him there was light. He spoke like singing: 'My Life is such that all earthly beings and growing things belong to me. Your **Father, the Great Spirit,** has said this. You must say this.' Then he went out like a **light in a wind.**"

CHAPTER 5
Silver Plume

St Patrick's Church in Silver Plume was built in 1876, the same year Colorado became the Centennial State. Four years later on Tuesday July 6th Alice Griffin, then a young 17 year old, married Jeremiah (Jerry) Buckley who was 8 years older, and had been lured to the Rockies by gold fever. He left Saranac, New York a town in the foothills of the Adirondacks to follow a dream and strike it rich with Colorado gold. Sometimes the dream is better than the reality. He discovered his lungs weren't cut out for working underground in dust filled silver mines. Consequently he had to get creative and he opened up and operated a livery stable in Silver Plume. Jerry's livery business was kept constantly busy delivering supplies and miners up the steep and winding mining road climbing up the Seven-Thirty Mine Road with its many hair-raising curves and switch backs to the Ashby Tunnel, Dives-Pelican, the Terrible, Baxter, Dunkirk, Dunderberg, Smuggler, Mendotta, and Seven-Thirty mines.

He turned out to be the first of many in the Buckley lineage to be a successful entrepreneur. Alice had herself quite a catch and everyone was excited as the wedding day approached, especially ten year old Mary, the younger sister of Alice. It was considered bad luck by the superstitious Irish to be married on a Saturday or in May, consequently the Tuesday, July 6th date. Of course, it was always good luck if the sun shone on the bride. The dawn sun was shining brightly on the top of Sunrise Peak when Ellen was awakened by her two smiling girls. It was a lucky day indeed for the Irish in Silver Plume, Colorado. This marriage was particularly productive, resulting in a family of thirteen children, eight boys and five girls. One of these boys was my father, Robert Emmet Buckley (Black Bob), who was the 7th boy and 11th child. Can't get any luckier than that!

Sometime between the 1880 census and 1883 Owen Feenan passed away having never fully recovered from the severe injuries suffered in the mining accident in Central City. For those keeping score, this is the second time Ellen has become a widow due to the untimely death of a husband. Having this happen wasn't as unusual as you might think due to the risky nature of life in the Colorado Mountains. Disease and mining accidents and getting shot took their toll. Today if you visit the local cemeteries in Central City and Silver Plume you can't help but be struck by the number of headstones for those who were young husbands or very young children from that era.

One can only imagine the strength she had to call upon to face life alone again. For Ellen though, she knew in her heart that she truly wasn't alone and trusted God in all circumstances to bring her through another one of life's trials.

God does provide and Ellen married for the third time on August 16, 1883 in Our Lady of Lourdes Catholic Church in Georgetown, Colorado. Her new husband was John Hickey. Father Nicholas Matz was the resident pastor and he had persuaded William A. Hamill, an Episcopalian, to donate a 1400-pound bell for the church, quite a spectacular addition to a small town church and a wonderful compliment for special events like weddings. The peel of the bells could be heard all the way to Silver Plume, which is two miles away as the crow flies, or as sound travels. Instead of rice, an Irishman probably threw an old shoe over Ellen's head for good luck when the Hickeys exited the church. Goodness knows she needed it! The Hickeys, and Ellen's children that were still at home, returned to Silver Plume to resume life and run the boarding house.

A train whistle was heard March 11, 1884, loudly announcing the first steam powered narrow gauge locomotive arriving in Silver Plume. As Silver Plume sits more than 600 feet above Georgetown and was reachable by train travel only by going over two miles of a steep and narrow canyon with Clear Creek loudly tumbling over rocks and boulders below, this was no small accomplishment. Railroad engineers designed a route similar to a big spiral staircase connecting the two mining towns by slowly gaining the 600 feet in elevation at a 4% grade. The crow's flight of 2 miles is extended to a 4.5 mile distance with horseshoe and hairpin curves and turns crossing back and forth bridging over Clear Creek four times, including the famous giant Devil's Gate Bridge.

This engineering marvel was known as the **Georgetown Loop** and was completed March 10th 1884. All the trains going into the Colorado Mountains at this time in history used a 3 foot narrow gauge track instead of the standard track of 4 feet 8 ½ inches. The narrow gauge was cheaper to build and could make the sharp turns necessary in the many mountain canyons. Although not as fast or as stable as the standard track trains in that era, they were the most practical for train travel in the mountains. Sometimes their instability presented problems, as in 1885 when an eastbound passenger train was blown off the tracks and into the Georgetown Lake.

That could say how unstable the narrow gauge train was or possibly how strong the winds were blowing down from the high peaks of the Continental Divide. Those winds are called chinook winds and the train engineers were well aware of the danger for trains travelling over the high Devil's Gate Bridge!

The Georgetown Loop was a major tourist attraction at the time, and continues to be even today. Back then the round trip ticket price from Silver Plume to Denver was an affordable $3 dollars. Having scheduled train service going through Silver Plume meant that the world had just opened up for the residents of this small mining town. People could now travel from Silver Plume across the country east and west to both coasts in the relative comfort of a train car in just a few days.

As Ellen thought back on her trip west in the oxen drawn covered wagon, she must have marveled at what amazing progress had been made in Colorado in her lifetime. Not only could people travel faster, but so could the mail. In one of these deliveries, Ellen received the sad notification from Ireland of her mother's death. The funeral card that was sent said, "*In Memory of Alice Taggart Short. Mrs. Short died July 20, 1884 and lies interned in the Old Mains, Dundee, Scotland.*" It had been 24 years since Ellen had seen her mother and now she would never see her again. The funeral card is still in the possession of the family (Sharon Haskins Kennedy).

On November 4, 1884 all the bells were ringing out a warning for everyone in Silver Plume of an emergency. There was a major fire burning in Pat Barrett's saloon. Before the fire could be extinguished by the Silver Plume volunteer firemen, most of the business district was destroyed. While the men fought the fire using 100 canvas water bags filled from Clear Creek and passed along by a water brigade, the women and children prayed together outside of St. Patrick's Catholic Church and it was credited to their prayers being answered, that **The Miracle of Silver Plume** spared the lives of the brave volunteers fighting the fire, although Pat Barrett was killed in the fire. The Church, Ellen's boarding house and all the homes in town were spared! Not a spark was blown onto the roof of St. Patrick's from the nearby burning buildings. The prayers of the women were answered not only by God but by the Georgetown pumper and crew who came up the hill to help their neighbors (*Ghost Towns of the Colorado Rockies, by Robert L. Brown*).

Too bad those women and children were not there to pray for the town when the Buckleys' red brick barn was razed, not by fire, but by the new construction of an Interstate Highway and the peaceful horse meadow was gone! Progress and ease of travel had reached the mountain town again. When I returned from the Peace Corps in the summer of 1970 and entered Silver Plume from the east on the newly completed four-lane highway, I was shocked seeing how Silver Plume had been changed! Silver Plume used to have a very dramatic entrance from the east and gone was the original train station, and the original red caboose of the Colorado and Southern

Railroad which all the kids used as their playground. Gone was the red brick train repair shop and parts warehouse which was purchased by the Buckley Bros. Store across highway six for its own warehousing needs.

The beautiful open mountain meadow in which the livery horses of Jerry Buckley were pastured in days gone by, and in more recent days the Haskins' horses were happy eating the mountain grass. It was now four lanes of paving. Like the Joni Mitchell song *Big Yellow Taxi* goes, "Don't you always seem to know, you don't know what you've got till it's gone. Paved paradise. Put up a parking lot." Today, seeing the thousands of Front Range skiers trying to get back to Denver after skiing at one of the I-70 corridor resorts, I-70 really does look like a parking lot! It was a sad day for me, and if Jerry Buckley had been alive, it would have been a sad day for him as well. All of my life up to then I had taken for granted, and had come to be comfortable appreciating, the dramatic entrance to Silver Plume from the original road level of Highway 6, instead of whizzing by 20 feet above ground on an elevated four-lane highway.

The tourists, and the new industry they would foster, were on their way. I always harbored disdain for this concrete and asphalt intrusion until one early morning in Vail when my wife shook me awake. "The baby's coming! My water broke and we need to get to Denver fast!"

We just barely made it to the hospital in time and only thanks to the new tunnel under Loveland Pass and yes - I-70. My wife knows what Alice Buckley felt like going to Denver on the train in 1902 when her water broke and my father was born on the train and sometimes you have to give credit to progress even if at first you aren't sure it is a good thing.

In 1892 John Hickey died and was buried in the Silver Plume Cemetery. Ellen Short, at the age of 57, has lost her third husband after nine years of marriage, but over the years the Lord had blessed her with children and grandchildren and they were there for her. Her faith and love of Jesus gave her the strength to look forward to another blue sky day, but not likely another husband after the pain of burying three. She had learned to take life one day at a time and to not get too comfortable, except in the Lord, because this world is not our final destination. Change is inevitable and there is more on the way.

Silver Plume had been booming in large part thanks to the 1890 Sherman Silver Purchase Act which by government law doubled the purchase of silver. But the repeal of the act in 1893 brought an end to the silver boom and began a decline in the mining era prosperity in Colorado. The Georgetown Loop to Silver Plume was attracting visitors from the entire country, and even from as far away as Europe. Tourism to Colorado was just beginning to fill in for the declining mineral revenues. In December of 1898 the Colorado and Southern Railway Company was chartered and acquired the Georgetown Loop. My father, Robert Emmet Buckley Sr, was born on the train between Silver Plume and Denver September 29, 1902. It was most likely a very uncomfortable train ride for Alice and Jerry!

This train provided passenger service from Denver to Silver Plume until 1939 when the original Loop was dismantled for the steel needed for World War Two. (Cordillera Press, *Guide to the Georgetown Silver Plume Historic District,* one of the authors Christine Bradley, the Archivist for Clear Creek County*)*

Amid the new reality of a decline in the economy, the bells in Silver Plume echoed again between the high mountains. Tons of snow had thundered down off of Sherman Mountain and buried the homes on the west side of the tall brick Silver Plume Grade School. Tragically, ten people were buried and killed, including an entire family. *The Georgetown Courier* wrote:

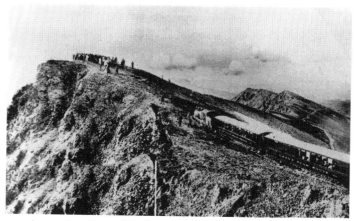

Argentine Central Railroad on top of Mount McClellan.

"The most disastrous snow slide was that on February 12, 1899 which resulted in the death of Domenico Destafane and his wife and son and two daughters. The snowfall that winter was one of the heaviest of which there is any record. The immense hoods of snow on the crest of Sherman Mountain broke away at 8:45 in the morning, and sent an avalanche of snow down Cherokee and Willihan Gulches that did not stop until a short distance of the schoolhouse in Silver Plume…The body of Destafane was not recovered until April, when Peter Vigna discovered a finger protruding from the ice in Cherokee Gulch." At the top of the hill in the Silver Plume Cemetery stands a tall monument marking the burial site of the ten Italians killed in that slide with a metal plaque reading: "SACRED TO THE MEMORY OF THE TEN ITALIANS, FEBRUARY 12, 1899 ERECTED BY THE PUBLIC."

In 1905 the Argentine Central Railroad incorporated and began to build the highest railroad in the U.S. going beyond Silver Plume to the top of the 13,587 foot high Mount McClellan; and on August 12, 1906 the first tourists were riding in two C&S passenger cars to the top from which you can see four mountains over 14,000 feet above sea level- Mount Evans and Mount Bierstadt to the east, and Grays and Torreys Peaks to the west, and to the north the smaller, but steep and avalanche prone, Mount Kelso at 13,164 feet high.

I have hiked to the top of Mount McClellan and Argentine Pass with my Forest Service trail crew from Silver Dollar Lake above Georgetown, and I imagined what those passengers felt that August day- enclosed in a slowly moving train and looking down with nervous stomachs. The train had to back down off the precipice further enhancing the frightening ride. The following year the 6600' foot long *Sunrise Peak Aerial Tram* was built from Silver Plume to the top of Sunrise Peak climbing 3300 vertical feet and opening for business July 15, 1907. This would make Silver Plume the first town in Colorado to have an aerial tram, but no skiers yet came to ride. My uncle Ray Buckley worked there when just a young boy and you can still see a few of the towers high up on Sunrise Peak.

On March 6, 1909 Jerry Buckley died suddenly and unexpected of natural causes, probably a heart attack related to his weakened lungs from mining and living at 9200' feet above sea level. Not spoken much within the family was his enjoyment of relaxing in the saloon after a hard day's work much to the consternation of his wife! (I can relate as I would stop by the local Vail bar to enjoy the camaraderie of my fellow ski patrolman before heading home much to Donna's disapproval!) Alice lost a loving husband, their children a wonderful father, and Silver Plume one of their bravest leading citizens. He was buried in the Silver Plume cemetery. My father was just seven years old when he lost his father. Alice became a widow with 13 children from ages two to twenty-seven.

Although her mother Ellen had words of comfort and advice as she had been in this situation three times, it was a true test of her strength and faith as she tackled this challenge life had handed her. God doesn't give us more than we can handle, and Alice showed this to be true. There was a lot of family support from her mother and sister Mary who had married David Collins, a former deputy sheriff in Cripple Creek, Colorado and was living directly across the street from Alice in the Windsor Hotel which they owned and operated. Ellen, now known as Grandma Hickey, was living with daughter Mary across the street and was there to embrace her Alice.

Alice Buckley looked to God for comfort and guidance, just as her mother did before her. In 1923 after living a good long life, experiencing much joy and sadness, it was Ellen's (Grandma Hickey) time to go home to the Lord. "In this world nothing can be said to be certain, except death and taxes" (Benjamin Franklin)! But Ellen knew better than Benjamin Franklin. She knew with certainty that she had finished the work, "Thou gavest me to do" and loved her and prepared a place for her in Heaven as pretty as a mountain meadow in springtime.

Died in Silver Plume, Colorado
April 15, 1923

Mrs. Ellen Hickey
Aged 88 years
Born in Belfast, Ireland

The funeral services will be held at the
Catholic Church
Tuesday, April 17, 1923
at 10 o'clock a. m.
Internment at Silver Plume Cemetery

Friends are invited to attend

Ellen died a happy and content woman! She spun her spell binding stories to her grandchildren sitting around a hot coal stove in Silver Plume, Colorado about her early life in Ireland, crossing the Atlantic in an immigrant ship, marrying Dan Griffin who together they jumped off into the Wild West on a covered wagon, and ultimately raised her children, and married two more times in the high mining towns! Her guide posts during her long life were the Ten Commandments which she could not read, but knew by heart, and passed down to her children and grandchildren. Commandments to love God first then to love her fellow man served her well throughout a long life of unswerving trust and love in God that she was never alone and always listened to her prayer, "I trust You Jesus." **I'll simply sleep in peace until you come to me!**

CHAPTER 6
Buckley Enterprises

Joseph Emerson Smith, writing for the Rocky Mountain News, wrote on *Mother's Day 1946:*

***

"As we celebrate Mother's Day this Sunday and remember the wonderful work mothers do, we think of Mrs. Alice Buckley of Silver Plume. Because hers is a thrilling and pleasant story of an unusual woman's struggle to bring up her 13 children, we want to share it with our readers.

***

'Dear God, look down on me here and help me to find an answer.' Alone in St. Patrick's Church in Silver Plume on a June day in 1909, Mrs. Alice Buckley knelt in prayer. Jeremiah Buckley had died three months before, leaving his 36 year old widow with 13 children to support. Alice Buckley's inheritance amounted to little more than a neat frame cottage, and a livery business which had been shrinking in proportion to the steady decline of mining. A housewife sheltered by a devoted husband, she had no business experience.

The once-busy mining town no longer heard the daily thunder of giant powder reverberating from the mountain walls. The glory of one of the world's great silver camps had departed with the demonetization of the white metal in 1893. There were more men than jobs in Silver Plume now, and the means of providing food and clothing for 13 children and keeping the younger ones in school would have to be created. Mother Buckley had taken her problem to the church.

***

Kneeling in St. Patrick's Church where the June sun was turned into rainbows by the tinted glass windows, the Widow Buckley found her answer. As she stepped out into the sunshine she said: 'One for all and all for one. In union there is strength.' That night Mrs. Buckley called a council of her children, and the famous family corporation of the Buckley's was organized. 'People need food, fuel, shelter, and transportation,' Mrs. Buckley told her brood. 'Let's call our corporation Buckley Brothers and make the livery business our first department.'

William, the oldest boy, and Jerry were assigned to the livery business consisting of stable, 12 horses, three carriages, fringed surrey, coach and wagons. 'We can also start a fuel department,' Mrs. Buckley went on, 'Will and Jerry can use the horses to bring in fallen timber, and the other boys can help saw and cut it for sale.'

***

The other boys were told to find jobs of their own choosing after school and on Saturdays. The girls would help their brothers whenever possible, and work in the home. Before the first meeting of Buckley Brothers broke up, Will had a suggestion to make: 'Shouldn't we kids have a working chart, a kind of agreement on what we're doing, to keep us in line?' Before the first meeting of the Buckley Brothers broke up, mother and children drew up the following document, doubtless one of the most unique on which a business ever was started:

1. Obey the Ten Commandments always.
2. Keep clean in mind and body and stay strong. Be neat in appearance.

3. Speak the truth in even the smallest matter, so you can look straight into every man's eyes with your chin up.

4. Keep your mouth shut unless you are sure of what you say.

5. Be tolerant. Don't fly off the handle. Remember there are always two sides to a dispute, and you may be in the wrong.

6. Don't promise unless you can deliver.

7. Give the best in you, so people will stick by you.

8. Be fair to both your customers and yourself. Give the customer the edge whenever possible and make him a friend.

9. Be thrifty. Save every cent to salt away in a reserve.

10. Put every cent into the till. Never carry money in your pocket.

11. No debts. Count ten before deciding to buy anything not absolutely needed.

***

The next day, the Buckley Brothers set out to find after school jobs. James, who was interested in storekeeping, got a job in Ed Cowel's meat market. Part of his wage was in meats to take home.

Edmund, ten, helped in the livery stable, taking care of the horses and doing other odd jobs. Robert, seven, also when he was old enough, began to work at the livery stable.

At the start of the corporation, Raymond, one of the older boys, took a job as night watchman at the Mendota Mine. He also worked as a mill hand at the Burleigh Tunnel near the Mendota, totaling $2.75 for his 12 hours' work each day.

John, always interested in mechanics, left school at 15 to work for Dick Milne, blacksmith, horseshoer and wheel-wright at Georgetown.

Ronald, the youngest brother, was to help with the driving and hauling or wherever help was needed in Buckley Brothers enterprises.

***

Mrs. Buckley, in addition to supervising the work of all her children, and providing them with the good cooking which made them strong and well, organized her own 'real estate' department.

As the family bank account began to expand, she bought up abandoned houses for taxes and began to fix them up for sale or rent. Any surplus profits were invested in endowment policies for the children.

Buckley Brothers' business, founded on faith and well planned as it was, grew rapidly. Most of the time it was thrilling and fun, but on occasion, it was grim and frightening.

Will and Jerry often found their work hard and dangerous in the winter as they scoured the canyon sides and Loveland Pass for fallen trees. Once Will was kicked in the head by a burro, and his jaw was laid

Bob Buckley is holding the horse and cousin Marguerite Collins is holding the reins.

open. Robert, when he was 13, drove Tom Henehan, state mine inspector, to the mines on an inspection trip. The boy guided his horses so expertly and cautiously over the steep, deep-rutted roads that the mine inspector gave him a monopoly on the three-day, twice-a-year job.

***

When James enlisted in the army in World War I, Robert took his place at Cowel's market, later changing to Morris Neuman's general merchandise and grocery store, and the Roberts Brothers grocery and hardware store. From the mine work, where he nearly lost his life in a snow-slide, Raymond moved on to attend an electrical school in Kansas

City, specializing in automobile work. Following service in World War I, he opened the Buckley Brothers Studebaker sales agency and repair shop in Denver, now at 660 S. Broadway.

John worked at the blacksmith shop until he had accumulated enough to buy out the aged proprietor, Mr. Milne.

In 1923 with the increasing popularity of automotive trucks, he bought the old brick two-story Georgetown post office building, then abandoned, and remodeled it for a garage and shop, which does a flourishing business.

While the Buckley Brothers branched out into businesses of their own, the home institution of their family corporation through the years has been the Buckley Brothers store at Silver Plume. The store had its inception when James returned from World War I and opened a meat market, Robert going with him. Morris Neuman, the storekeeper, who wanted to retire, sold out to them.

The Buckley's new modern store building has become the "nerve center" of the entire community. Evenings, townsfolk gather around the big oil heater, sit in comfortable chairs and talk or listen to the radio.

William remained as head of the hauling and delivery department of the corporation from its start until his death June 11th, 1945. Jeremiah stuck with the daily job of hauling supplies from Denver, making himself the "lifeline" of the store. Edmund looks after the filling station and assists in the store.

Other projects the Buckleys acquired through the years include a dynamite agency in Denver, serving several states, and a contract to carry the mail between Denver, Empire, and Silver Plume and points in between when train service on the mail was abandoned.

Through the years, Mother Buckley saw to it that her boys and girls had play to offset their many duties. They learned vocal and instrumental music and had their own orchestra.

The boys learned sportsmanship through baseball, and the Buckley Brothers baseball team was noted for having eight members from one family.

✳✳✳

The children learned kindness from the example set by their mother. The great snowstorm Easter Sunday, 1944, caused many busses and cars to be marooned because of slides and four foot snow.

William Buckley directed the rescue work, and the Buckley Store was used as rescue headquarters. Without charge, hot coffee, fruit, sandwiches, and other food were furnished from the stock. Blankets were unwrapped from the shelves and women and small children were bedded down.

✳✳✳

Mother Buckley is 85 years old now. Recently she has been seriously ill, but with gentle care, she is recovering.

She is looking forward again to the time when friends can stop in for some of her coffee and layer cake and homemade chokecherry jelly. And she wants to be ready for the time this summer when an aged wayfarer or a young hitchhiker will knock at her door for a snack. Mother Buckley would mother the whole world if she could." *Rocky Mountain News*

Will Buckley organized the team and recruited the coach, top left, and Father Walsh to say a prayer for the team. Eight Buckley brothers are Ray, Jerry, John, Will, Bob, Jim, Ed, and Ron.

Silver Plume baseball team with eight brothers and a cousin

Successful Trip Is Made
Over Loveland Pass
By Motorists.

Georgetown, Colo., Oct. 9.—Promise of an early opening of the Loveland pass road thru Georgetown and Dillon to Leadville and the Holy Cross district was given here when William, Fred and Robert Buckley, Donald Marshall, William Buxton and William Taylor of this city made a successful auto trip over the pass to Dillon.

The men reported that the route could be opened with concerted efforts of the two communities, and a party of volunteer workers from Dillon and Georgetown will go to the pass Sunday and attempt to make the road passable for tourists before the coming of winter.

The distance between the two towns by the new route is twenty-eight miles. At present, traveling via Silver Plume, Kremmling and Berthoud pass, the distance is 120 miles.

Along a part of the route the men who made the trip over the pass had to cut away willows and move fallen timber on the old wagon road which leads to the pass from Dillon. They covered the distance in a little more than three hours, and waited a part of the time for a steam shovel working at the top of the pass to let them get by.

The Silver Plume baseball games were celebrated by the entire town and after the game there was a sharing of food, drink and camaraderie and on occasion the Buckley's orchestra would play for a dance the night after a big game. Will and Jim Buckley were the pitchers and talk around the County was that Will Buckley was the fastest runner and many a wager was lost betting against him! You wouldn't have won a wager betting against him running for Clear Creek County Commissioner, a position he served for twelve years.

Many notables would share time fishing Clear Creek with one or more of the brothers and display their catch for the camera in the Buckley Store. As a young child I remember a photo hanging in the store of Governor Ed Johnson displaying his catch of fish with my Uncle Ron. It wasn't too far to ride their horses up and over the Continental Divide to go fishing.

Bob Buckley with several brothers and friends from Silver Plume drove a Maxwell over Loveland Pass in 1926. Bob's the photographer. .

First car over Loveland Pass driven and photo by Bob Buckley

Dave Collins, who was closest to my dad in age and was a close childhood friend as well as cousin, told me that "Black Bob" was always up for that practical trick. My dad was known as "Blackie" because of his coal black hair and "dastardly pranks." One time when Dave was walking on the train station boardwalk he took a sprawling fall when one of the boards had been loosened and somehow mysteriously raised up tripping him at just the right moment. He instinctively knew who was behind the prank; "Where's that damn Black Bob?"

Bob could be found most of the time working in the Buckley Bros. Store up on Main Street Silver Plume where he was the butcher, the baker, and the main troublemaker. When eggs would spoil or tomatoes would spoil in the vegetable section, they would become his hand thrown missiles from the side of store at poor unsuspecting targets of opportunity. Many stories have been told of people on the main wooden sidewalk looking around for the person who had just hit them with a rotten tomato. His targets were not strangers and always knew it was Black Bob probably hiding on the side of the store and eyeing his next target!

It was almost a common occurrence for Dave to be ambushed from behind with a rotten egg or an over ripe tomato and not be able to see who had thrown the messy missile. But he always knew who the culprit was! Dave told me that one of Black Bob's favorite targets was Ben Bosco a town eccentric bachelor and fur trapper who was an old man when I knew him. Dad would always check in on him making sure he was ok. I was impressed by the chickens and goats that had free roam of his house. And Cousin Sharon Haskins said she was impressed by his having a log that was burning in his stove that extended out his front door and having a donkey and coyote that were best friends.

When I returned back to Colorado from my service in the Peace Corps and was applying for a job at the Vail Ski Resort, my Uncle Ron who then was managing the Buckley Store asked me to take a can of beer into Pete Seibert's office (Pete was one of the founders of Vail) and shake it up and spray it all over. A trick Pete would perform in the Buckley Store after my Uncle had cut off his tie.

Pete would come into the store after a business trip to Denver still wearing a business suit. Needless to say I didn't shake a can of beer and spray it in his office as Uncle Ron wanted; thinking he might get away with that, but it wasn't for me when pursuing a job!

In Pete's Book *Vail Triumph of a Dream*, "Both of us (Earl Eaton, co-founder of Vail) had spent the winter of 1957 working at the Loveland Pass ski area. I was the area manager; Earl was a mountain maintenance man and ski patroller. During the days we worked to serve the trickle of skiers (only one hundred to two hundred on weekdays, perhaps a thousand on weekends) who dared to drive the slick, twisting fifty miles on U.S. 6 from Denver to Loveland. Nights we spun dreams around a potbelly stove in Buckley's store, down the road in Silver Plume. Always the talk was of skiing: how to do it, where to do it, how to build a money-making ski resort."

Pete had laid out the ski runs and lifts at Loveland Basin and built a great ski mountain there, as well as the Vail and Beaver Creek Ski Resorts, the largest and most popular Ski Mountain complex in North America.

Although Pete would always point out that it was a team that built Vail and Beaver Creek. I am still very proud to be able to say Pete Seibert was a friend.

One time we were looking at a ski resort in Idaho together and were invited to dinner in a private home. One of the guests had been an Army Ranger and served in the first Gulf War and noticed that Pete's face was a patch work of scar tissue. He asked Peter if he had been wounded in World War II when in the famous Tenth Mountain Division, whose ski troops trained near Vail, Colorado.

Peter related that "He had been shot up pretty badly in an assault up Riva Ridge (a name for a famous Vail ski run) on Mount Belvedere in the Apennine Mountains in Italy. He was a sergeant leading his platoon up the steep snow and icy mountain when he was hit in a hail of bullets."

Peter was evacuated down a ways on the mountain where a triage area was set up for the wounded. An army medic was bent over Pete and attending to his wounds when a mortar shell exploded above all the wounded in a tree. Knocking Pete unconscious! When he returned to consciousness, he knew he was terribly wounded and looking for the medic who had been attending to him, Pete rolled his head over to the side and all he could see was a "shoulder!" I can tell you there wasn't a dry eye among the dinner guests! War is hell!

The Colorado ski resorts are noted for their deep and plentiful dry powder and Colorado sunshine. With 300 days of sunshine, on average, the clear and cold days in the winter give way to a clear and frigid night sky. Sounds great and what's not to like about sunny skies and light as a feather powder snow during the day and a star studded night sky with the stars seeming so close you could reach out and touch them.

When I was on the Vail Ski Patrol one of my duties was avalanche rescue and control co-leader with the responsibility to assess the avalanche danger and send teams into slide areas to blast or ski cut potential avalanche prone slopes. The Colorado clear and frigid cold nights in addition to great star-gazing meant the development of a very unstable layer of snow at the ground level of a snowpack called depth hoar. Depth hoar behaves just like marbles.

This isn't a problem on the flat ground of a mountain meadow, but put this on a Colorado mountain slope of 30 to 45 degrees (where most avalanches will occur) and you have nature's recipe for an unstable snowpack and an avalanche.

This natural phenomenon poses a very serious threat, especially if new snow accumulates on top and is accompanied by high winds causing a heavy wind slab riding on top of the loose marbles. Colorado is notorious for leading all other states in avalanche deaths thanks to depth hoar. A dubious honor to be sure. And the ski patrols all over the state use explosives extensively and ski cutting in the early season to knock down early season slides.

As the season progresses into the heavier snow months the deeper new snow on the ground will hopefully insulate the warmer rock and ground from the cold sky, and preventing the warmer snow/water vapor to escape and rise up through the snow pack to the cold sky leaving the build-up of the depth hoar layer. This process is called sublimation and is unique in nature where a solid changes to a gas without going first through the liquid stage. One thing about depth hoar, Black Bob wouldn't use it for making snowballs. The depth hoar crystals don't stick together.

When my father was very young, an avalanche hit Silver Plume demolishing and burying homes again in the Italian part of town west of the Silver Plume School. My young father could hear crying below the snow and the rescuers shoveled out a family buried under the compacted snow. A frightened young girl who was rescued and found with her mother under the kitchen table would be the future mother of the Ski Patrol Director at the Loveland Basin Ski Area.

He employed me when I was eighteen to be a ski patrolman at Loveland. I used to tell him he had to be nice to me or I would tell his mother! Sadly avalanches were a common threat in the Rocky Mountains killing many in the area around Silver Plume and claiming the young life of Eddie Collins, the oldest son of Mary Collins and brother of Dave and sisters, Mary (Ellie) Ellen, and Marguerite Collins, and a cousin of the Buckley children. The following is a local newspaper account of the avalanche which killed Eddie and Arthur Osborne, and my father's brother Ray Buckley barely escaped with his life.

The Idaho Springs Mining Gazette, Friday January 8, 1916 reports, "Georgetown was stunned by an appalling disaster Thursday Jan. 6th which resulted in the death of Arthur H. Osborne, U.S. Deputy Mineral Surveyor of Georgetown and Edward Collins of Silver Plume, who were engulfed in a snow slide from Kelso Mountain. Mr. Osborne was engaged in surveying mining claims for Edward Collins and Ray Buckley, who were assisting. The three had partaken of their noonday lunch and started up A.P. Gulch (probably Sonora Gulch) which is about 30 feet wide with precipitous sides. Suddenly the snow broke away from the smooth mountain side, not more than 50 feet above them. It came with such a rush that it carried Osborne and Collins from their feet, the former carrying a transit and the latter an ax and tape line. Buckley who had nothing to impede his movement, scrambled out of the snow. The last he saw of Osborne and Collins they were sitting on the snow and being carried down the steep and narrow gulch by the rapidly moving snow slide, which stopped about a half a mile below the starting point. Buckley, being unable to find his companions, went to the Josephine Mine about one mile away for assistance. That night found about 40 men on the ground. The slide was from 5 to 7 feet deep. On account of the precipitous sides of the gulch with no place to throw the snow, it was deemed best to commence at the foot of the slide and work up the gulch. The men engaged all night long shoveling snow, and all day Friday. No news had been received from the rescue party up to six o'clock Friday."

Georgetown Courier Saturday January 15,1916, "The bodies of Arthur Osborne and Edward Collins were found Saturday morning about halfway up the avalanche. The body of Osborne was found under five feet of compact snow, and that of Collins under eighteen inches of snow. Both were lying on their faces, head down. Collins' neck and back were broken. The transit, ax, and the tape line were found near the bodies, which were about 15 feet apart. Osborne had been engaged for several days in surveying mining locations for Edward Collins (19 years old) and Ray

Buckley, who were assisting him in the work. Thursday noon they started across a ravine on the mountain side which was covered to considerable depth with snow. Buckley was in the lead, followed by Collins, and then by Osborne. On reaching the middle of the ravine, Buckley sank into the snow up to his waist. He told his companions to watch out, as there was a hole. Just as he got out Collins dropped in the hole, and in his efforts to get out, started the snow slide, which broke away about 50 feet above him. Buckley was on the edge of the moving snow and saved himself. Collins and Osborne were immediately engulfed in the slide and in a few moments, carried out of sight. The snow slide, instead of piling up at the foot of the ravine (Sonora Gulch) made a sharp turn and continued down the gulch (Stevens Gulch) for a distance of nearly 2500 feet." *Georgetown Courier*

This was an incredibly sad loss for the family; Mary Collins who having lost her husband, David, in 1905 from pneumonia, was now confronting the death of her oldest son, Eddie. He was a young father figure to his younger brother and sisters as well for his younger Buckley cousins. Grandma Hickey was there to console her daughter and hold her tight. Simply nothing in life is sadder or harder to do than to bury one of your children or grandchildren; and she was also there two years later to hold her first born Alice who lost her daughter Elsie who perished in the Great Flu Pandemic in 1918.

My cousin, Sharon Haskins Kennedy, tells of Grandma Mary Collins, "When Uncle Dave Collins was a little boy Grandma Hickey used to send him to the saloon up on Main Street to buy her a bottle of Red Eye Whiskey. He said he had to keep Grandma Collins from finding out because he would get into a lot of trouble when she did. I think she probably found out more than not. I used to think Grandma Collins had more than one set of eyes as she always used to catch me on the way home from playing up on the hill with the my friends and she would get me by the ear and make me come in, sit in her platform rocker, and say the **WHOLE** ROSARY."

"She always said 'you should be home helping your Ma with the work, not playing.' I am sure in her day there was not much playtime and lots of work. In order to avoid Grandma and play with my friend, I had to climb up the mountain to the right of the Bulls Head go down the other side and come out on the Ashby mine dump right above my friends' house. It was a lot of work and not much play time after a long climb, Grandma Collins always seemed to catch me on my way home anyway."

Back in the early winter when I was ski patrolling at Loveland Basin the ski patrol received a call that a big slide from the Seven Sisters Slide on Loveland Pass had swept across Highway 6 possibly burying several cars. This was just past the Loveland Basin ski area parking lot. The ski patrol set up a probe line and it wasn't long before one of the probe poles hit something about seven feet below the surface. Dave Collins was following the ski patrol probe line with a steel shovel, and furiously dug down to a side window and we were able to rescue alive the two very frightened women passengers trapped inside their car. Dave was 64 years old at the time and a lift operator at the ski resort. I'm sure he was driven by the memory of his brother Eddie killed in the slide just a few miles east of Loveland Pass.

Dave's and Eddie's nephew was also caught in an avalanche while working on the Vail Ski Patrol. Gerry Haskins and I are cousins and as close as brothers and both went to the same college at the same time, worked on the Loveland and Vail Ski Patrols, and have a lifetime of shared family, friends, and stories. Gerry that day was working with an avalanche control team of the Vail Ski Patrol out in the China Bowl area, and I was assigned to the team of Vail Ski Patrolmen providing protection to President Ford alongside the Secret Service.

That bluebird Colorado morning I was riding up the mountain on a chairlift with one of the Secret Service Agents. We were in the lead of the Presidential detail and I was wearing a radio earpiece in one ear monitoring the Vail Ski Patrol radio channel, and another one in my other ear listening to the Secret Service channel for the protective detail. The Ski Patrol channel came alive with an urgent transmission that a Vail Patrolman was caught in an avalanche off the top of China Bowl Cornice (now known as Genghis Khan), one of the largest slide paths in the Back Bowls of Vail!

The avalanche patrol leader on the team, standing at the top, was giving a live two-way radio play-by-play account of a huge avalanche hurtling down the mountain carrying Gerry with it. The cornice on which he was standing had broken off behind him and he had already dropped about 20 feet straight down with the huge broken chunk of cornice and causing an avalanche on the steep slope beneath the overhanging cornice (a cornice is a buildup of wind driven snow). He was helplessly trapped in the rapidly tumbling snow and travelling at a very high rate of speed down the steep mountain side. "He's in view flying past the trees on the downhill left hand side of the slide; he's disappeared under the snow; he's popped up; he went out of sight again; I see his arm, on and on like this for what seemed an eternity." I began silently praying a Hail (Ave) Mary and pleading for Mary's intercession to save Gerry so we wouldn't have another avalanche victim in our family. "He's surfaced again! He is sitting on top of the avalanche sliding on his butt. THANKFULLY the slide is going past him!"

Gerry was able to drag his hands and feet to slow down enough to allow the slide to release him from its grip. Clearing his mouth of the snow and trying to get his breath getting up slowly and feeling like he had been run over by a train, he waved back to his ski patrol team mates back on top that he was alive!

I think the late Eddie Collins, Grandma Collins, and especially his late mother Marguerite, and Grandma Hickey were all praying for Gerry on that bluebird day! Gerry was spared to also ski on the protection ski patrol detail for President Ford and on the protection detail for then Prime Minister Pierre Trudeau of Canada, who specifically requested that Gerry ski with him. We were all lucky to have Gerry survive one of the biggest avalanches in Vail's China Bowl!

As I was riding up the mountain listening to the play- by- play of the slide with one radio plugged into one ear and tuned to the ski patrol frequency and another radio plugged into the Secret Service frequency and riding with Secret Service Agent Perry, who I let know what was being transmitted on patrol's frequency. The other ski patrolmen who also were listening into the patrol frequency relayed the information to President Ford and to the following lift chairs in the detail. We were all silently praying for Gerry. When I heard that Gerry had escaped from the terrifying slide, I was just so thankful to God and filled with joy and emotion I started waving my ski poles. Lucky for me that the agents didn't shoot me! They probably would have if they weren't celebrating themselves! They all knew Gerry from his recent days also being assigned to the President's protective detail and he was highly liked and respected by everyone on the United States Secret Service detail.

L to R ski patrolmen are: Don (Dozer) Johnson, Joe Macy, Bill Hudson, Dick Peterson, Jim (Jake) Jacobsgaard, Brian McCartney, Chuck Malloy, obscured unknown, President Gerald R. Ford, Vince Ferraro, and far right my cousin, Gerry Haskins. The picture was taken at Vail Ski Patrol Headquarters on of top of Vail Mountain in Vail, Colorado. *Vail Associates Photo*

***

The Buckley family experienced a major blow and sad but also happy news that Grandma Buckley after living a very full and a very rewarding and challenging life passed onto the Lord, Who answered her prayers that long ago day in Silver Plume's St. Patrick's Church.

"Mrs. Alice Buckley, Mother and Founder of Famed Family
Corporation," Dies at 85:
Rocky Mountain News
(By *Joseph Emerson Smith*)

"Clear Creek County lost a widely known pioneer in the death of Mrs. Alice Buckley, 85, of Silver Plume. Friday, November 21, 1947, at the home of a daughter, Mrs. Alice (Leonard) Reichwein, 415 South Clay Street, Denver. Her life story of unusual achievement has been the subject of newspaper articles; and last May the Rocky Mountain News featured her in a full page as Colorado's outstanding mother.

She was born in Nevadaville, November 8, 1862 where Daniel Griffin had brought his young bride, Ellen Short, from St. Joseph, Mo. The following May, while attempting to rescue his mining partner from being shanghaied into the army, Griffin was shot and killed by a provost marshal. The widow married Owen Feenan who, prospecting on Republican mountain, above where Silver Plume now stands, discovered a promising silver claim. Returning to his work in a mine at Central City, he was so seriously injured by the fall of the bucket that, in the belief he was dying, the secret was disclosed to Thomas McCunniff, a friend, who promised Feenan he would take care of the wife and Alice, his stepdaughter.

Feenan recovered, but by that time McCunniff developed the discovery into the famous Pelican mine. He placed Mrs. Feenan in charge of the miner's boarding place, the Pelican House, and employed her husband as the driver of an ore wagon. Alice married Jeremiah Buckley, after attending St. Mary's Academy in Denver, and helped him build a transportation business. When he died March 6, 1909, the decline of mining just about emptied Silver Plume of its population, and the widow, with small means, faced the problem of how to provide a livelihood for her young children, eight sons and five daughters.

She formed a 'family corporation' to provide the village with food, fuel, shelter, and transportation. William Francis, the oldest son and Jerry took over the livery stable; with their wagons they brought in down timber which was cut into firewood. James D., showing interest in store keeping, worked in the meat market after school. The other boys obtained jobs while keeping on with school. All turned their wages into the corporation pool. Hay, grain, coal, was added to the livery business. Raymond was a night watchman at the Mendota Mine. John worked for Dick Milne, blacksmith, horseshoer and wheelwright in Georgetown. This kept them out of debt, taught thrift, honor and kindness. James and Raymond saw service in the First World War. On their return, the Buckley Brothers Corporation started a grocery and meat market, a dynamite and powder agency, and branched out into the automobile business. Today they have a large sales agency and complete auto repair establishment in Denver, operated by Raymond and Robert Buckley, the explosive branch sells over eight states and is operated by James; John has his auto business at Georgetown; Jerry has the transportation end; Ronald and Edmund run the grocery and meat market and look after the oil business in Silver Plume. William, county commissioner, died June 11, 1945. Elsie, a daughter, died in 1918.

Mother Buckley saw to it during the years that her boys and girls had plenty of play to offset the hard work. The Buckley Brothers baseball team, eight brothers playing, is still remembered in the county. Her daughters, all married, are excellent cooks and housewives. The children were taught music, vocal and instrumental.

Her health began to fail a year ago. In October she was taken to Denver. Requiem Mass was said at St. Dominic's Church Monday morning and internment was at Mt. Olivet. Eight priests were in the chancel, among them Rev. Christopher Walsh, formerly pastor at Georgetown, and Rev. Francis Potempa pastor of Idaho Springs and Central City. Fathers Harold B. Campbell, Manus P. Boyle, Richard Heister, Charles Jones, John Moran, and Michael Maher were present. The great church was filled, many coming from Clear Creek County. Father Walsh in his sermon expatiated on her victories over apparently insurmountable obstacles, her faith and piety, her charities, and the influence she exerted in the community.

Mrs. Buckley is survived by her seven sons, Jerry, James, Raymond, Robert, John, Edmund, and Ronald, and four daughters- Alice, Ellen(Nell), Bernadette, and Eloise. There are 24 grandchildren, six great grandchildren, and one great-great grandchild." *Rocky Mountain News.*

I have a hope chest filled with newspaper articles and pictures of the family, mostly accolades about Alice Buckley, her sons, the Silver Plume baseball team, the Buckley Store, the other business ventures, and the Buckley brothers' accomplishments. But missing is anything for Alice Buckley's five daughters and it seems strange to me now going through the memorabilia for this story of my family and knowing how really special were my aunts. My father was the eleventh child out of thirteen and the seventh boy which means that he had 10 other siblings older than him and two younger. My father had such great esteem for his sisters who were much more than just sisters. They were his caregivers when he was a baby, and a young child, especially when his mother was busy having two more babies and the responsibilities of managing 13 children and a husband.

After his father died when he was only seven, his mother had to be overwhelmed. Of course there was the deep grief she felt from the loss of her husband, but she also had a house full of children, many of whom did not understand what had happened, and all needed to be reassured that they would all survive this tragedy and continue to be loved and cared for. It was the "cared for" part that her daughters were essential to the family, They had to roll up their sleeves a little higher and tend to the younger kids and all their needs, help in the kitchen, clean the house, wash and dry the clothes without the modern appliances, clean the floors and stairs, and spend little time on themselves and their own grief. There was no fame or glory in this- just hard work and love. When the boys were older they would eat first on the limited sized table and after they ate their meal, which was prepared by Ma Buckley with the girls assisting, the girls could sit and eat. All the boys insisted that their vegetables be served on separate plates, a habit they carried into adulthood.

The girls were last to eat and then responsible for hand washing and drying the dishes. They tried to live *Matthew 22:34-40*: **The Greatest Commandment,** "When the Pharisees heard that he had silenced the Sadducees, they gathered together, and one of them tested him by asking, Teacher, which commandment in the law is the greatest? He said to him, "You shall love the Lord, your God, with all your heart, with all your soul, and with all your mind. This is the greatest and the first commandment. The second is like it: You shall love your neighbor as yourself. The whole law and the prophets depend on these two commandments." My dad knew how important his sisters were to the Buckley Brothers, even if they got little credit, and loved them all dearly.

While the brothers were out doing the "business" work, the girls were the support team. Reflecting the endless hours the girls and Ma Buckley were in the kitchen cooking and baking, innocently one night my dad inquired, "What kind of pie for dinner?" He received the curt reply from his tired Ma from cooking all day. "It's pie damn ya eat it!" Ma Buckley's total trust in God was passed down to her children and grandchildren, as well as her delicious pie recipes!

Top row from left are the Buckley Brothers: Will, Ed, Jerry, John, and Ray, bottom row from left: are Jim, Alice (Ma Buckley), Ron, and Bob.

Ma Buckley and daughters Alice, Eloise, and Bernadette
(missing in picture are Ellen and Elsie)

Will and Jim Buckley

Verona Chapel, Eva Buckley (Will's wife),
Josie Marshal, and Alice Buckley

Avalanche demolished and buried many homes in
Silver Plume west of red brick school house.

Ed Buckley is standing by the Buckley Bros. truck
which later broke a bridge over Clear Creek.

Bob Buckley is standing next to a monument in the Black Hills near Custer, South Dakota while delivering a load of dynamite for Buckley Brothers. The plaque reads, "General Custer camped here July 1874."

Custer's Dakota Expedition included 1000 soldiers from the Seventh Cavalry, 110 covered wagons, 70 Indian scouts, 4 reporters, and **two gold miners**. The Black Hills had been invaded and the Treaty of 1868 broken purposefully because the government of President Grant wished to take the land from the Sioux, Cheyenne, and Arapahoe Tribes. Gold was discovered on this expedition leading to another gold rush, but Indians were few and far between. Custer found them two years later in July on the Little Big

Horn River in Montana!

"Over the next hundred years, more gold would be extracted from a single mine in the Black Hills (estimated $1 billion) than any other mine in the continental United States.(*The Last Stand*, by Nathaniel Philbrick)

**Will Buckley who ran Buckley and Sons Livery
after his father's death.**

Bob Buckley, left, heard the cry of a small child below the avalanche debris. The child and her mother were found alive under the kitchen table. The child is later the mother of Rich and Ron Lane. Rich was my Ski Patrol Director at Loveland Basin and Ron is a very good friend from early age, and a brave and lucky combat Vet who survived in Vietnam's jungle and rice paddies. He still suffers from the defoliant Agent Orange.

Will Buckley is standing by wagon and Windsor Hotel where Mary Collins, Grandma Hickey, and family lived. What's with the car?

Bob Buckley Sr. found a truck load of pretty girls in front of the Kneisel & Anderson Store in Georgetown, Colorado. This store is family run and still in operation today.

CHAPTER 7
Moving On

The torch of life had been passed from Grandma Hickey to her daughters Alice and Mary and then down to their children, grandchildren, and great-grandchildren. Family names are always important, but in my immediate family there was a big element of confusion where names are concerned. My father and mother, Bob Sr. and Donna Buckley, bear the same names as myself and my wife, Donna. What are the odds of that happening? My mother came from a long line of five girls, with mom being the youngest, and was surprised by a boy when my oldest brother was born.

He was named Robert Gary Buckley after our dad, but strangely he was called by his middle name. But after having three successive boys she thought it was important to give one of her boys the full name of her husband, so I became Robert Emmet Buckley Jr. and was called Bobby. Gary has a daughter he named after mom. So the official name count was three Roberts and three Donnas. Call out either name and you would get someone, maybe just not who you were planning on. Gary was eight years older and has passed away and is buried alongside mom and dad in the Silver Plume cemetery.

Curious visitors that know me will think it is me that is buried there. My other brother, Donald Edmund, is 5 years older than me and much wiser and smarter - at least that is what he has always told me. During the sixties after college my brother Gary joined the Air Force and my brother Don joined the Colorado Air National Guard. My sister Sheila graduated from Colorado University and I graduated from Regis University in Denver.

My dad and his older brother Jim were operating the Buckley Store up on Main Street in Silver Plume where dad met a cute 18 year old blonde tourist from the flatlands of Kansas. Love at first sight, they soon were married on March 10, 1935 in Wichita. My mom found it difficult adjusting to being walled in by the high mountains towering over both sides of Silver Plume and being sometimes isolated by the scary road up Clear Creek Canyon which was a very narrow and twisting mostly one lane dirt road all which inevitably made the flatlander nervous. It was not uncommon for the road to be closed due to avalanches, rock and mud slides and cautious drivers had to always keep a wary eye out for falling rocks and mountain lions crossing the narrow road. The road followed the old Ute trail which had been widened to one and two car lanes where permitted which wasn't often and driving around blind corners the horn was sounded loudly to warn oncoming traffic. Backing up to a widened area was the only solution to a standoff. I have a picture of the Buckley Brothers truck carrying a load of logs over one of the wooden bridges over Clear Creek with the front end of the truck having made it over the creek onto the roadway and the rear of the truck and the broken timber bridge resting in the creek. My Uncle Will was driving, and his wife Eva and brother Ron were along for the excitement! *I know my aunt had to be hysterical; I lived with her in Silver Plume when I was a Loveland Basin ski patrolman and she was a nervous wreck when we drove to Denver on the dry modern roads!*

It didn't take my mom long to know that Ma Buckley ran the Buckley Brothers businesses and she and Dad had to account for every penny spent on their own personal things. Between feeling penned in by the towering mountains and the long cold winters and her every move judged by her mother-in-law across the street, she wasn't too happy about life in Silver Plume. She did make some very exceptional friends in Silver Plume. Verona Chapel, Josie Marshall, and Vivian Rowe were sitting in the parlor with mom when her first born toddler, Gary, was admonished from putting his hands again into the candy serving dish. My brother looked at her and then smiling leaned over the plate with his hands behind his back and put a piece of candy in his mouth. Verona admonished my mother not to dare spank him! This would not be Verona's first time over the years to come to the rescue.

If you have ever seen the TV sitcom "*Everybody Loves Raymond*," mom was like Deborah whose nosey mother-in-law, Marie, was always critical of everything that Deborah would do or say. My young mother exerted great pressure on my dad to join his older brother Ray in the car business in Denver when asked, not because she was just feeling trapped by Silver Plume's 9100 foot elevation above sea level and its steep surrounding peaks, and having to drive down to Denver through twisting rock canyon walls on the narrow dirt road. One time she bragged that she must have set a world speed record escaping through the canyon to Denver.

The highway above Silver Plume wasn't much better than the road through Clear Creek Canyon. The road was still very narrow and the wooden bridges were only wide enough for a single vehicle and not built for heavy loads as demonstrated by the Buckley Brothers truck which collapsed the wooden bridge carrying what would be considered a fairly light load.

Will, wife Eva, and brother, Ron learned
not to trust the wooden bridges crossing Clear Creek!

The newly weds, Bob and Donna Buckley, hiked up the Seven-Thirty Mine Road to the **Clifford Griffin Monument** overlooking Silver Plume far below. The Seven-Thirty mine road was the same steep winding road that my young father delivered supplies to the mines above Silver Plume for Buckley Brothers Livery. The Town of Silver Plume is sandwiched in the valley between the high mountains in the background of the picture and the high mountains on the Monument's side of the Valley on Republican Mountain. A classic avalanche path is seen in the background.

If you are from the flatlands of Kansas as my mother, a real sense of clausterphobia can develop! Especially when the drive to Denver and the wide-open prairie was a scary trip. There were no two lane paved roads or tunnels and strong bridges or I-70 back then down to Denver. Mom felt stifled and short of breath by the cold thin air and a mother-in-law that kept track of every dime she would spend!

Buckley Bros. Motors was formed and judging from the fact that my uncle and dad were partners for over 35 years in business and never had a major disagreement would say much for their upbringing and my mom's perseverance to live where she could breathe freely! Their dealership was located at 660 South Broadway in Denver across the street from the Merchants Park baseball field and was originally a Studebaker dealership. Dad was proud of the fact that his grandparents had crossed the prairie in a Conestoga Covered Wagon built by Studebaker, and in his show room he had a picture of a Conestoga wagon. **My cousin Sharon Haskins Kennedy has two wooden stools that Dan and Ellen Griffin used on their covered wagon journey to Colorado.** And when Studebaker folded its tent Buckley Brothers Motors became a Mercedes Benz dealership and a Toyota dealership. My father worked literally night and day providing for his family; and the Buckley chart of doing business that was written years ago was the foundation of Buckley Bros. Motors' business plan.

I can't help but think back fondly about growing up in the fifties and sixties. I didn't have to watch someone else's sad version of reality on TV. Wholesome TV shows abounded and you didn't have to have parental blocks. *Leave It to Beaver, Father Knows Best, Ozzie and Harriet, What's My Line, Gene Autry, Roy Rogers, and the Ed Sullivan Show,* and my parents' favorite, *Bishop Sheen's "Life is worth Living"* were some of the popular shows then. Of course, special just for the kids, was the unforgettable *Howdy Doody!* But my favorite was *Sea Hunt* with Lloyd Bridges and it kindled in a Colorado mountain child an early interest in the ocean.

Kids could ride their bikes to friends' houses and play in parks until dark without fear. Kick the can and hide and go seek were nightly affairs. The kids in Silver Plume would play on the Town's bandstand and climb up to the Bull's Head and crawl on the smooth grandma's cradle behind the old stone jail. My father and my uncles Jim and Ray, retired members of the famed Silver Plume baseball team, had box seats behind the first base dugout and every home game of the Denver Bears their seats were full with

Buckley children sporting their baseball gloves hoping to catch a foul ball. The Denver Bears were a Triple AAA farm team of the New York Yankees starting in the mid-fifties and I became a lifelong Yankee fan by watching future stars in Denver like Bobby Richardson, Tony Kubek, Marv Throneberry, Don Larsen, Ryne Duren, Ralph Terry, and manager Ralph Houk who all moved up to the Yankees. Elvis Pressley and Pat Boone and the Everly Brothers sang the songs I liked to hear on my bedside radio while I was daydreaming about the girls in my grade school classes. The kids from this generation grew up to be called "baby boomers" because there was a huge increase in the birth rate of babies and 4,000,000 babies born yearly. For the most part we were blessed to be living in a peace time strong economy without hunger or a great depression. World War II was over but the Cold War and Korea were present dangers. In the early 1950's Leroy Buckley was the eldest child of my uncle John who owned the Buckley Garage in Georgetown and when I was very young, I remember Leroy leaving for Korea and my parents praying for his safety. Leroy's sister Phyllis was the pride and joy of the entire Buckley family studying to become a doctor and growing up in Georgetown.

When Leroy safely returned from Korea he worked for my uncle driving the Georgetown Buckley Garage tow truck and one cold winter night Leroy was driving over Loveland Pass to help a stranded motorist in the midst of a whiteout blizzard when his tow truck was hit by a huge avalanche from the Seven Sisters slide on the east side of Loveland Pass. His tow truck was swept off the road like it was a toy and rolling end over end until stopping at the bottom of the slide path trapping a bleeding Leroy in his truck. Buried under compacted snow at the bottom of the slide path, the tall lean six-footer stuck a rag in his bleeding neck wound and hand over hand tunneled out of the slide and crawled back up to the roadway. Luckily a highway patrolman found him there unconscious but still barely breathing!

On another occasion in 1980 he was struck by a car while putting chains on a car marooned in a blizzard between Silver Plume and the Pass. He was saved by a passerby car of Black Americans who would take turns lying on top of Leroy in the brutally cold temperatures keeping him warm until an ambulance arrived. Leroy was severely injured with multiple fractures and serious internal injuries, but he later recovered well enough that he and his loving wife, Vivian, put both of their sons John and David through college. I remember that Leroy faithfully shoveled out our Aunt Eva, Will Buckley's widow, in Silver Plume when there was new snow covering her walkways to the road and to the coal barn in the back of the house. No matter how deep the snow Leroy could always be depended on to deliver coal and the propane gas from the Buckley Garage to Aunt Eva to keep her house warm!

Leroy Buckley

He was a third generation Colorado pioneer living the pioneer spirit in the 20th century building his family and businesses in the heart of Colorado snow country. He flirted with death twice in his 76 years. Once surviving a massive snow slide on Loveland Pass that demolished his tow truck and in 1980 overcoming all odds to recover from a near fatal hit and run accident while helping a stranded motorist on I-70. In the community, he retired as a volunteer fireman after 20 years of service and received the Georgetown Citizen of the Year award in 1990. He was a man of great faith passed down through the generations from Grandma Hickey, Grandma Buckley, and his mom and dad, my aunt Ivy and Uncle John being an inspiring example of faith, integrity, hard work, humility, and compassion for the entire Buckley family and the many who knew him. Leroy's death came suddenly as the Hepatitis C that he contracted, from an emergency blood transfusion after the 1980 accident, finally overcame him. Leroy was remembered at his overflowing funeral service in Our Lady of Lourdes Catholic Church in Georgetown by many of the town folks grateful for the countless times he pulled them out of a snowbank, repaired their cars, and when it was time to pay would say, "Leave ten bucks on the counter!" Or more often than not, just say, "No charge." And that is what he said to me when I picked up my Jeep which ran like new after he tuned the engine!

Leroy Buckley was quietly generous and much beloved in Georgetown by the town folks and by the entire Buckley family, and especially by his loving wife Vivian and devoted sons John and David, and his beautiful daughter-in-law Laurie, and grand- children Sean, Emily, and Anna. He always loved helping people whether after a difficult accident in a blizzard, or washing the bugs off their windshield on a warm summer day, or repairing a difficult automotive problem. He attended Regis University, my alma mater, as well as Denver University.

When my family moved to Denver we lived in a tall three bedroom house on 26th Avenue and St. Paul Street, just across from the Denver City Park Golf Course. The house lent itself to my older brothers' shenanigans when my parents were away and Verona was down from Silver Plume and taking care of the four of us. Sometimes Verona would innocently answer the front door and be confronted by angry winter drivers loudly complaining that they had been hit by a barrage of snowballs emanating from the backside of the house and wanting to find and report the unseen culprits guilty of throwing the snowballs presumed from the backyard. Verona innocently and unsuspecting would point out to the rightfully angry motorists that the boys were upstairs doing their homework. She then would call out upstairs to my older brothers who would politely answer, "What can we do for you, Verona?" Unbeknownst to Verona, there was an overhead trapdoor in my sister, Sheila's closet to an attic which had a dormer window opening onto a small flat roof on the backside of the house- a natural snowball throwing area for tossing up over the peaked roof to 26th Avenue below. My brothers had dialed in the range.

Another time that Verona was taking care of us when I was five and my 10 year old brother, Donny, made a child-like stuffed dummy and placed it at the bottom of our long steep driveway awkwardly twisted underneath my overturned tricycle and smeared with ketchup. We hid in the bushes and watched as a car pulled over on St. Paul Street and a crying woman and her husband approached what she thought was a badly injured child. Her laughing husband carefully picked up the dummy and the two carried the injured dummy to the back door and rang the bell. Verona looked at the dummy and knew instantly the two culprits behind the stunt. We were caught "red handed!" By the funny look on Verona's face when she was looking at us, she knew **the real dummies**. Growing up with Black Bob in Silver Plume, she also knew that apples didn't fall far from the tree!

One episode in 1957 which highlights the forgiving nature of Verona and the sharp wit of my older brother Don was when four of my fellow 12 year old buddies and I decided that we would take Donny's pride and joy 6 cylinder spotless used 1954 Studebaker Champion out for a little spin around the neighborhood. He was at work and had driven my parent's car to work as mom and dad were on a business sponsored trip. Unfortunately for me, my older brother took the Friday afternoon off from his job as an assistant service manager at Buckley Bros. Motors. It wasn't exactly like I was the only driver because my friend Ronnie was working the clutch, brake, and gas pedal while I handled the steering wheel and the shift lever. About three blocks from home I heard a car loudly honking its horn.

Uh! Oh! I pulled over and it wasn't long before Donny was opening the driver's side of the door and with a- **I gotcha-** grin on his face announced, "End of your joy ride boys. Give me the keys. You can walk home!" He bought his shiny 1954 Studebaker Champion for a great price off Buckley Brothers used car lot. It was like brand new and his pride and joy. Even today he still thinks of it as his favorite car. Lucky for me I didn't cause any damage or get it dirty! But even luckier for me was that I was protected by Verona who was caring for us while my parents were away. But for insurance, I locked my brother downstairs while he was cleaning up.

On another occasion that my parents were away and Verona was taking care of us, both Don and Gary bought the exact same color and style of shoes on the same day from the wholesaler that Buckley Brothers used for the Silver Plume Store. Neither knew that the other had been to the wholesaler and had bought the same style shoes. Gary got home from his job and stopped Don in the living room on his way out of the house and told him to "take my new shoes off." Gary had finally had it with his younger brother repeatedly wearing his clothes without asking. Donny replied that he was "wearing his new shoes and he wasn't taking them off." Next thing, Gary tried to physically remove the shoes and Donny and he ended up wrestling in the living room. Younger brother Don finally pinned his older brother on the floor. Sheila and I were spectators, and I thought Verona was going to have a heart attack!

Thinking it was over and he was late for his date, Don started for the front door when his brother spun him around and placed his nose under his right eye. Bleeding all over the place he and Gary went down to their basement bathroom and tried to stop the bleeding. Down in his bedroom Gary discovered **his** shoes where he left them earlier in the day. By this time very remorseful but belatedly, Gary took Don to the doctors to straighten his nose. Of course, my mom and dad returned that day from their trip to witness Verona cleaning up the blood on the floor. Our sister Sheila met my parents at the front door to warn them of the altercation and bloody scene. Verona thought it was quite amusing that my brothers had bought the same shoes unbeknownst to each other and assured my folks that there was just a small fracas and not to worry.

I followed my older brother Don into working for my dad in the summers after I turned 16 and between semesters at Regis Jesuit High School. After attending summer school at the Colorado School of Mines, I had been accepted to work as a Loveland Basin Ski Patrolman starting in December. So I was still an auto part shag boy for my father's parts department at Buckley Bros. Motors on November 22, 1963.

I remember, as if it were yesterday, returning back to Buckley Bros. Motors and having an interruption over my truck's radio tuned to KIMN rock and roll radio station blaring loudly the latest pop hit, the announcement that President Kennedy had been shot in Dallas, Texas. Arriving back at the business just minutes later, I went to inform my dad who was in his office in a meeting with a German Mercedes Benz factory representative. I interrupted them, apologizing, but I thought they would want to hear what I had just heard on the radio minutes earlier. My dad always had time for me no matter what he was doing, so he waved me into his office introducing me to this big burly German who spoke with a strong accent.

I told both of them that President Kennedy had been shot in the head and taken to a hospital in Dallas. Immediately the German began saying: "Gut, Gut! I hope he is dead!" My dad and I were both stunned both by the news and his reaction. My Irish Catholic father coolly responded, "This meeting is over!"

I enrolled at Regis University the next year after ski patrolling at Loveland Basin Ski Resort for the winter and living in Silver Plume with my widowed Aunt Eva who was a retired school teacher. Her family had immigrated to Eagle, Colorado from Montreal, Canada when Aunt Eva was just a small child and speaking fluent French. In my junior year at Regis College I enrolled in advanced French after learning that I would need one year of a modern language before I could graduate and this was the only class still open to me. But I wanted to speak French with Serge Coutet, the Loveland Basin Ski School Director, and my Aunt Eva.

It was by lucky chance that I had Professor Dr. Charlotte Donsky, a French immigrant who had married an American serviceman and moved to the U.S. after the war with her GI husband. For some reason she took me and another transfer student named John under her wing and privately tutored us, understanding we were going to be lost trying to keep up in her advanced French language class. We would join her at lunch for our extra tutoring, and at one of our lunch lessons we encountered a quietly sobbing and shaking professor. She was totally distressed after being in her office and one of the German professors in her office was talking in German to another German speaking man who had replied to Dr. Donsky in an angry tone evoking a flashback memory of her childhood in occupied France. Her fear was registering in every muscle of her face and shaking body. I was reminded of the German Mercedes Benz factory representative.

My teacher's unwanted flashback was to a very fearful time in her youth hiding from the German Gestapo who had rounded up most of her Jewish family, including her father along with many of his immediate family to never be seen again. He came from a family with thirteen children and her mother a family of six children. Over a hundred family members were lost with only four survivors, including Charlotte and her mother. Just before Charlotte died, she finally broke her silence after hearing someone claim that the Jewish Holocaust was a hoax, and before she died she recorded her frightening experiences, *"Let me tell you about the Holocaust*(Marc Donsky, her son)! She and her mother were hidden from the authorities and masqueraded as Christians constantly frightened and warily looking over their shoulders. Dr. Charlotte Donsky, at Regis Jesuit University in Denver, would not have enjoyed meeting the Mercedes Benz factory representative nor would she have tolerated a comment made to me by a Jesuit Padre on Punlap Island that the Holocaust was a hoax! I am sure she didn't hear anything that ignorant at Regis which is a Jesuit University. I know I didn't!

My senior year events in Southeast Asia were daily in the news with the 1968 Tet Offensive and mounting casualty figures for Americans killed in combat. The students in my graduating class of 1968 were from all over the country and holding draft cards which exempted them from military service, for the time being. Suddenly after graduation it was another matter! The odds were high that if a Regis University student wasn't headed to graduate school, law school, medical school, or the seminary he had to seriously think about enlisting in one of the armed services. It was almost certain he was going to be drafted and likely headed to a very deadly war zone in Vietnam, or quit like the many thousands who had already fled to Canada.

I was forced to think about the near term future after graduating in June of 1968 from Regis! The young men and women of my generation were sent to fight a war in faraway jungles and cities of Vietnam! *What's my Line's* Garry Moore might have said, "Will the **real lying politician** (the war monger label was tagged on Barry Goldwater in the 1964 presidential campaign) please stand up!" *You Bet Your Life* that a loud Texan who spoke with a **forked tongue stood tall**! Chief Black Kettle would have recognized **President Johnson** who must have been asleep when President Kennedy spoke in his Inaugural Address, "To those new states whom we welcome to the ranks of the free, we pledge our word that one form of colonial control shall not have passed away to be replaced by a far more iron tyranny. We shall not always expect to find them supporting our view. But we shall always hope to find them strongly supporting their own freedom-and to remember, that in the past, **those who foolishly sought power by riding the back of the tiger ended up inside."**

Pat Hannon (August 03, 1946 to September 04, 1966) was a classmate of mine at Regis and a native of Littleton, Colorado. Pat was a marine and shot through the neck and killed in combat in Vietnam and his death certainly made the draft question very real for his classmates. (Patrick J Hannon is on the Vietnam War Memorial Wall at Panel 10E, Line 67.)

The 1960's was an amazing decade for America with revolutions in music, pop culture, politics, war, body bags, violent demonstrations in the streets, race riots, burning cities, assassinations, the Beatles, The Graduate, Creedence Clearwater Rival, the sexual revolution, and successful peaceful demonstrations leading to de-segregation. Nearing graduation from college in 1968, I thought that odds were really high that such a small mountain county, Central City's Gilpin County, would probably make me immediately available to be inducted into the military soon after graduation.

That winter there was a Peace Corps display in our Student Union Building and pausing on my way to lunch, I browsed at the brochures and took up a casual conversation with the recruiter standing by his display. Ironically there was a peaceful anti-war prayer vigil taking place at the same time in the lobby where the recruiter's display was standing. The recruiter was a Returned Peace Corps Volunteer (RPCV) who could answer from his own personal experiences in the Peace Corps the many questions that I and other students had for him.

Later in the afternoon he was holding a test and an application session for anyone who was interested. Definitely I was intrigued by this new opportunity and later returned to fill out the application and take his test, along with a roomful of other interested seniors. The test was mostly a timed language aptitude examination demonstrating an ability to learn a new language. You had to memorize a made up and unrecognizable vocabulary in a time certain and translate a dialogue written in the very strange vocabulary. Not new to me after taking advanced French.

You also had to sign a release that allowed the FBI to do a background check. The Peace Corps application asked me to choose three countries which interested me, and I listed Micronesia first, after looking at all of the handouts and listening to the recruiter. I placed Nepal as my second choice, and then as my third, South America. Peace Corps Service was only a temporary deferment for the Selective Service for the years served in the Peace Corps. I was very attracted and fascinated by the proposition of helping people and was a young altruistic admirer of the Peace Corps and President John Kennedy's "**New Frontier.**" About a month later I received an invitation letter to the Micro Seven Peace Corps Staging in Escondido, California in early June. Until the Peace Corps recruiter had come to Regis University, I didn't know or was aware of the word Micronesia and now I am heading there! What a world of surprises in the midst of such confusion and violence to find yourself graduating from college.

Micronesia was a collection of 2000 plus small islands which had been colonial holdings of Spain, Germany, and Japan. America occupied the Spanish Island holdings after the Spanish/American War. At the start of World War I, Japan's powerful navy took the Truk Lagoon from Germany, and later The League of Nations created a South Pacific Mandate to be administered by Japan for the remaining German holdings after World War I. After World War II, the U.S. Navy initially administered the Japanese held islands from a base on Guam. In 1947, the United Nations formally established a strategic Trust Territory of the Pacific Islands to be administered by The United States Department of Interior from Saipan in the Marianas. The Trust Territory of Micronesia encompassed more than 3,000,000 miles of Pacific Ocean extending from Polynesia to the Marianas Islands.

Some Democrats stood up to President Johnson, and were opposing him in the 1968 presidential primary election, including Democrat Senators Eugene McCarthy, and President Johnson's outspoken nemesis, Robert F. Kennedy, forcing the unpopular President to step aside in 1968. A fellow Regis student and I witnessed Bobby Kennedy's motorcade in springtime Denver being mobbed by a predominately African American crowd. He was standing up on the back seat of the convertible with Olympian Rafer Johnson and waving and brushing his shock of auburn hair from his blue eyes. His limo slowed down about 20 feet right in front of where I was standing with my friend and the surging crowd forced it to a stop, completely surrounded by the excited crowd. Our presidential political candidates are exposed to extreme physical danger and hoping that this charismatic leader would avoid his brother's fate that day in Denver.

The friendly crowd must have remembered how he had reached out to another mostly African American crowd of 5000 in Indianapolis after learning of Martin Luther King's assassination. Bobby Kennedy spoke from his heart as someone who knows from the pain of a white man killing his own brother. He spoke these words, "What we need in the United States is not division; what we need in the United States is not violence and lawlessness, but is love and wisdom, and compassion toward one another, and a feeling of justice toward those who still suffer within our country, whether they be white or whether they be black." And he quoted his favorite poet, "He who learns must suffer, and even in our sleep, pain that cannot forget falls drop by drop upon the heart, and in our own despair, against our will, comes wisdom to us by the awful Grace of God"(Aeschylus).

On June 5th, 1968 Robert Francis Kennedy was assassinated in Los Angeles, California. My parents, Bob and Donna Buckley, drove me down from Central City to the airport in Denver for my long departure on my two year Peace Corps assignment just days after his assassination. I must confess it was for me a bittersweet moment filled with anticipation for the Peace Corps experience before me and I wasn't likely going to see my mom and dad for two years! Also I had a very deep sadness in my heart for the sudden and tragic loss of Bobby Kennedy!

I had planned a stopover in Fresno, California before travelling onto Escondido, California and Micro 7 Peace Corps Staging. Pediatrician Phyllis Buckley, my cousin, and Dr. Al Reschke's wife, and mother of baby Shawna and older sister Terri was in the last days of her losing fight against cancer. Al had told me how much Phyllis was looking forward to my visit!

She put up an amazing fight trying everything that modern medicine could offer at the time including surgery, heavy chemo, and radiation. She had everything in her husband and children to live for and courageously waged her uphill fight. I saw her the summer before when she returned very sick to climb for the last time Grays and Torreys Peaks above Silver Plume, the two high beautiful mountain peaks. The two fourteeners were next to Mount Kelso where 19 year old Eddie Collins was killed in an avalanche, also near Mount McClelland where the Argentine Central Railroad climbed high touching the sky. The mountains were in her DNA as well as her ancestors who had made Colorado High Country home after emigrating from Ireland.

Her husband and partner in her pediatric practice, Dr. Al Reschke, met me at the airport, and on the way to the hospital informed me that Phyllis had fallen into a deep coma and wouldn't be able to communicate. Al and I entered her hospital room and we walked over to her bedside and to our mutual surprise and astonishment, Phyllis awakened and welcomed me with a weak smile. We then had a wonderful hour long conversation touching on our family and my upcoming Peace Corps opportunity. She recounted with me her climb the previous summer up Grays Peak(14,258'high) and Colorado's 10th highest peak and crossing the connecting ridge to Torreys (14,267'high), and slid down a snow field to the base of the two peaks, all on her bucket list before she died. Just weeks earlier before her incredible brave climb my Forest Service trail crew had maintained the Grays Peak Trail.

We also discussed her impending death and what it would mean for her two young daughters and husband. I felt a deep and profound gratitude for my recent Jesuit Education at Regis University and being able to share the wisdom of my senior year Theology Professor, Father Edward L. Maginnis, S.J. I know our private sharing was deeply appreciated by both Phyllis and her husband. I received a letter from Al in September thanking me for my taking the time to stop and meet with Phyllis who had died early in the morning on September 16.th He had been awakened from sleep by a Statue of Mary falling off Phyllis's dresser and breaking on their bedroom floor. Minutes later he received a call from the hospital that she had just died.

Phyllis is buried within a stone's throw of Grandma Hickey and next to her father and mother, John and Ivy Buckley, in the Silver Plume Cemetery.

Phyllis is holding Shawna and Al's holding Terri and the family puppy.

Don't Get Too Comfortable

BOOK TWO: PEACE CORPS YEARS-
THE MUSICAL

OUTRIGGER CANOE IN THE PISERAS ISLAND LAGOON

CHAPTER 8
Peace Corps Training

On a sunny a warm day in June of 1968, I arrived at the San Diego Airport and met up with some of the other Peace Corps candidates for the start of Micro 7. We boarded an old white school bus which took us up to the Escondido Peace Corps staging camp which was a former nudist colony. Approximately 700 of us were checked in and given our schedules for the next week of meetings and medical and dental appointments. A big part of the medical review was interviewing with Peace Corps psychiatrists; my interview was very casual and comfortable. Some others must have had a different experience and were gently eliminated in this process at Escondido. World War II and the Japanese occupation had stripped some of the Micronesian Islands of many century long held traditions and family anchors. I came to understand that there were some definite problems in the Western Pacific paradise! Consequently, there were some candidates that voluntarily removed themselves from the program at this early stage and some were asked to leave, including an attractive girl who had been raped in college. The Peace Corps psychiatrist thought some of the young men in Micronesia, in the event of drinking too much hard liquor (sakow), could easily cause a very frightening and dangerous flashback for her. I thought that it was a real loss and twice again an innocent victim, later I learned differently.

The assignments for the different districts and the programs we would be working in were given to us in Escondido. I was assigned to Truk (Chuuk) and the *TESL* program. *TESL* stands for Teaching English as a Second Language and most of the candidates were slated to be teachers. The other program was *Omnibus* which was for the engineers, lawyers, architects, carpenters, marine fishery, agricultural, and business specialists, mechanics, and other skilled professionals which would be useful in Micronesia. I was later transferred over to the Omnibus program because of my background working for the Forest Service as a trail construction crew boss. I personally thought that I would be better suited for some type of construction management, and I was pleased when the Peace Corps came to that same conclusion.

The medical doctors and dentists in town were kept busy all week, although some of their care was suspicious. I remember going to their dentist, as required, and the next thing you know I was having some of my teeth filled that I knew didn't have cavities. I had gone to my own very competent dentist at home and had received a clean bill of health. We were inoculated for every conceivable tropical disease, including *cholera,* which was rampant in Micronesia and would come to play a big part of my eventual service there.

I survived being cut or quitting at Staging and the day soon came when we were bussed up to Los Angeles (LAX) International Airport dressed in a mandatory suit and tie for the flight to Hawaii and then on to Guam. My group boarded a chartered stretch DC8 and flew to Hawaii. Aloha! This was my first time in Hawaii and during our short layover I remember drinking cups of complimentary fresh pineapple juice from a Dole pineapple stand and breathing in the warm fragrant air. I was tired, but excited, when we boarded the same jet for another long flight over the Pacific Ocean on to Guam.

After landing on Guam we were transported to Navy barracks at the Agana Naval Air Station to await our flights on Air Micronesia shuttling us to our respective districts in Micronesia. My flight schedule allowed for a couple days on Guam which was mostly spent playing tourist and doing some last minute shopping in the local stores. I bought a short wave Japanese transistor battery operated radio and a tape recorder and a raincoat. All the while on Guam noisy B-52 bombers were flying overhead to and from Vietnam on bombing runs from Anderson Air Force Base about thirty miles away on the opposite side of the island from the naval base.

It brought home to me the long distance the Vietnam War was from the American West Coast, about 8 thousand miles away from where I began my long flight. I heard that more bombs were dropped during the Vietnam War than were dropped on Germany and Japan combined during World War II, and many of those were dropped by the B-52s flying from Guam.

Travelling around Guam a taxi driver pointed out two separate military funerals of young Guamanian boys killed in Vietnam. I asked myself at the time whether it was because English was their second language and they didn't understand, "Duck" or "Watch out"! (70 boys from Guam were killed in Vietnam.) Also memorable was when I and three others hiked up a trail to the Talofofo Falls where a holdout Japanese soldier was hiding in a nearby cave. Four years later he was discovered by two Guamanian farmers that he made the mistake of attacking. He was quickly subdued.

Shoichi Yakoi had been living and hiding in the jungle cave near the falls for 28 years following the end of World War II. We must have walked right by his hiding place and thankfully didn't come upon the fanatical warrior from WW II who must have been relieved to have his lonely war come to an end. Later back in Japan, he was welcomed as a hero although he personally was ashamed and apologized that he didn't fight to the death for the Emperor.

Finally the time came to fly down to Truk (Chuuk) on Air Micronesia and begin Peace Corps training. After what seemed a short flight from Guam, our Boeing 727 flew low over the Truk Lagoon and I could see out of my window a few of the bombed Japanese ships partially submerged and rusting near the shore of Moen, the capital of the Truk District of Micronesia. Upwards of fifty sunken Japanese ships turned the lagoon into a graveyard of ships and men sunk during Operation Hailstone launched from American carriers February 17, 1944. The jet then buzzed over the postage stamp size packed coral runway to check the state of the art modern wind sock!

The jet airliner landed in cloud of dust and roar of the jet engines with full reverse thrusters and slamming on the brakes with loud unnerving rattling sounds inside the plane. It seemed like we were going to scream past the end of the runway and directly into the lagoon before we came to a screeching halt that pulled tightly against my seatbelt. What an exclamation point for finally arriving at the final leg of the long journey to Micronesia!

Moen was an extinct volcanic island and one of eleven within the world's largest natural lagoon. The Japanese turned the huge lagoon into a heavily fortified naval base in the Pacific- their Japanese Pearl Harbor. Upon stepping foot for the first time in Truk, I was struck by the humid heat which was unbearably hot for someone used to the high cool mountain air of Colorado and feeling like I had just survived a very close crash landing on the packed coral runway. Waiting around the small terminal in the hot sticky air was a delegation of Peace Corps staff and volunteers who welcomed us to the Island of Moen and the Truk (Chuuk) District Center. Looking around I didn't see Amelia Earhart in the crowd who I half suspected had been captured and taken to Truk during her worldwide flight over the Pacific Ocean in 1937 and would be among our friendly greeting party.

Our group of candidates hadn't yet reached our final destination that day. After gathering up our luggage we were transported by taxis, small Japanese pickups with small benches on the side of truck bed. We travelled on a mud-potholed dirt road to the harbor where we were all loaded onto a World War Two LST invasion landing craft for the trip over to Uman Island.

It was a slow boat ride and the fresh air of the open lagoon was welcome relief. Passing more rusting shattered boat hulks which had beached themselves in shallow sea water before sinking into the deep water of the lagoon, we finally reached our Peace Corps training Island. Uman (pronounced ooman) was truly beautiful from the LST and proved to be very pleasant once we landed.

After a smooth ride in the calm lagoon, we pulled up alongside a volcanic stone jetty which extended into the lagoon built to handle larger ships during the war. The LST's crew tied up and our hungry and thirsty group unloaded our suitcases. I was looking forward to getting something to eat and drink. We were welcomed by locals and Peace Corps staff and directed to tables in the grass school playground to handle the newcomers' host family introductions and were also given a training schedule. My host father, Fumuo, and his 13 year-old son Domingo, led me to their house just a short distance away where I would be living for the next two months of training assuming I wasn't sent home early.

I met a fellow Peace Corps candidate roommate who had preceded my arrival in our temporary quarters in Fumuo's family tin house. Whew! It was hot and muggy and I was famished and exhausted. So I asked my new roommate if there was any place I could get a bite to eat, "Go look for yourself, like I did when I first arrived!" Is this the Peace Corps way? So alone I walked back up to the school playground and soon found a Peace Corps cantina where I learned rice and canned mackerel were the standard fare for breakfast, lunch, and dinner.

This was immersion into a new culture without hot dogs, hamburgers, fries, and a coca cola and without English being spoken, modern roads, electricity, street lights, telephone, and modern plumbing. The Uman islanders were gracious and friendly to their new Peace Corps arrivals and while walking along the path little children would bravely walk up to me and say, "Ran anim (hello)" and happily run away giggling. Young boys and grown men would walk along the path customarily holding hands.

Peace Corps organized us into smaller groups according to the Trukese dialect we needed to learn. Later that afternoon, each assigned group met at one of the classrooms in the grade school with our Peace Corps Volunteer Advisor to begin our training sessions and to learn what to expect in training. Language classes started early the next morning and the teaching method would be much different from language classes in high school or college where grammar and sentence structure were just as important as actually learning to speak the language. The language instructor, we were warned, would pronounce a sentence or phrase and continually repeat it until everyone could repeat it back correctly, not worrying about the translation. "First you will memorize the dialogue and later learn the meaning. Later I learned that what I thought was just one word would in fact be a phrase.

We would not be taught sentence structure, spelling, or individual word vocabulary. The focus was on proper pronunciation! Some words were hard to get your tongue around and others sounded like four letter words in English. Language classes would take the entire morning, and after lunch we would disperse to our TESL or Omnibus training sessions. The TESL trainees became quite adept at doing the Hoki Poki! "You put your right foot out, and shake it all about! You do the Hoki Poki and that's what it's all about!" I was happy to be in the Omnibus Program.

Late that afternoon I returned to my new home and enjoyed our first dinner of rice, canned fish, and breadfruit and adopting the custom of eating with the fingers of one hand while waving my other back and forth shooing away the horde of flies from the food. I was surprised that we were eating canned fish instead of fresh fish as the fishing was poor in the Lagoon. The host's children were watching every move and took quite a delight in the two newcomers sharing their home. Domingo, the oldest at 13, spoke very passable English he learned in school, and very proudly was the translator for the two trainees that first night. Confident that our language classes would soon teach us the basic rudimentary language skills to survive, but Domingo was a big help that first week of training.

Without electricity our light was provided by a kerosene lantern. I had my flashlight which I used to walk the plank out to the latrine (benjo) overhanging the lagoon. You had to be careful not to step on the open hole in the wood floor which you would squat over. No fur lined toilet seat available! Special benjos were constructed by the Islanders utilizing Peace Corps supplied plumbing materials. A new water system was constructed to deliver surprisingly cold water from the many small creeks rushing down from high up on the mountain piped directly into the tin sided showers provided for the trainees, most not accustomed to taking cold showers- not a problem for a former Forest Service trail crewman used to bathing in the cold waters of Bear Creek. The water pressure was exceptionally strong and the pipes would frequently break apart at the joints and have to be repaired by the Omnibus trainees. My first night sleeping was incredibly uncomfortable sleeping under a mosquito net!

Language classes were held in the small 15' by 15' foot newly framed huts open on three sides for small groups located up and down the length of the island from one village to the next. Our classes attracted a crowd outside our hut, and at first provided interesting and exciting entertainment for Uman Islanders with the volunteers being quite a novelty to behold!

My group of lagoon trainees and the outer island trainees were located in separate villages with some further down the pathway and had a long walk going up to the school. The pathway was previously a Japanese narrow gauge railroad bed with the tracks and ties ripped up and strewn to the side. There were no bridges spanning the many creeks flowing off of the mountain; so in the dark, and even during the day, the walk could be challenging and dangerous for the trainees and instructors navigating through the creeks, stepping on wet slippery rocks, and climbing up steep banks. Just the project for a Forest Service trail construction crew boss, and I soon found myself building bridges again. The concrete bridges were reinforced with the ample steel narrow gauge rails strewn along the side of the path with the Peace Corps supplying the cement and my host father organized the laborers. I became instantly a hero to those Peace Corps candidates who had the longest walks up to the training center. Two of the reinforced concrete bridges built by Peace Corps on Uman Island are pictured below.

Total immersion into the culture of Uman Island and profusely sweating under the hot tropical sun, and breathing in the humid air with the new smells (especially from the benjos) soon began taking a heavy toll on a number of trainees some quitting voluntarily when the full reality what the next two years would be like. But most of those trainees leaving were 'deselected' and asked to leave. Not too surprising to me that my unfriendly roommate was one of the early de-selections, as he was totally consumed to have sex with anyone of the young teenagers hanging outside our house. He wanted to be in the Peace Corps for the wrong reason and potentially could have become a sexual predator camouflaged as a Peace Corps Volunteer! Back in the United States, his acting on his compulsion would be called statutory rape! I was surprised that he got as far as he did thinking he maybe mistook the word **Peace** for another spelling in Peace Corps.

Stu and Judy were two Peace Corps psychologists who monitored each of the trainees on a continuous basis mentally and psychologically to see how they were holding up to the stresses of adapting to the new culture and the new environment. I was queried, "Is this really where you want to be and what you want to do for two long years?" The last thing you would want is to be isolated on an island when it really wasn't working for you. There wasn't a bus to catch home! Some newlywed couples decided that their marriage was not working and left to get a divorce, and some left to save their marriages which were under stress in the new culture and training.

One of my married friends and his wife discovered that their new marriage was just not working and decided to go back home and get divorced. He returned later and was assigned to the outer Caroline Island of Satawal where he found his true love was working in fisheries and the woman of his dreams. He married a local girl and spent many years working on Satawal becoming an authority throughout the Pacific for fishery resource management. Also one of his Satawal Island in-laws, Pius "Mau" Pialug, was a traditional Caroline Island navigator who became famous navigating the Polynesian Voyaging Society's outrigger canoe, Hokule'a, to

Tahiti and back using only the ancient traditional island navigational methods. The story was told in the 1976 U.S. Bicentennial PBS Special-*The Navigators: Pathfinders of the Pacific*. Another candidate found out he couldn't live without following his San Diego Chargers football team-duh! I might have been more sympathetic, if he couldn't follow the Denver Broncos!

Finding Stu and Judy to be most helpful in my decision to stay, I felt no pressure from them to stay or leave. "Let's make the best decision for you and the Peace Corps. If you were going to be unhappy, you would not in the long run make a good Peace Corps Volunteer." Personally, I drew strength during training by attending daily Mass at a nearby chapel offered by Bill Suchan, S.J. (who would say his name rhymed with 'soup can'). He was a newly arrived teacher at the Jesuit Xavier High School on Moen and was attending our language classes. After World War II, the Jesuits had taken over the former Japanese Fleet Communications Center to establish a highly respected college preparatory high school for young men from all of Micronesia. Later it was opened to female students as was my all male Regis High School.

Domingo, the 13 year old son of my hosts, led me on climbs in my free time up to the mountaintop on Uman Island. There we explored Japanese concrete bunkers and anti- aircraft gun emplacements facing out to the lagoon. We found empty sake bottles strewn about the abandoned bunkers appearing Japanese soldiers had just left after a night of drinking and would return any time soon. It seemed a wise choice that the American Military chose not to storm the island beaches in the Truk Lagoon. Japanese defenders would have likely fought to the last man from the Lagoon's fortifications.

A dentist friend back in Vail served on an American submarine during the war which was one of many stationed outside the passes of the Lagoon to bottle up the Japanese Navy, preventing access and egress to and from the large naval base and army garrison now trapped.

The hungry Japanese confiscated most of the local food supply of breadfruit, taro, and coconuts. They used explosives in the Lagoon to kill large numbers of fish which resulted in destroying much of the coral reef fishery habitat, and I heard stories that some even resorted to cannibalism of Trukese. Near the end of the war the brutal treatment by the Japanese left deep scars in the culture. Hopefully President Kennedy's Peace Corps can help to heal the culture.

One afternoon our Peace Corps advisor showed up for our usual meeting and was nearly unrecognizable with a very grotesquely swollen face from a centipede bite while sleeping. I made a point of checking my sleeping area and tucking the bottom of the mosquito net tightly under my sleeping mat. Years later I saw a centipede crawling on my seven year old son's shoulder when awakening in the middle of the night on Punlap Island.

The lessons and experiences of the Peace Corps Volunteers who were **advisors** to the Micro 7 candidates were incredibly helpful to the future volunteers. One thing that stuck out in my mind was to always work with the elected official of the island, called a magistrate, and **respect the traditional chief on the island** who really held the power. And be cautious when drinking sakow (whiskey) and a home brew called **yeast** known for causing **fiti go-go** (craziness) and possibly creating very dangerous situations for a Peace Corps Volunteer! By the end of training, I was feeling more confident in the language and cultural training to begin to get my feet wet as a new Peace Corps Volunteer working and living in Truk. It was a bittersweet day saying goodbye to my host family and the gracious people on Uman Island! It's time to roll up my sleeves and go to work knowing it wasn't going to be a walk in the par...adise !

Truk Lagoon (from Xavier High by Donna Buckley)

CHAPTER 9
On the Mark

I found a small home to rent in Mwan village on Moen which I shared with two other volunteers who were working in the fisheries program. We rented the home owned by the godfather of Mwan Sop(village) redesigned and improved by the Peace Corp architect and his wife. He had been my mentor in the Omnibus Peace Corps training program and he and his wife had organized the Mwan Village Youth Club which used the house for their weekly meetings.

The youth club was a very positive organization helping to give direction and purpose to the youth of the neighborhood. There were always enthusiastic kids hanging around the house that were most helpful to me moving in and seemed to have answers to all of man's problems. At first I thought it wise to watch them like a seagull, but I quickly learned to trust them to watch and protect the three us in Mwan Sop (village). One of the new Micro 7 PCV young ladies, when first living on Moen, was attending to her bodily functions in a benjo (Japanese for a potty overhanging the lagoon) when a peeping Tom popped up in the same hole in the open floor that the young lady was squatting over. AHHHHHHH…CRAP!!!!

Words are not adequate to describe the surprise and fearful shock felt by our new Peace Corps Volunteer! When I heard about what happened I was horrified! I also thought of the girl who had been a victim twice in

Escondido Staging and the difficult, but proven to be wise decision, made then by a Peace Corps psychiatrist to gently deselect her from Micro 7.

One of my passions was soccer from playing in college and I had a goal of forming a youth soccer league on Moen similar to a very popular youth softball league set up by a Peace Corps Volunteer. Some of the village boys and I would go down to the local grade school and kick the ball around and have pick-up soccer matches. I was at a disadvantage having injured my right knee senior year in a college soccer game keeping me from ski racing in the winter. The kids showed no mercy and ran circles around me on the field.

We developed a very friendly camaraderie, and they watched out for their new Peace Corps buddies. It didn't hurt that our landlord lived next door and the mayor of Moen Island, Petrus Milo, lived just a couple of houses down from us. I was off to a good start on Moen, but my Peace Corps assignment would change dramatically and soon! As the saying goes, *"Don't Get Too Comfortable!"*

Jesse R. Quigley, the newly appointed, District Administer (Distad) of theTruk (Chuuk) District, had just returned to Moen from a district wide personal and governmental tour of all of the outer islands. He wanted to introduce himself and get to know the chiefs and people of each outer island getting acquainted with their individual needs. He resembled John Kennedy in appearance, temperament, and intelligence and was traveling on the *Truk Islander* with his department heads, including the director for Community Development and Howard Seay, the Peace Corps Director for the Truk District.

They learned that the chiefs of Ono, Onari, and Piseras on the Namonuito Atoll were very unhappy about their languishing dispensary projects. Some building materials had been transported to their islands the previous year and had been haphazardly dumped off with most of the cement on one island, the lumber on another, and steel reinforcing bars (rebar) on the third island. There were also no plans for on-site construction supervision for each of the buildings on Ono, Onari, and Piseras Islands that had participated in a fund matching program.

Each of the islands raised money from copra sales for a down payment matching the government funding. It was being administered by the Community Development and the Health Services Departments to address a **cholera epidemic** in the outer islands.

Each of the Islands had sent a representative to live and study for two years at the Hospital on Moen to be schooled in health care learning to be a health aid technician for their own island. The three Islands of Ono, Onari, and Piseras now had trained health aids but no sanitary facilities. The dispensaries would provide an emergency room like facility to administer immediate lifesaving oral and/or intravenous rehydration for severe cholera victims who could die within hours if left untreated and a sanitary facility for emergency care for other emergencies.

Peace Corps Director Howard Seay requested that I attend a meeting in the Distad's office accompanied by Marvin Kretchner, a new volunteer like myself, who was an experienced professional and talented master carpenter. So what does this have to do with me? Jesse Quigley said he needed someone to be the onsite supervisor for each dispensary and would I be willing to take on this assignment? I would have to pack up and go out to the Namonuito Atoll in four days on the regularly scheduled *Truk Islander* Field Trip ship and supervise the construction of the three dispensary projects on Ono, Onari, and Pisaras Islands.

Marvin was revising the old drawings and also adding a large concrete water catchment to the dispensary. He was also drawing the working construction detail plan and a new materials list. The new building materials needed to be purchased and delivered to the *Truk Islander* before it departed the following Monday.

"Wow! Four days? I need a little time to think about this!" "Yes!" I immediately answered, "I will go!"

The Distad said that because the materials which were delivered last year were simply dumped haphazardly, Community Development was going to make available to me one of their motor boats from the boat pool that would accompany me out to the outer islands. I then could equally redistribute the materials around from one island to the other.

This was a project that had been screwed up for a long time and no wonder the chiefs jumped all over the new District Administrator Jesse Quigley. He personally promised the chiefs that he would make this a priority to straighten out the mess and get those three dispensaries built as soon as possible. I was honored to be considered for this project and I knew that Howard Seay was pleased by my positive response. With no time to waste after the meeting, Marvin and I left knowing the short time frame to get organized. He would redesign the dispensaries and materials list. I would get ready on a very short notice to pick up and move to the Namonuito Atoll, as well as purchase the new construction materials and deliver them to the Field Trip Ship.

The Namonuito Atoll is 170 km (106 miles) from the Truk Lagoon. It is a triangular shaped atoll with Ulul and Piseras (Piherah) forming the base of a triangle, and Magur Island is located at the top of the triangle. And moving down the northern side of the triangle along the submerged reef from Magur Island are Ono Island, Onari Island, and finally Piseras Island at the eastern base of the triangle. The reef connecting the islands is mostly submerged between all of the islands in the atoll. Ulul is fifty miles along the base to Piseras. Like the Hawaiian Island Chain, the relatively small islands in the Namonuito Atoll are separated by the open and deep waters of the Pacific Ocean.

The Outer Islanders' subsistence economy and culture were similar, or akin, to the early Native Hawaiian and Native American economic and cultural lifestyles. The people of Puluwat, Punlap, Pulusuk, Satawal, and the Namonuito Atoll lived both off the land and the sea and, except when buying certain staples from the field trip ships, they didn't have as much need for money as we have in the United States. What a wonderful Country that has a Peace Corps that sends their citizens half way around the world to help others in need. In truth, this was an experience of a lifetime.

Men wore loin cloths or just a cloth wrapped around their waist and some would wear pants or shorts. Women sometimes wore a long wrap around cotton skirt called a lava lava or a pull on skirt and wearing nothing on top. When it was cool a short sleeved colored tee shirt. I never saw a true grass skirt but the little girls and women attached coconut palms at the waist over their lava lava skirt when dancing at feasts. For travelling to the District Center on the Truk Islander the women would wear the customary pull over dress (muu muu) when on Moen. Most men and women had usually walked around the island bare footed. The food was mostly breadfruit, taro, coconut, pandanus fruit, and fish mostly consumed with pounded breadfruit or taro called po (like Hawaiian Poi) along with some rice, and bread (pilewa) when available. The outer island used outrigger sailing canoes utilizing the traditional navigational skills and boat building technology of the traditional South Pacific culture. These islands were the last place left in the Pacific for the traditional seafaring culture using stars, ocean currents, Trade Winds, bird flight patterns, chants, and lately a compass.

Many of the same traditions of Hawaii and Tahiti, before Captain Cook, were alive and still a way of life on these remote Micronesian Islands. The Namonuito lifestyle must have been similar to that of the proud Colorado Ute culture of Chief Colorow in the 19th century walking around the island with no fences or walls between the thatched homes and depending on natures' bounty in a food gathering subsistence economy. In some ways, I was following in my great grand-parents footsteps facing unknown challenges, dangers, and an uncertain future. One of my challenges was to make arrangements with my roommates on Moen to take over the Mwan Youth Club and assume the lease on our house, and pack up my suitcase and store it at the Peace Corps office. The volunteers in the outer islands wore the traditional loin cloth (afitita), so I could leave my suit packed in the suitcase! But I would need the Peace Corps health kit and the book locker reserved for the outer islands volunteers.

The basic food stuffs like rice, sugar, and coffee could be bought from the stores on the field trip ship. Marvin was working on the drawings and material list so when that was completed, I could begin purchasing the additional building materials and tools from the Truk Trading Company and Co-op Store and transport them to the dock in the next two days. Marvin's services were in great demand on Moen, especially by me now, so I stayed in close contact with him. And once I received the material list the work really began in earnest. I barely made the *Truk Islander* field trip ship before it departed. There was another Peace Corps Volunteer who was also travelling to the Namonuito Atoll, as well as the Catholic Padre whose parish consisted of all the Western Islands and the Namonuito Atoll. The majority of passengers were Namonuito Islanders returning back home from having taken the opportunity for a quick turnaround trip resulting from the Distad's trip. The Catholic priest, called Padre, had taken this opportunity to buy additional necessary building materials to complete the new Catholic Church on Piseras. The outer islands didn't have a handy Ace, True Value, or Home Depot Hardware store to quickly run to when you needed something.

September was still a good time to be traveling on the open ocean as the strong trade winds hadn't yet begun to blow in earnest. This was still considered the rainy season which usually started in July ending in November. If we didn't run into a typhoon, it looked like a smooth trip. This being my first time to be on the open ocean, I was looking forward to the trip but wasn't sure if I would get seasick. I grew up on skis and not sailing or living on a large lake or the ocean. However Colorado has wonderful high mountain lakes - nothing like the Oceans or Great Lakes. Peace Corps volunteers from the Midwest or the coasts likely grew up ski racing in the winter and sailboat racing in the summer. Much like some of my friends from the Vail Ski Patrol who were incredible ski racers on the Snow Pigs (Vail Ski Patrol) town race team and were jolly boat sailing racers as kids growing up on sailing water, some of the outer island volunteers were familiar with sail boats and the open ocean. I was soon to meet a veteran Peace Corps Volunteer from the Midwest who had just returned back to Truk after a vacation following his two years working on Magur and had extended his Peace Corps service to build a school on Magur Island. He had mastered open-ocean sailing on his own outrigger sailing canoe and **routinely sailed** past Ono Island on his way over to Onari Island from Magur. I called him **Red Sail** for his distinct **red sail** on his wa (outrigger canoe) and was a very skilled sailor from what I would soon observe. Sadly, I didn't have the chance to know him better, but I assumed that he brought his sailing skills with him from the Great Lakes. I brought no such skill with me, just a Colorado Ski poster with the picture of Georgetown friend, Johnny Kruger, skiing at The Winter Park Ski Resort- an instant **ice breaker** with people who had never seen snow.

CHAPTER 10
Namonuito Atoll

The Truk Islander was no Love Boat! The government run fieldtrip transportation service was a **vital** link connecting the outer islands to the Truk (Chuuk) Lagoon. It provided passenger service, health care, mail service, and even the delivery of cargo, such as my shipment of building materials which was carefully stowed in the hold. A government runabout for my use was lifted by a crane on deck alongside the ship's own runabout, and I was determined that the dispensary materials would be properly unloaded on each of the three Namonuito islands.

The Truk Islander also served as a financial center for the islanders. They would sell their bags of dried coconut meat, called copra, to The Truk Trading Company and The Co-op Store for money using their new found income from these transactions to buy goods from the same stores at highly inflated prices. By far the most popular items to buy were cartons of cigarettes, coffee, sugar and bright colored cloth fabric that were used for lava lavas and loincloths. A field trip ship was a very big deal and a highly anticipated event for each island; the circus came to town.

Breathing a sigh of relief that Marvin and I had accomplished the impossible, I was actually gliding smoothly out on the turquoise blue waters of the lagoon on this sultry afternoon enjoying the welcome sea breeze and the offshore views of some of the other islands within the lagoon. Before leaving Mwan Sop, I took the opportunity to write my parents back home in Central City, Colorado to let them know about going out to the outer islands and to let them know there was going to be a long mail delay between our letters and how sad, yet expected, the news about my cousin Phyllis dying on my birthday, September 16.

I'm sure there must have been some added worry on their part upon receiving my letter. It was bad enough that their youngest son was halfway across on the other side of the world, but now they weren't going to hear from him for months at a time.

The crowded stern deck of the ship was quickly filling in with people and their pandanus mats that were covered with peeled fresh coconuts and woven bags of native food for the passengers spending the night on the rear deck. Padre was sitting comfortably on a mat among the women and children passengers as he motioned me over to him. Introducing himself, he warmly suggested that I should put my sleeping mat down while there was still room for it.

The Peace Corps volunteers and the priest didn't have cabins and slept on the back deck with the islanders. Padre pointed out that it was actually more comfortable out in the fresh air instead of riding in a hot and stuffy passenger cabin, usually reserved for government officials. It was mid-afternoon when I began to feel the open ocean swells when the ship departed the smooth waters of the lagoon through the pass and into the open ocean. This was the first time for a mountain boy from Colorado to experience the open seas, and I was thrilled. The ocean was in my Irish DNA.

There was both an up and down motion as well as a new, side to side, rolling motion. Deciding to move forward so as not view where the ship had just left, I could now see where we were headed. This proved to be beneficial in other seafaring ways. On the bow of the ship, the fresh sea breeze replaced smelling noxious engine fumes belching from the smoke stack and also ended the rolling from side to side sensation.Probably it would take a while for the seasick feeling to subside.

The Peace Corps did provide meals on the ship, and I joined some of the crew members already eating and slowly drank a Coke which thankfully did settle my stomach. After eating a late lunch, I introduced myself to **Red Sail**. The Peace Corps Volunteer extended for an additional year because he had been successful in securing a Peace Corps *School to School Partnership Grant* to build a new school on Magur Island. Listening to him talking to a group of people from Magur, including the chief, he was very impressive by how fluently he could speak **"Weito."** But it sounded forced and unnatural-not having the same rhythm or tone of the native speakers.

For me it would be like learning to swim by being thrown into the deep end of a swimming pool where you will either sink or swim. Having learned the speaking basics of Lagoon Trukese during Peace Corps training, the people of the Namonuito Atoll could understand my limited Trukese allowing me to speak to them, yet not able to understand most of their reply. It really wasn't so much 'sink or swim' but 'tread and swim.' And unlike the volunteers who were TESL teachers that spoke only English during class hours, I would be speaking the outer island language all day with the workers.

The ship was taking a short detour up to East Fayu where an ocean freighter had run aground on a reef a couple of weeks earlier. East Fayu used to be known to the nearby Hall Islanders for its abundant sea turtles and birds and occasional turtle hunters, but now it was known for this giant ship resting on its reef. The *Truk Islander* arrived off the island early the next morning, and a boarding party was sent out on the ship's runabout to explore the scuttled ship.

The sight of the huge freighter stuck on the reef was both awesome and eerie at the same time. It was a little like looking at the Titanic, but this abandoned ship wasn't going to sink anytime soon grounded on the reef. Surely in this modern time of radar and sophisticated navigational equipment, the captain and the navigator had some SERIOUS explaining! I later went ashore on East Fayu and thought what it might have felt for the crew on this uninhabited island out in the middle of nowhere with only seabirds, white sand, and waves. Surely they were happy not to be the captain!

What was the *Truk Islander* doing there? Perhaps the captain was thinking he might still salvage valuables from the reefed freighter. Late in the afternoon, the ship weighed anchor and headed for Ulul on southwest corner of the Namonuito Atoll. Red Sail was trailing thick mono-filament fishing line tied to the railing of the back deck. It wasn't long afterwards that he had pulled a large tuna onto the deck.

This was my first but not last taste of raw sashimi soaked in lime and soy sauce and eaten with rice and pounded breadfruit brought aboard the ship by his friends from Magur. Sleeping soundly on the hard deck, I awakened to the sound of a change to the ship's engine and heard the clanking sound of the dropping anchor off Ulul Island. Still before dawn, I rolled over and awaited for the sun to rise over the island. The sunrise soon greeted the *Truk Islander* bobbing up and down off the shore of what could have been one of the Technicolor scenes from Marlon Brando's movie *Mutiny of the Bounty,* and on cue were two outrigger paddling canoes of topless beautiful young teenage girls circling and waving greetings to friends and family on board. The bright sun revealed a sparkling turquoise sea and the green island with its lush forest of tall coconut and breadfruit trees, brilliant long white beach, and several large gray and brown thatched buildings that I soon learned were boat houses (oots).

There was a colorful throng of waving Islanders including naked children excitedly running up and down the wide beach. A day that was anticipated by the people of Ulul with much excitement had arrived, and I could hardly believe that this scene was even real. After the ship's runabout ferried the passengers to the island, the ship's crew began in earnest the offloading of the cargo in the hold, while I watched intently that the building materials bound for Ono, Onari, and Piseras (pronounced Piherah) weren't mistakenly dumped onto Ulul. With that over, I eagerly went ashore looking for my friend Lewie from Micro

7. He was a TESL English teacher with a passionate dedication to being a successful Peace Corps Volunteer in the outer islands. Talking to him during training envious of his opportunity, here I was going to meet him and share my excitement of joining him on the Namonuito Atoll. We would be just 50 miles apart when I would be living on Piseras. He couldn't believe his eyes, when I had finally found him. Lewie introduced me to

Steve Hayden

a veteran Peace Corps Volunteer from Arizona, Steve Hayden, who impressed me for his gentle and respectful manner with the islanders. Steve spoke softly, with a natural flowing command of the language. From his friendly, generous, and helpful advice, I gained an important insight into a new culture. His example would inspire and serve me well for my two year assignment on the Atoll. Steve was leaning on the lee platform of an outrigger sailing canoe (Picture was taken by Kent Weidemann (wife Jan) a PCV working on Ulul).

Talking to Lewie that night about the beautiful young girls in his eighth grade class, he commented that he was bound and determined not to take advantage of his young attractive students. He didn't want the parent teacher conferences to be about his behavior!

Ulul was the largest island and the most populous on the large Namonuito Atoll and just about the coolest place I had ever seen. The village was very different from the loud hubbub of the District Center on Moen. I was struck by just how quiet it was and immediately knew how special this experience was going to be with these strong attractive people. To this day I remember just how memorable my time was on Ulul and pinched myself making sure I was awake and this was real. Ulul may have had the same feel of a Colorado Native American Village where there were no fences and confident and happy children running and playing without any fear of offending the neighbors, and drying racks for salted fish like the drying meat of buffalo, deer, elk, or bear in a Cheyenne or Ute Indian village!

The men wearing their loin cloths and women wearing their lava lavas, and topless, were dressed in the customary and acceptable fashion for the Namonuito Atoll. There was nothing provocative, sexual, or immoral about it! This had been standard wear for Caroline outer islanders for a thousand years although the textile material came from the pandanus tree. Also it was customary for the women to stoop their heads and shoulders and lower themselves at the waist when walking in front of a brother, a chief, or group of men as a sign of customary respect.

Land ownership on the outer islands and the all-important clan designations (inong) came from the mother. So even though women would stoop and lower before men, this was a matriarchal society and the women controlled the wealth and the roost. Chiefs were determined by which clan that they belonged to and that was determined by their mother. A beautiful girl in the eyes of the island men were overweight girls. (fokun kitinoop)

The next afternoon the *Truk Islander* lifted anchor and headed up to

Magur Island to dispense the field trip magic on another Namonuito island. I walked around Magur before the ship weighed anchor for the next stop at Ono Island where one of the dispensaries was slated to be built. We anchored offshore of Ono Island on the deep front side of the island where large waves were not hindered by a coral reef from breaking onto the front beach and went ashore and like everyone else soaked from head to toe getting out of the ship's runabout. I met Ono's Chief Sak (below) for the first time, a very big man who graciously welcomed me with a strong handshake and welcoming smile. He was most thankful and relieved to see me and that the new District Administer honored his promise.

We stored the boat pool's motorboat in the thatched canoe boat house (oot) along with two fifty gallon drum cans of gasoline and the new building materials joining the previous materials. As the business of the field trip ship progressed, Chief Sak walked me around his village taking me to meet my host family and the islanders of Ono. The elderly host couple walked me back behind the thatched village to a wooden grey frame house with a tin roof. The sound of the waves crashing loudly onto Ono's beach was a sound I hadn't heard in the Truk Lagoon.

The ship weighed anchor and the field trip moved on to Onari Island only a short distance away.

Chief Paulus of Onari Island introduced himself and personally welcomed me to the island. I remember him asking me to stay and wanting me to first start on his island. It was very frustrating not being able to understand this new language. I could understand that there was a slim to no chance to get any of the chiefs to voluntarily give up any of the haphazard earlier offloaded materials on the three Islands.

Onari had a hospitable Peace Corps Volunteer who put me up for the night who was a TESL teacher. John lived in a small elevated wooden frame house no bigger than twenty-by- twenty and four hundred square feet with a great view of the ocean from both the front and rear of the house. The village on Onari was located on the narrow spit of the island (like the panhandle of a frying pan) and with a path running down the middle from the beach and entering into the wider forest of breadfruit and coconut trees beyond.

Despite the constant roar of the ocean waves breaking loudly on the island's outer reefs, the little house was very comfortable with a constant breeze blowing through the large screened-in windows. Natural air conditioning breezes kept most of the mosquitos away making this a most comfortable abode. Mosquitos and comfort were the reason for locating all the Namonuito villages situated in locations where the tropical trade winds blew. Reading his fresh pile of mail and trying to write responses to all his letters before the ship departed in the morning, my new Peace Corps friend was completely absorbed writing letters home.

Walking about the island and outside nearly every thatched home, Onari's families were gathered around eating their evening meal. I was invited by their waving of a hand to join them for dinner. 'Feito monga, feito, feito'(come eat, come, come). Or 'feito oon nu'(come drink coconut). It was customary to invite anyone walking by, but the people of Onari certainly wanted me to know how much I was welcome! All the little children were running around naked playing and laughing and were confident with no fear of strangers. Mostly the food was cooked octopus and or small reef fish freshly speared and cooked whole on a fire with pounded breadfruit and with coconut milk liberally squeezed on top. I did the same back in Colorado with ketchup.

Coconut is the preferred drink at all meals and men or boys will climb a tree and cut down a bunch or just toss a few down at a time. These fresh coconuts are opened to drink by the islanders whacking open a hole in the side of the husk with a machete, or peeling the outer husk and exposing the light colored nut whacking off the top of the nut to open it for drinking.

After spending the night on shore at John's house, the next morning it didn't take long for the copra to be traded and the islanders to spend their money with the ship's stores for mostly coffee and cigarettes. It was time for me to say a short goodbye (olela) and board the ship for Piseras, the last stop for me in the Namonuito Atoll. The sea between Piseras and Onari was very rough and with no visible reef it certainly gave me pause to think just how safe or wise it would be navigating and operating the motor boat between the islands, and what if there was a mechanical breakdown? One of the concerns creeping into my mind was a conversation between a PCV friend of mine from training who was a master mechanic working at the boat and motor pool. He laughed at just how poorly the government equipment was maintained. I wasn't sure whether he was seriously discouraged and thinking of tossing in his oily rag or excited by the challenge. **Now** this concern was no laughing matter to me. If he was right and the motor failed on the runabout between Ono, Onari, and Piseras, I was sure that I didn't want to float across the Pacific because of rock hard bags of cement and warped two by fours already making up my mind before seeing what was stored on Piseras.

The *Truk Islander* entered the large lagoon of Piseras from the Northwest with one side of the reef pointing back in the direction of Onari and the other side of the reef pointing west and towards Ulul Island. Piseras Island was the southeastern corner island of the large Namonuito Atoll. The surrounding reefs formed a very large V shaped long lagoon, which I was to learn was teeming with fish (chamong eek) and had tremendous spear fishing. There also was great trolling for tuna from sailing canoes outside of the lagoon. The chiefs of Ono and Onari were worried I wouldn't want of leave with so much food on Piseras, surely getting very fat (fokun kitinoop)!

What a beautiful turquoise lagoon the Truk Islander was smoothly cutting through as we approached the verdant green tropical island. The travelling circus had come to Piseras and the white sparkling beach was teeming with expectant children and adults alike. The Island was much bigger than both Ono and Onari combined. After anchoring and the last of the dispensary materials were off-loaded, I boarded the ship's runabout for my next Island greeting and the beginning of my Peace Corps dream. On shore I examined a huge stack of hard sacks of cement and the story was the same with a small pile of warped lumber. I talked with the Trukese Community Development representative accompanying the field trip about the situation and we agreed that we should make a replacement order to be delivered to each of the dispensary projects on the next scheduled trip out to the Namonuitos and not compound the earlier mistake.

Fortunately Marvin's new plan had added a huge concrete water tank to collect fresh rain water from the corrugated aluminum roof. The extra cement for this large project was part of the materials we had just dropped off on each of the islands and would be sufficient to be used until the replacement construction materials arrived. Most the plywood and straight two by four's went into the roof and we get along with what we had until replacements arrived. I made up my mind that I wasn't going to transport damaged goods in a questionable motor boat between the three Islands without Bill the PCV mechanic along for the ride. A plan developed and the decision now was to send the motor boat in Ono's Oot back on the next field trip ship. I informed the Trukese Community Development representative accompanying the field trip ship to make arrangements to deliver fresh bags of cement and lumber to the three islands of Ono, Onari, and Piseras and to have the motor boat picked up from Ono and taken back to Moen on the next field trip ship.

The good news was that there was still plenty of money left in the dispensary account so ordering more materials wouldn't be a problem. I also ordered more steel reinforcing rods which I didn't want to move around on an outrigger canoe. The chief (hamol) of Piseras introduced me to my host and his wife initially who were to be my caretakers on the island and who were providing me with a small thatched hut to call home. Upon entering it took me a moment for my eyes to adjust from the brilliant sunshine to the dark interior. After laying out my sleeping mat and putting my clothes and toiletries on a small shelf at the end of the hut, I hung my mosquito net. There wasn't room to hang my ski poster.

The ship was to remain for two more days. Before it departed for Truk, I had to buy some necessities for myself including: enough cloth for loin cloths (afitita), some toiletries, several towels and wash cloths, two big plastic tubs for washing clothes and dishes, a plastic bucket for carrying water from the common pump to my hut, a kerosene stove, two cans of kerosene, soap, and some food including bags of rice and flour, sugar, and instant coffee, a tea pot for boiling my drinking water, a few pots and pans, some metal dishware, and an assortment of spoons, knives, and forks. The ugly American has moved to Piseras!

Dan and Ellen Griffin's supplies filled their covered wagon for their journey from St. Joseph to Denver. My supplies filled my small thatched hut. When it came time for the ship to depart and cut my ties to the modern world, I realized that I was really on my own. No electricity, plumbing, phones, communications, or any of the modern conveniences of home. But my summer job working for the Forest Service trail crew in the Colorado back country prepared me for living in the backcountry, but this was much more than living in the Colorado backcountry for two years. It could be a risky and lonely challenge fulfilling John Kennedy's vision for the Peace Corps.

The island prepared a feast (likipin pari) to welcome me and to celebrate their priest's return to finish their new church. 'Padre' was a Jesuit missionary from the New York Province and Fordham University. We sat together eating and enjoying the celebration and sharing friendly conversation by two fellow Irish Americans in remote islands in Micronesia.

Padre had many useful construction tips unique to the outer islands. Some were as simple as to begin stockpiling the coral sand and aggregate near the building site. The sand and aggregate piles would need to be washed of the sea salt, leaves, and dirt by rain and by having the women dump buckets of fresh water on the piles. Padre offered for our use his stacks of individual block wooden pallets. We would have had to build pallets before making the individual cement blocks with our steel mold block machine taking over a month to make enough blocks to build a dispensary.

Padre asked if I knew how to make sure the foundation was square. Since I had already graduated from a Jesuit High School and College, I allowed Padre to answer his own question. "It's the *three, four, five triangle*, of course!" Connect three lines with those lengths and you would insure a right or perpendicular angle for the larger of the angles or using any multiple of those sides. Basic geometry! But the answer to his next question was more difficult. "How do you cut the proper angle and length for roof rafters on a 3/12 roof pitch using a carpenter's square to mark the line for your cut so the rafters butt properly together at the peak of the roof? And what is the measurement using the square to determine the length of the rafter for the 3/12 pitch to the intersection of the notched cut at the wall of the building where the rafter rests? And how do you measure the notched cut so it fits perpendicular to the top of the wall? And how do you measure the cut at the end of the rafter so it's pointing perpendicular to the ground?" **He lost me at rafters!**

Make sure to keep the new block wet for at least one month and covered from the hot tropical sun. He shared how to bend your rebar and cut it without a bending tool or a rebar cutter and how to best smooth the mortar joints with a bent 3/8" bolt which he later gave to me, and also he gave me some of his extra line levels to make sure the block walls go up level. What is the proper proportion or ratio of cement to the coral sand, aggregate, and water when hand mixing the concrete in the tropical climate and what technique is best to hand shovel the mix? I could learn all the techniques observing the laying of the church's concrete floor over the next week. This and much more unsolicited construction advice he shared with me. One of his favorite sayings about the frustrations of living in the outer islands was, "We may be chagrined but not surprised!"

Life began to stir before dawn with roosters crowing and the church bell ringing loudly. The bell was an acetylene tank that floated onto the beach and hung by the church and rung by hitting it with a hammer. The bell was rung about 15 minutes later with a pause, and then 2 separate rings of the bell. I got up and rolled out from under the mosquito net and splashed some of my previously boiled water on my face, hoping to resemble someone awake and presentable to attend Mass in 15 minutes. Joining the full church of islanders just as the bell rang loudly announcing the start of the service in the new church, I was more than self-conscious!

Men were arranged on one side and women on the other side of the church sitting on the packed sand floor with harmonized singing between the two sides of the church. The service was conducted by the Padre in Lagoon Trukese which was difficult for me to understand as I hadn't heard any ecclesiastical vocabulary during language training. But I had a hard time understanding him when he spoke his New York version of English, and his Trukese was impossible for me to decipher. Immediately after the service, Padre, the elected magistrate of the island, the traditional island chief, and I met to discuss plans to finish the concrete floor of the church and coordinate the start of the construction on the dispensary.

Padre was expecting a sailing canoe from Puluwat (in the Western Islands) to come and pick him up and take him back to his parish headquarters on Puluwat Island in about ten days. The last thing left on Piseras Island was to pour the concrete floor, thankfully because Padre might not be back for months. A plan for building all three dispensaries came together in my mind knowing now that I could proceed with the three projects without having to waste a lot of time moving building materials from island to island. My initial thought was to start the essential first stages of construction one at a time on each island. We had to start with the gathering of sand and aggregate, build the wooden pallets for the cement-block manufacturing, construct the foundations on each island, and pour the concrete floors so I would have a solid platform to lay block on and from. It would be a slow process of manufacturing and stockpiling enough of the block and supplying enough sand and aggregate for the entire project on each island.

I reasoned that all three islands could start on the necessary **first phase** beginning with Piseras and when finished with phase one, I would repeat it on Onari and Ono Islands. Finally when finished on Ono Island with the phase one, I would then return back to Piseras Island to start phase two which was building the vertical structure and water tank. When finished there I would leave and go build phase two on Onari. And when finished with phase two on Onari, I would move to Ono Island completing the last dispensary.

My hosts were terrific, and every morning after Mass, Emere would drop off fresh coconuts to drink and some fresh fish to eat with rice, breadfruit, or taro and bananas for my breakfast. I was somewhat concerned that I might become a *fatty*! I was just beginning to learn about the wonders of the coconut tree and what a vital role it plays in the life of the islands. After draining the refreshing coconut water and chopping the green and gold fresh coconut in half with my new machete, I would spoon out the soft fresh meat forming on the inside of the nut with a scraper cut from the husk of the coconut. Dangerous with my unfamiliar machete, I came close to singing on the women side of the aisle. Mature coconuts and the fiber from the husk are used to make copra, cooking oil (deetka), rope, kindling, and toiletry usage.

Putting on a loin cloth with Emory's help, I ventured forth timidly to meet the brave new world and fit into the culture with my lily white legs.

The island chief and the elected magistrate and I went on a tour of the possible locations for the dispensary. They picked a site that was very close to the beach with a view of the ocean and the sound of waves breaking on the outer reef two hundred yards away. What a neat place to go to work. The nearby grade school was just a short distance behind the site, and I could hear the classes being taught in English by the Piseras teacher. The white plastered school was like the one room school house of *Little House on the Prairie*. All grades shared the one teacher in the one room school house built of block construction with large open windows and doors taking advantage of the ocean breeze.

This school was a Peace Corps School to School project built by the previous PCV, Joe, already legendary on Piseras, who had recently completed his tour of duty and returned back to the States. From what I heard he was loved by the people on the island and was an incredible spear fisherman. Also behind the dispensary site was a large open grassy area used for the school playground, island feasts, and children catechism classes on Sundays. Bordering the grassy field were thatched homes, including the home of the traditional chief and his family and the framed house and tin roof of Padre's very small house.

Along the same side of the dispensary were many coconut palm thatched huts with young parents of many small children. One 6 year- old, when I was living on Piseras, would later become a priest and build a church on Ono Island. As the two chiefs and I walked by these thatched homes, we were always beckoned to join those families having breakfast outside, or in their cook houses. Curious children would surround me wherever I would walk on the island. I was always impressed by how happy all the children were and how comfortable and loved they were by their entire extended family. Some of the young boys would go on to be skilled navigators and boat builders. Traditional navigation and boat building skills were passed down orally from one generation down through the ages by memorized rhythmic chants-because there wasn't a written language. The ancient design of the tough and very versatile outrigger canoes were adapted to the ocean and weather conditions of the South Pacific and custom designed and built using only natural building materials found on these island.

This same culture developed a navigational system capable of making long distance journeys of thousands of miles across the Pacific. The boats of Micronesia and Polynesia were sailing around the Pacific before Columbus discovered America. The wide body of knowledge was passed down orally and memorized from teachers to students for thousands of years. There is another separate and ancient language used by the navigators called the language of old (kapasen lamalam) much like our old language roots of Latin.

Star courses, wave and swell patterns, ocean currents, bird flight patterns, and whatever other useful physical observable information such as using back sights to get pointed in the right direction when leaving an island (I used the same technique as a Vail surveyor marking ski lifts on Vail Mountain) when leaving an island were passed down through ancient chants and songs from one generation to the next. Taboos and superstitions **and curses** were not passed down anymore, or so I thought! I later found out that Padre used them to control some superstitious outer islanders' behavior! Also, it was pointed out to me that Padre took a nap every afternoon and was accompanied in his closed up house with small young girls. I was not fluent yet to understand all that my fellow worker Bogey, who had a small daughter, was saying. But I sure caught his drift and concerned look. He was seemingly perplexed at me for not reacting, but I was literally and figuratively at a loss for words in his Weito language, or in my English!

Padre had a generator and projector and showed an old WW II movie, **The Sands of Iwo Jima,** one night under the stars. The next day all the young boys were reciting the dialogue word for word and gesture.

My friend Bogey and his wife and daughter on Piseras Island

Maybe it was because of their youth and with my challenge to learn their island language, I was very impressed. The role of Sgt. Stryker was the most popular and was repeated by almost every young boy on Piseras Island- talking and swaggering about like John Wayne. The people of the Namonuito Atoll thought of themselves as the "people of the sea" or **re-metau**. The word that they used to describe me was **re-wan** which meant literally a person on top or a **superior,** and this word described all Japanese and Americans-especially Padre being in charge of their spirit world. Most Peace Corps Volunteers tried to discourage the notion that **re-wan** applied to them. This name really didn't apply to how I felt about myself. To be truthful, I admired how accomplished and self-confident all of the outer islanders were in their own skin. The young children and my co-workers would become my best language instructors. At night I would struggle with my new host family to master essential words in the outer island language which were really important to know when experiencing **total immersion** in the culture. **Yes, I am still hungry! Or no thanks, I am full! Don't spear that fish!** There were many words I was discovering were actually phrases instead of the one word I was hearing. So I became focused on learning what was being said and how it sounded than piecing together each individual word. Quickly I comprehended that some words I knew in Lagoon Trukese were understandable by replacing certain sounds with a different pronunciation. For example the word for *Chamong (many)* was changed to *Rhamong*, or the word for Truk was *Chuuk* in Lagoon Trukese and *Ruuk* on Piseras. The words that had the *"s"* sound would change with a soft *"h"* sound. Like *set(sea)* would become *"het"* on Piseras. The letter *N* became the letter *L* as in *Neboganim* (good night) to *Lebogalim*.

The Weito language in the Namonuito Atoll was much softer sounding and spoken with a quiet tone much like Hawaiian; and the word for canoe, *wa*, was the same word in Hawaiian. The small children who you met on the island path with friendly smiles and slow pronunciation of words of good morning, good afternoon, good evening, and good night were the best of my tutors. They spoke slowly and loudly and proudly wanting me to hear their every word. And with their limited vocabulary, I quickly learned basic pronunciation. And without fail they would put a smile on my face cracking me up with their theatrical antics. It was for these special little people that the islanders and I were working so hard to build their dispensaries! And nobody wanted them to learn the words **cholera or anumaumau** (strong superstition or curse). These children of Piseras are memorizing the old Catholic Baltimore Catechism and the Word of God in their catechism class. The boy on the left didn't know the correct answer to the question and was very upset! As you can tell from the picture, clothing is optional for the small children. Tops are optional for women in the outer islands who wear lava lava skirts and sometimes the women opt to wear a full light dress or a Hawaiian moomoo. The men wear loin cloths and on occasion a pair of trousers or shorts and a shirt.

There was not an alphabet developed for the outer island languages and memorization was just a fact of life for the culture from the earliest times that the islands were inhabited. These children will memorize their catechism lessons just like their fathers and ancestors had to memorize all the navigational information important to know to survive voyages on the open ocean and all the important steps and methods to build the outrigger sailing canoes. In past years before Christianity was introduced to the islands, there were many customary superstitious taboos and rituals that were passed down through the generations of seafarers. Fortunately these children won't be tested on the navigators' sacred rituals and taboos of old (lamalam).

Although my Peace Corps training was for the Truk Lagoon and not the outer islands of the Truk District, I would be in a situation where English would not be spoken to me. Surprisingly, I was able to communicate in my limited Lagoon Trukese.

Piseras Island had a trained work force which had just built a new church. Already skilled in cement block manufacturing, mixing and pouring concrete floors I was able to make quick progress. Block pallets were already available thanks to Padre, and there was also the opportunity to observe the island technique in mixing and laying the concrete floor of the church. It was very interesting to witness Padre's adaptions to building in the outer islands compared to Marvin's professional construction background and the construction handbook I picked up in the Community Development's construction office.

Living in my thatched hut showed me how important it was to build a dispensary facility easy to keep clean. Upon waking in the morning, I found my toiletry hand towel, which I had laid out flat on my little shelf, covered with pepper looking cockroach droppings. There must have been thousands of cockroaches living in the walls and ceiling and the same small black droppings would cover the top of my mosquito net in the morning. These cockroaches were not just these little things that were annoying. They were the size of my thumb and quite ugly.

When nature called I would walk about 100 yards to the beach where there was an overwater benjo that was provided for Padre and a coconut tree plank you had to negotiate without falling into the lagoon. I soon learned that most islanders relieved themselves either in the forest or in the shallow waist deep water near the shore of the protected lagoon, or at low tide on the edge of the beach. The strong ocean current would carry the human waste out to sea.

When I availed myself of this method I would think bombs away, "Remember Pearl Harbor!" as the ocean current flowed towards Japan. When the trade winds blew in the winter months I learned the hazard of this method one night when a blue-bottle jellyfish washed across my ankle and stinging like I never felt before. If you have never had this experience and are curious how it feels, take a hot knife and slide the blade across your ankle, but I don't recommend doing this without screaming, "**Wi-yo**"!

Besides the church there was a community well with a hand operated pump. You could fill a bucket to wash off the sea water after swimming or, if you were a small child, you could stand underneath the cascading water while your mother pumped the handle. This fresh water well was used for cooking, washing clothes, or bathing. Back in the forest, there were hand dug separate bathing areas for the men and women, which I used only once, as there were small creepy critters swimming all around your body in the green slimy water. I learned to bathe at the pump using buckets of cold water I poured over my head. Since the air temperatures were in the high 80's and 90's, a cold shower felt great.

The islands collectively went to bed early. There were no automobiles on freeways, or loud ski patrolmen exiting bars to disturb the quiet, or sixties TV programs to stay awake and watch. Except for the wind swooshing loudly through the coconut fronds, and the constant pounding of waves on the nearby reef, and an occasional baby's cry the island was really quiet! Occasionally, you would hear a very loud crashing of a giant wave that hit with such force on the reef it would startle me up out of a sound sleep.

No need for an alarm clock. The roosters did the job. Their crowing was followed by the loud ringing of the church bell next door. Padre was only occasionally on Piseras and everyone attended his daily Mass to start the day. The island bell ringer, a smallish man with a hunch back and wild curly hair, would start by ringing the bell three times around 4:30 AM. By my standards, this was a little early to start the day, but when in Rome....This was a warning bell followed about ten minutes later by two bells and then finally by one. By this time you had better be dressed in your loin cloth and on your way to Mass, if not already there. Everyone - men, women and children- sat and/or kneeled on the sand floor. This was an important part of the day for them and they attended happily.

The average medium age of these Micronesian Pacific islanders was only 20 years, and living like the soldiers in combat on the edge of death every day focused their minds on life and death. Ernie Pyle, The World

War II correspondent, had been attributed as saying, "There are no atheists in a foxhole." Whether he said that or not, I observed first hand that there were no atheists on the Namonuito Atoll.

Just a few weeks after my arrival, I was suffering from an upset stomach and was trying to sleep off a fever in the hot and humid confines of my hut. The bell ringer, who also served as the traditional island medicine man (sausafay,) had heard I was ill and came by to offer me some traditional island medicine. It was chopped up with a lime peel and came tightly wrapped in a small white rag. I was told to suck on this for a few minutes. Unlike Western medicine, it came with no list of ingredients, possible side effects, or other warnings. I felt bad enough to throw caution to the wind and did as the medicine man directed. Whoa! This put me into a dream world and upon awakening my symptoms were entirely gone, as well as the entire day. I never did find out what it was he gave me, but it did the trick.

After waking up I walked over to the dispensary site and was impressed with the new piles of sand and coral aggregate. More impressive were the women who were carrying the copra bags full of sand and rock from the beach and the full buckets of water to wash the sand. This heavy lifting phase was the responsibility of the women of the island who are truly the unsung worker backbone for the school, the new church, and now the dispensary project.

I was in awe of the behind the scene absolutely necessary heavy lifting the women performed in starting to stock pile sand and aggregate. They carried the heavy copra bags balanced on their heads. There were no front end loaders and dump trucks to move the tons of sand, aggregate, and water. Amazing all this was done with such dignity and strength of purpose. They knew all about the cockroaches and they wanted a sanitary building where the health aid could administer sanitary life-saving measures to help in keeping cholera or open wounds from killing their loved ones.

"Never on Sunday" from the 1960 Greek film described life on the outer islands! Saturday was reserved for making food preparations for the Sunday Sabbath. The 4th Commandment, *Remember the Lord's Day* was a day of rest for the Lord and also for all the people of the Namonuito Atoll. Making of food and fishing were considered work in their subsistence lifestyle economy, although the fishing looked more like play to me as the men obviously enjoyed their **work,** like the Utes and Cheyenne hunters of the 19th century in Colorado hunting elk and deer. Or I might add my father taking his only day off of his hectic week to go fly fishing with his three sons. So there was a halt to pouring Padre's floor and my dispensary tasks on Saturday. Some of the men took the opportunity to go open sea fishing on their sailing canoes, and others would go fishing in the lagoon with their paddling canoes and drop hand lines (lifilif) straight down catching red snapper. Some went spear fishing (ligipur) in the lagoon along the edge of the reef which on the south side of the island dropped straight down like a sheer cliff from the bright turquoise waters above the surface of the reef to the dark black depths of the Pacific. The first time I floated over it while spearfishing, I had the eerie feeling like falling off a mountain cliff in Colorado.

Other men went with their wives into the interior of the island where large breadfruit trees grew and gathered breadfruit (mai) from high up in the trees using a special "V" shaped on the end long wooden pole for knocking the hard unripen breadfruit down to the ground below. A ripened breadfruit wasn't suitable to boil and cook which was how breadfruit was commonly eaten. Some men walked around high up on the limbs of the tree, monkey like and as easy as if they were on the ground, but carried a rope when falling was feared. Others smoked out tree crabs by building a fire in a hollow base of old giant breadfruit trees.

But the most curious of all was watching some men put some breadfruit sap, which they had been chewing, and attached the sticky mass onto the end of a long pole. Then they climbed carefully up a coconut tree which had a sea bird resting comfortably at the top, quietly and stealthily slipped the pole between the coconut branches and finally poked the bird on its underside. Frantically the bird tried flapping its wings to fly away but it was firmly stuck on the end of the pole and pulled down to its captor who wrung the bird's neck. The sea birds resting in the treetops, when thrown on a fire feathers and all, tasted a lot like a Cornish hen to me.

The food preparation on Saturdays was serious business and the entire island participated. Many of the women went into the taro (pula) fields, really more like bogs, and dug up the yellow leaved tuber. Later the women boiled the breadfruit and the taro in big steel pots sitting on a fire. And some of the cooked breadfruit and taro would go onto a big wooden block to be pounded with a hand held coral pounder into mashed potato consistency called **po** or in Hawaii **poi** while some would be cut into pieces and have coconut milk squeezed on them. The men or women sat on a low stool (pwager) with a sharpened shell or piece of metal on one end to scrape out the coconut meat from a split opened coconut, and the shredded white coconut meat was squeezed releasing the milk.

Old hard grey coconuts that had ripened on the coconut tree and fallen to the ground were gathered up by grabbing them by their green shoots. These were mature coconuts which were used for making copra and coconut milk. The nut or seed inside is like the ones you would see in an American super market, hard and brown on the outside with three pores like eyes on the shell with hard meat on the inside wall of the nut. There was a very soft and spongy ball like food (apwil) that was a child's (actually everyone's) favorite dessert in the middle of the nut.

The shucking of the hard coconut shell is performed by the men taking a sharpened hard wooden spike or a metal spike anchored in the ground, and forcefully thrusting the shell against it, and prying the pieces off the dried husk like peeling a banana. (This was also the way a fresh coconut was shelled and you have a light colored hard nut to drink the coconut water inside. And this was how many drinking coconuts were dropped off at my hut everyday by my host, along with a bunch of bananas. Some of the old coconuts fibrous peels were tossed into a water pond to cure the fibers for making rope, and others were used for making fires to smoke the coconut meat drying it for copra production, and others for making fires on the sailing canoes to cook fish in a wide metal bowl, or for making fires at the cook houses.

Man could not have survived on these Pacific Islands without the coconut tree providing building materials, drink, food, string, rope, and a wine called falluba or ari. When Padre was on the island the chief, for good reason, would halt the production of the falluba, but the non- fermented and very sweet form called ari mum was harvested for a drink for the children. The coconut trees had spaced notches for feet cut out by a machete to make it easier to climb the tree. A younger man or boy could easily climb a coconut tree with or without the notches. I became adept at climbing the coconut tree either way, but would learn the hazard of climbing in the rain.

The bottoms of the native islanders feet were very tough from walking barefooted and it took time for mine to toughen. But the bottoms of my feet never did toughen enough to walk without tennis shoes on the reefs like the islanders which was necessary when hunting octopus at low tide on the sharp coral.

The young girls even at 6 or 7 were caring for their younger brothers and sisters instead of playing with dolls. It was not unusual to see small girls with young babies straddling their hips and walking on the paths in the forest with their parents. Young boys were mostly playing down at the beach and around the boat house and being watched by the grandfathers who were passing down their stories. These men were happy reliving some of their life stories and of course there was some embellishing for the eager young audience and plenty of humorous punchlines to keep their attention.

Sometimes a loud high-pitched wiyoooo wiyooo signaled the sighting a white sail or sails far out on the ocean bobbing in the waves. There was a rush of all the islanders down to the oot (boathouse) to await the safe return of loved ones and a fresh catch of fish. You know it was a good sign when the outrigger canoes would drop their sails offshore a short distance to enjoy a quick meal of pounded breadfruit, or cooked rice or both, wrapped in banana leaves with freshly cut slices of raw fish (sashimi). The fishermen knew that once the fish were hauled ashore the chief took control of the catch and begin to divide it up with all of the families according to each family's needs. And indeed the canoes arrived shortly and the fish were brought up to the oot and laid out on freshly cut coconut fronds. The young children excitedly danced around as the chief began to butcher the large fish and cut off fresh filets. He carefully strung a number of the choice pieces together with a coconut frond and began to hand the string to each family representative almost always with friendly banter over the choice pieces. Everyone was having a great time and smiling and laughing. A fire was started next to the oot and the fish skeletons were placed on the fire along with the heads of the fish. The roasted eyeballs were a special delicacy which I admit never caught on with me. And the fishing stories began to be told by the equally happy fishermen. "You should have seen the fish that broke our line and got away. It was at least 6' feet long!" Sometimes only a large fishhead would be all that's hauled in after a shark poached the catch. The head enhanced the proof of the story of the one that got away.

A very similar scene played out on the plains of Colorado when Native American buffalo hunters successfully returned to their hunting camps and told of the buffalo that escaped, or when my dad and his flyfishing partners gathered on the banks of the Williams Fork River in Western Colorado. We have original 8mm home movies so there is an actual record of the original size of the fish. My father tried to make his fish longer by stretching them holding the trout's head and pulling on the tail.

After the impromptu barbecue the men laid thick palm branches down on the sand beach from the beach up to the oot like railroad ties. The heavy sailing canoes would be pushed up onto the line of branches and every available man would push in unison to the chant "n-a-hoy"and pushing on **hoy**. "N-a-hoy" was called out all the way into the oot, and reminding me when I was stuck in a snowbank with my friends pushing my car out on the count, "**One, two, three- push!**"

Sunday began with Padre saying Mass accompanied by singing, the women's side of the church harmonizing with the men's side. The music was loud, joyous, and spontaneous. Toddlers stumbled from one parent to the other sitting on the right or left side of the church separated by a three or four foot space forming an aisle. In some cases, the toddler would be intercepted by another playful relative who would grab the child and put it on their lap before releasing it to continue on its journey. Sometimes to get a child's attention a tiny pebble would be tossed hitting a small child on the back of the head or making a whistling fetching noise or a clicking of the tongue to get the child's attention.

It was very common seeing children just naturally nursing from a mother's breast in church and really anywhere. Padre's sermon was delivered in a harsh staccato cadence in Lagoon Trukese and not in Weito, even after living in the Western Islands for so many years.

After the service everyone dispersed to their thatched homes and gathered up their contributions for the prepared feast and met in the open grass outside the school. Family groups sat cross legged on the short grass awaiting Padre's blessing. This was a summer season of plenty with large amounts of breadfruit, taro, coconuts, fish, lobster, and tree crab. "Feito Monga" (come eat) with a waving to sit and join. I surely wasn't going to starve on Piseras nor want for a friendly welcome feast including singing and dancing and laughter all around!

Thinking I would never read all the books in the Peace Corps book locker, Sundays turned me into a bookworm. I even read some real snoozers like *The Memoirs of Victor Hugo*, the *History of Vietnam*, and *The Rise and Fall of the Third Reich*- down to every last word in every last book. Wandering down to the boat house a group of men and women were playing cards and telling stories while watching their kids playing on the beach and running in and out of the lagoon. I joined in a swim with some fathers and mothers who were teaching their toddlers how to swim. The children were introduced to swimming and playing in the lagoon at a very early age because it was a necessity of life, as well as fun. One of the men pointed out a stone fish and warned me not to step on it as it was very poisonous and could kill you.

Swimming was for the islanders a necessary skill to learn and the laughing children were like ducks taking to water; a young palu (navigator) from Piseras jumped off a Japanese war vessel fifty miles from his island in the open ocean to escape a brutal slavery and swam back to Piseras and later lived to tell the story to me. When I arrived on each Island of the Namonuito Atoll, a feast was prepared to welcome me with food, coconuts, singing, and dancing. Everyone clearly was having fun and enjoying the day, especially the children and me!

Women welcomed Bob to Ono with a feast and performing traditional Island dancing similar to the Hawaiian hula.

Welcoming feast on Piseras with dancing

Puluwat Outrigger Sailing Canoe for Padre

The dispensary footers and concrete floor were poured and the block manufacturing was in progress and it was time for me to begin the same process on the other Islands of Ono and Onari. My goal was to get each Island making block and having their foundations and floors poured so each chief felt that there was progress on their own island and they weren't being left out. The anxious chiefs from both Ono and Onari had separately sailed down to Piseras and paid a visit to inquire when I would be starting on their islands. All three chiefs were reluctantly agreeable to the plan given their focus on just their own island. Two men from Onari came and helped me load my few things (pisek) on their outrigger canoe (wa) to move up to Onari, just when I was getting comfortable on Piseras- Rhamong eek (lots of fish), mai (breadfruit), and pula (taro) just what worried the other chiefs that I wouldn't leave.

It was hard to just pick up from the beautiful island where I had made good friends and inroads into the culture and the new language, but I was really excited to be on the ocean in an outrigger sailing canoe. There just aren't that many people in the world that have the opportunity to have the authentic sailing experience of Oceania and Polynesia. These Caroline Islands were one of the last places remaining on earth where the proud tradition was still a way of life. I had absolutely no sailing experience growing up in Colorado being a skier not a sailor, but I imagined the experiences would be similarly exhilarating. "It runs in the Family."

Our canoe was met at the beach on Onari by Chief Paulus and dancing and singing women wearing lava lava skirts festooned with coconut fronds. What a welcome! I wasn't expecting this and enjoyed every minute of this special day from my first trip on a wa to the happy feast. Smiling young children were imitating their mothers' dancing to the music of Island chants. I sure appreciated the grand welcome. I now had a better idea of how important the building of the dispensary was to these people, and couldn't let them down!

John, the Volunteer already living on Onari, was one of two teachers in the school and was gracious letting me move into his tiny house with him. The one- room framed house was tight and uncomfortable for the two of us always being in the way of the other. This just added to the motivation, if I needed any, to complete phase one as soon as possible.

Although not in Hawaii, it was the type of beach property many surfers dream about. There was a benjo (the coconut-palm thatch enclosed toilet space built for Padre when he was on Island) out the front about 200 feet away in the lagoon. Walking the plank to the benjo at night was tricky, but I could go around the back to the beach behind the house at night taking care of business next to the lapping waves. The tide would come in and all was nice and cleaned up in the morning. Occasionally there were others on the beach. I think I was the only one bothered!

This picture was taken from my window on an Air Micronesia flight directly over Onari Island. The green is the island shaped almost like a frying pan surrounded by the reef and smaller islands. The village is located on the narrow part or handle and when the wind blew the village was free from mosquitos and was naturally air conditioned.

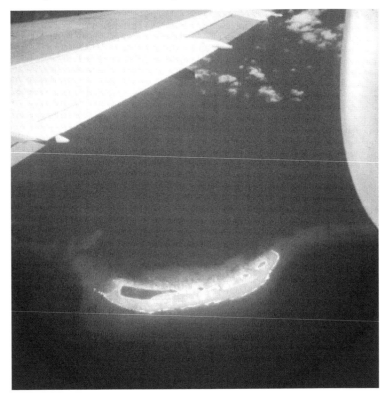

I learned from John that you had to have water proof containers to keep things dry. I also learned from John how hard the Peace Corps TESL teachers worked! Their day didn't end when the kids left school for the day with preparing his lesson plans, correcting papers, constructing visual aids, and preparing his dinner. There was no signing in and out on a time clock, but for a young college graduate like John, it was exciting to be putting to work the things he had learned in Peace Corps training and seeing the progress of his students. Unlike tenured teachers who have a backlog of old tests, assignments, worksheets, and sometimes ideas as well, John was a wellspring of new ideas. His enthusiasm and energy was contagious. At night when we would talk over our day, I was always impressed with how I would be finished and able to relax and he would still be working on something.

There weren't any cement block or concrete structures on Onari so building a dispensary was a new learning experience for everyone on the island. The block manufacturing began slowly but the islanders were fast learning the process. After a few failures and frustrations soon Onari was cranking out growing neat stacks which were then covered with wet copra bags to keep the blocks from drying out too rapidly during the curing period.

Also a delegation of eager men from Ono sailed over to observe the block making and took their new found knowledge back to Ono and started manufacturing block on their own. The women of Onari started stockpiling sand and aggregate by the dispensary site and rinsing the piles with fresh buckets of water. Mother Nature had been giving them a helping hand providing copious amounts of fresh rain water to wash the salt out from the sand and coral rock. These islanders were excited about working on the project and there was never any need for me to plead for or push the workers. None of us punched a time clock and we didn't work under the pressure of a deadline when we would finish the project, just the sooner the better.

My friend Adjubwah took me under his wing and gave me a spear for spearfishing and a koomy, surgical elastic tubing for a hand held sling to propel the spear through the water much like a sling shot. He took me out into the lagoon for my first lesson teaching the basics of diving down on the reef fish and spearing them and safely removing them from the end of the spear. It's not like back in Colorado when you remove a trout from a hook and banging the back of its head on a rock and tucking it nicely into your wicker creel. You are floating in the open ocean full of hungry sharks attracted to blood and the wildly flopping fish want to stick you with sharp-spiked venomous spines sharp as razor blades.

You CAREFULLY grabbed the fish still on the end of the spear with your free hand without touching the fins or the spines holding the fish still and inserted the back of its head and neck into your mouth biting down hard crushing its brain. Carefully you then pulled the dead fish off the spear and tucked it in between the folds in your belly pouch formed by folding a loin cloth in half and tying it around your waist. But you had to tie it in such away it could be readily untied and removed if a hungry shark became too interested in your belly and punching it in the nose didn't detract it from attacking your stomach from where the smell of the blood emanated.

A hungry bear might cause a Colorado fly fisherman to hand over a full creel of fish. Same principal!

While free diving and snorkeling you are aware of a very strong current washing around the island so you had to be careful not to be carried out beyond the reef. Adjubwah had no problem swimming deep and against the current wearing only his homemade wooden goggles. I came with swim fins, mask and a snorkel so I was able to keep up with him. He could drop down easily and stalk the fish while staying underwater for a long time. At first I was like a balloon and had to exert a lot of energy just forcing my body down under the sea surface and holding myself below without popping back up to the surface. I learned to take many deep breaths on the surface and expel the breath from my lungs before diving. It was always a struggle to swim back to the Island against the strong ocean current akin to swimming upstream in the Colorado River. But this was sure a fun way to go to the supermarket! And the new underwater world was as beautiful as it was dangerous!

Spearfishing was a great way to clean off the cement dust and sweat from working on the dispensary, and at the same time be a productive food gather for my host family. But you did have to watch out for sharks, eels, and barracudas all which wanted to snatch your speared fish. And I had to be careful not to step on the poisonous stone fish in the shallow water, or bump accidentally into a poisonous jelly fish, or the beautiful Lion Fish.

The underwater living coral reef was a rainbow of colors and home to an abundant variety of strange and colorful sea life. The turquoise green parrot fish, turtles, manta rays, sunfish, crabs, lobster, giant clams, and an incredible colorful variety of tropical fish weren't in a glass aquarium tank at Sea World but you were actually swimming in their midst. And the reef itself was a poison filled labyrinth of sharp stinging points and razor sharp edges. I must admit I didn't feel comfortable with the reef sharks suspiciously swimming around me at all times eyeing what I was doing.

Venturing forth by myself one day after work to spearfish, I spotted a head of what I thought was a fish poking out of a crack in the coral and pulling back on the koomy (elastic surgical tube) of the spear letting go with a perfect shot. Or I thought! But a large eel which had been shot through the neck came wriggling out of its hole trying to swim up the spear to where I was desperately holding on. Its menacing teeth were intent on biting me! Afraid to drop the spear, I kept the angry eel at bay by jerking the spear backwards sliding the eel's teeth away from my hand and body- again and again. Finally, I reached the safety of the beach after tiring myself out swimming against the strong current using only my free arm. Walking through the village with my trophy out of the water harmlessly spinning on the end of my spear, I felt pretty lucky that I wasn't bitten by the eel but also feeling pretty cocky. Until one of my friends told me that this type of eel was very dangerous and not edible. He looked at me with my brother Don's wide got-cha-grin and flung my trophy back into the ocean. **"I had a lot to learn"** and was thinking that same devil eel might be looking for me- the next time I swim into its domain.

On food preparation Saturday, a large number of men and women in a flotilla of small outrigger canoes paddled from the island paddled outside of the reef to the open ocean. The sea was like a smooth lake as there wasn't a breath of wind on this bluebird day and the reason the sailing canoes weren't fishing. The paddle canoes held large coconut palm branches and one canoe carried a long rolled up gill fish net. We paddled out on a side of the island where the sea bed sloped gently to deeper waters. Some of the canoes with the coconut branches were being paddled by laughing happy young girls enjoying the beautiful day.

I had no clue what was happening but was enjoying the blue sky day as well and the, "Live movie reel that was unfolding before my wide eyes." Several divers dove down about fifty feet to the sea bed and attached the long net to the bottom and with floats it stood about five feet tall above the sea bed. The outrigger canoes with the coconut palm branches formed in a wide arc began beating the sea surface and slowly closing ranks above where the net was placed on the sea floor. Just like the Colorado cowboys herded wild horses into a pen, a large number of large white fish were being herded along the sea bed into the gill net.

I was riding in one of the paddle outrigger canoes carrying the men who began diving down to the net holding the trapped fish. The divers dove down to the live fish caught in the net and killed them by stabbing them with a knife in the back of the head and then hauling them to the surface and thrown into the canoe. Initially being just an observer, I also dove down alone while the others were gathering their breath. At about thirty feet below the surface and above the net, suddenly something bumped hard into me from behind and turned me upside down! A very large blue shark had bumped into me and it was now circling me about ten feet away with another companion huge blue shark. Having been forewarned not to panic and desperately swim to the surface when encountering a large shark underwater, I made my best imitation of an angry chicken spreading my wings to show I was not as small or weak as I felt, waving my arms slowly up and down.

This seemed to be an appropriate time to pray a *Hail Mary* for a miracle. The very menacing sharks continued to slowly circle me when

Adjubwah dove down and joined me evening, the odds with the two sleek huge blue machines. Smoothly they retreated back out into the deeper waters! My whole body easily would have fit in either one! Only then did I force myself to swim slowly back up to the surface, and quickly I climbed back into the canoe finally filling my lungs with air! I watched my rescuer finish the job of harvesting the fish from the safety of sitting in the canoe. Admittedly, I was nervously trembling but feeling safe in outrigger paddle canoe! So much for macho man! But the danger couldn't spoil the blue of the sky and the deep blue of the ocean and the beauty of seeing the two open-ocean blue sharks. And **I was alive!**

Learning another very important lesson of the sea on Onari Island, I walked with Adjubwah and another companion out onto the reef at low tide. I was walking on the reef in my tennis shoes, and we were peering down in the deeper pools of standing water for targets for our spears. We came upon a hole with a large concentration of fish which had attracted us, or actually distracted us, and without warning we were all picked up by a giant rogue wave washing over the reef and flinging the three of us head over heels uncontrollably bouncing along the tops of sharp coral! Finally the wave slammed us onto the rocky windward beach. Battered and bleeding but no apparent broken bones, all of us had deep cuts where we tried to frantically to grab onto the reef. Never turn your back to the open ocean while standing on the reef!

I learned another lesson about the open ocean one day when I accompanied Adjubwah back down to Piseras Island starting out on a beautiful Saturday and not cloud in the sky in his outrigger sailing canoe. On our return trip back to Onari, we were suddenly caught in a powerful wind and rain squall nearly capsizing the outrigger sailing canoe. Luckily the canoe didn't flip totally over but the sail and the riggings were afloat next to the canoe and both of us desperately struggled pulling the riggings, ropes, and wet sail from the rough ocean. I helped as best as I could and learned not to stand on the tam (the outrigger) which started to sink fast. I was a skier not a sailor. What did I know in the open ocean? NOTHING!

Finally finishing up the foundation and concrete floor on Onari, it was time to move on over to Ono and start the process all over again. I was very thankful for the hospitality that John showed me while I stayed at his house on Onari. And I was especially grateful for the new Onari Island friends and was looking forward to the time I would return to finish putting up a dispensary on the recently completed foundation.

But it was time to pack up and sail again on another outrigger canoe short trip to Ono Island and construct the third foundation. The winds had picked up considerably with the early trade winds blowing and the trip to Ono Island on a small sailing canoe was now more than exciting for me. My last sailing trip on the open sea when a sudden and extremely strong squall had nearly resulted in disaster taught me to have at least two experienced Namonuito sailors aboard. Both Nargori and Adjubwah transported me over to Ono. Another lesson learned!

There are lots of ways to die in the Pacific Ocean, but being carried out to the open sea in the jaws of a blue shark, or breaking your neck on a jagged reef, or being blown away on a disabled sailing canoe, or being bitten by a sea snake, moray eel, or blue-ringed octopus, or bumping against a Lion Fish, or a blue bottle jelly fish while swimming were real possibilities for me!

Do you know how lucky you are?

CHAPTER 11
A Home on Ono

It was beginning to really dawn on me that 2 years was a long time to not see my family or friends, or go out on a date and have an honest to goodness cheeseburger with the works- French fries, and a Coke with a tall cup of ice! But I was now totally engaged and knew the rewards were worth the risks and sacrifices. And I was really beginning to speak more Weito.

And because of the challenge of my assignment and my close calls with the ocean, I was growing every day in my faith in God! But Chief Sak, who had been one of the first to welcome me when I arrived in the outer Islands on the Truk Islander, again welcomed me at the beach on Ono as we were pulling the canoe up on the sand. My two friends from Onari helped me unload all of my pisek (belongings). Santiago and Rufina and their young teenage daughter were my hosts and were also going to provide my housing down a small hill behind the village.

Seemingly everyone on the island followed us down to the weathered grey house sitting below the village. The thatched church was on one side and the common water well and an old weathered moss covered foundation on the other side. The people who couldn't squeeze inside the house jockeyed for a place at the door to watch their first Peace Corps Volunteer move in and hang a ski poster of my friend, Johnny Kruger, skiing at the Winter Park Resort, the first ski poster to hang on a wall on Ono Island.

Santiago and his family would be living in the village in their thatched home overlooking the ocean and I had the house to myself, a real luxury after being crowded in with another PCV on Onari. I needed to wash the sea salt off from sailing over from Onari before returning back up the small hill to where I was to be the honored guest at another welcome feast. I don't know why I am a big deal but I wasn't complaining, just getting fat!

Ono was a very small island with less than 100 people, including the women, children and elderly. It was so small that I was wondering how many workers were available to build the dispensary and also wondered how many people lived here before the cholera epidemic. I was going to miss spearfishing with my friend Adjubwah when he and Nargori left to return to Onari. He had become a close friend and he and his beautiful wife and their small children made me a part of their family, and I know he had saved my life – twice! I didn't know at the time that I wouldn't see the two of them again for many months. I did know that I would return back to Onari and finish building the dispensary where there was a completed foundation and neatly stacked cement blocks.

Hearing the waves breaking on Ono's beach that first night and trying to fall asleep in my new surroundings a sense of loneliness and missing home in Colorado came over me. It was nice to have Johnny Kruger to keep me company so far away from my home in Colorado.

BONG, BONG, BONG.......BONG!.... The loud ringing of the nearby church bell startled me awake from a deep slumber. Not feeling particularly prayerful when I bent low to duck into the small thatched chapel, I found a spot in the far back. Soon everyone was whispering and then everyone was looking and smiling at me, and I immediately felt at home among family. That is just how I felt as their warmth totally dispelled the melancholy mood of the night before. And, I remembered: "Where two or three have gathered together IN MY NAME, I AM THERE IN THEIR IN THEIR MIDST" (MATHEW18:20). The sun soon rose over Ono as the islanders and I started the day with song and a Rosary prayed in Kapasen Weito.

After having some rice and fish that Rufina brought me to eat for my breakfast, I heard the metal tank which had floated in on the tide being rung loudly. First day for work on Ono reminded me of the loud school bell at Regis High at the start of the first period of freshman year which put a fearful pit in my stomach; so with a gulp and putting on my game face, this freshman PCV marched up the hill to the meeting. Bastor greeted me with a huge friendly grin on his face while still banging the metal cylinder one last time to summon the last of the stragglers.

The chief spoke first and the assembled group discussed what would work best for each of them working during the construction of the dispensary. It was clear Sak might be the chief, but he wasn't a dictator. Each man contributed to the discussion of what the best way to organize among themselves to gather food and who would be available to work on the dispensary. This was not like a regular job with a time clock to punch in the mornings with a company or union rules. How many men could work on any given day on the dispensary would be decided each morning. The chief did make one rule which was the prohibition of the collection of ari (coconut wine also known as falluba), or the drinking yeast until the construction project was complete.

While building the dispensary the families still needed to provide food for their families and there was obviously a manpower shortage on the small Island. After the meeting, I was left with Bastor and Lucio and two others to begin to lay out the foundation. Bastor, Lucio, and I carefully marked off the approximate perimeter of the foundation with a string line. There was no fanfare or ground breaking ceremonial shovels when we broke ground on Ono's dispensary, and no photographers taking our pictures with a shovel for a press release! Ono had already started on manufacturing their cement block and there was already sufficient block to build the dispensary. We dug the trench for the foundation and built the forms to pour the concrete into, and made sure using the three, four, five triangle that the foundation was absolutely square. Padre would have been so proud!

Just to the side of the home provided for my use was a 4 foot tall foundation which the people had built on their own hoping in vain that

Padre would construct a new church on it. Unfortunately, it wasn't square and Padre respectfully declined. We weren't building a church, but I knew that if the foundation wasn't square the building sitting on it would be plagued with all sorts of problems, like windows and doors not fitting properly, and the roof would have to be altered to compensate. It's best to always start with a good solid foundation which is true for just about everything in life; especially learning a new language like the foundation of *Latin* helping me to learn French in college, and now *Lagoon Trukese* helping me to learn the language of the outer islands.

Chief Sak had called upon other possible helpers for constructing Ono's dispensary using the very powerful traditional custom of 'fanape' (small islands like Ono) called **tegnor**. It is asking for something as a family privilege, but more like *a family obligation*. I suspected that the elderly Rufina and the old Santiago may have asked Bastor for the sacred privilege of raising one of his beautiful teenage twin daughters. Santiago looked to be in his early seventies and possibly too old to father a child with Rufina who wasn't young herself. Bastor's daughter looked to be a twin. These girls were almost identical in beauty and were always together and nearly attached at the hip and whose thatched huts were side by side to each other.

I observed this custom as well on Piseras and Onari with families who had many children and would share a child with another family member who maybe had lost an only child or were unable to have children. The child would address both the actual parents and the adopted parents as papa and mama, and there was not a sense of abandonment only the sense of having more than one set of loving parents. And Rufina and Santiago seemed to me to be much too old to have a fourteen year old daughter. But how old was Abraham and Sarah?

The marriage custom in these islands was such that the husband usually went to live with the wife's family on her island. The husband received his property ownership, his island status, and his clan (inong) from his mother, and not his father. The outer islands are ruled by the mothers' lineage and the chiefs are determined by the mother's clan. So Sak could (tegnor) call on those men of his clan who live on other islands to come and help to build the dispensary. Chief Sak asked a member of the ruling clan of Ono and living and married to a woman on nearby Magur Island to come down to aid Ono in building its dispensary. He was special because he had attended PATS (Pohnpei Agriculture and Trade School) on Pohnpei Island and was a certified skilled carpenter who spoke English and after his graduation from PATS had worked construction on Guam.

He would definitely make a valuable addition to the Ono construction crew plus a huge help for me by having a professional carpenter with professional experience. Having sufficient laborers was a challenge for such a small island where hand shoveling and mixing concrete in the tropical climate was really hard, heavy, sweating, and exhausting. I would always take a turn with the shovel as did many of the women of Ono. We all pitched in!

It isn't just all work and no play. After spending the work day under the hot tropical sun getting dirty and sweaty, I would go spear fishing with a few of the workers who also wanted to jump in the ocean and cool off and wash off the dirt, grime, sweat, and cement from our worn out bodies. The tropical water was very comfortable compared to the cold Colorado mountain streams I would wash in after a hard day's work constructing trails in the Arapahoe National Forest.

Ono was interesting in that the front side of the island had no barrier reef but the ocean gradually became deeper and deeper the further away you swam out from the island. There were pockets of coral outcroppings of new reef teeming with fish life, although Ono did have a barrier reef around on the backside of the island. One Saturday, I was spearfishing with brothers Lucio and Aliphon on the front side of the island in about 15' of water just beyond the breaking waves. They were about 10 yards from me when I swam upon a hole in the submerged reef that contained a school of exceptionally large fish. I tried calling to my fellow spear fishermen to join me, but they were underwater and had seemingly not heard me.

So I began to stalk close enough to spear the smallest fish in the school of four or five fish. It was about four feet in length and a foot wide, and I was starting to pull back on the (koomy) sling getting ready to take my shot at the fish's head. Before I could let my spear shoot the big fish, Aliphon came out of nowhere and grabbed my right arm tightly preventing me from firing my spear. He motioned for me to surface and shook his finger at me. It turned out I was eyeing **a large grouper** and this fish could easily attack and drown me. Later back on the island he explained that it takes very experienced and strong men to spear and haul a grouper to the surface and was very dangerous! They leave them alone for good reason knowing from previous tragedies. There was much to be learned about surviving in the ocean that one doesn't learn fly fishing in the South Platte at Deckers, Colorado.

The deep waters off the front side of Ono were never dull. There were days when I would just follow along and watch the Ono Islanders and pick up pointers on spearfishing and their stalking technique, but even more satisfying was just observing abundant marine life. One day two awesome creatures of the deep glided by like big graceful underwater birds and the Giant Manta Rays seemed just as interested in us as we in them. My two friends dove alongside the swooping and graceful giants slowly flapping their wings and seeming to enjoy the company. The islanders could dive so much deeper than me down from the surface turquoise blue waters to the deep blue holding their breath underwater for what seemed an inhuman length of time.

Both the big mysterious animals and the divers were stunning to watch! So amazing I was shoveling concrete one moment earlier in the day, and I later was snorkeling in a Technicolor world seeing giant Manta Rays. One of the divers carefully grabbed a Manta and hitched a ride down even deeper. The big animal hardly even noticed him, and later when he surfaced he had a huge grin of a man who experienced something very wonderful and special!

Occasionally we would see large green turtles quickly swooping away from us and diving away to some mysterious destination not at all playful like the Manta Rays. This sea world was so fascinating and new I was transported from loneliness to a profound sense of awe words fail to describe. An old mountain man saying of Kit Carson seemed to fit the occasion, "Wagh!"

At night looking up at the South Pacific heavens having the same failure of words looking at the sky full of stars, I thought it really special watching the Southern Cross moving through the heavens just above the horizon. But sometimes you would see the distant bright lights of a big ship moving steadily through the night on its way somewhere to a modern world leaving you behind in the dark and going to somewhere unknown. Come back! I'm here!

On another day, unexpected danger showed its face again. There was an area of the beach on the back of the island that formed a half moon bay with pounding waves crashing onto one side of the beach and calm waters of a protected lagoon on the backside. A natural swimming pool with very clear warm water and a smooth sandy bottom was like a natural hot spring where I went sometimes to soak after a big concrete pour. The calm side of the sand beach barrier was also a great place to snorkel and view colorful tropical fish; angel fish, butterfly fish, and even the poisonous but very beautiful lion fish didn't seem very interested in my presence.

After work one hot afternoon, I decided to go spear fishing on the open ocean and the open ocean side of the half- moon beach. I foolishly went alone not finding anyone who wasn't already busy gathering food. I entered into heavy surf and began to swim out into deeper water. I snorkeled down below the surface wearing my face mask and fins where the visibility was still very poor. Close to the beach the water was very cloudy with suspended sand and air bubbles. I had swum here just days before when lazy waves gently broke on the deep sand beach and the water was translucent and a beautiful blue, but this was not one of those days.

The water began to clear at about 20 yards out from the beach when I spied in the corner of my eye a very large grey colored shark with a white underbelly closing and only five feet away and looking directly at me. It was so much bigger than any of the white tip reef sharks I had become accustomed to seeing. The huge shark had been totally obscured in the sandy bubble filled water and a surprise to have this scary monster following me and jumping out of the dark and going BOO! I knew I was in mortal danger!

I swam slowly underwater away from the shark angling to the right to rounding the corner of the island and staying in the deeper clear water while pointing the tip of my spear at one of its large eyes. I swam slowly around to the front of the island without retreating back the way I had entered. And luckily for me the big shark didn't follow disappearing back into its bubbly hiding place. I was breathing so hard when I dragged myself out of the ocean that I laid down flat on on the beach calming my pounding heart and getting back my breath. I learned another lesson and swore that never again would I go back there alone spear fishing when there were huge pounding waves clouding the water. The big mysterious shark became for me a **Great White Death,** which was a nightmare for nights to come! "Do you know how lucky you are?" Phillippe Cousteau warned me later at breakfast in Truk!

It was easy to make friends with the island people on Ono. The workers and their families would beckon me to join them to eat, "Feito monga," including Bastor who was the father of a very pretty teenage daughter who with Santiago's and Rufina's daughter made heavenly smelling plumeria flower wreaths for me every morning. Bastor always welcomed me with a cheerful smile whether at work or dinner.

I really enjoyed going from one welcoming home to the next and joining the families sitting cross legged around the dinner fire and learning more language and usually eating freshly barbecued fish, and occasionally lobster, off the fire with pounded taro (po), or breadfruit (mai) , or cooked white rice. We ate with our fingers off banana leaves instead of plates and always washed our food down with coconuts. (oon nu)

Only once did I go spearfishing at night for lobster! We paddled out in two canoes and attached water proof flashlights to our heads with a strong piece of rubber. When diving down from the surface with the flashlight turned on, the lobster stood out like they had a string of bright neon lights attached to their bodies making them easy to spot but not easy to spear. Surprising just how fast they could swim away. my spearfishing skills were no match for their speed. Plus I got a very creepy feeling diving in the dark not seeing but feeling what was behind me and beyond the beam of my light. It wasn't long before the skilled spear fishermen would surface with a lobster on the end of their spears and quickly filling our canoe. There was no question this was way over my head! They would dump lobster after lobster into a bag held by the paddler of the canoe and dive back down in the dark looking for more.

It was eerie looking at the light beams penetrating the dark water illuminating the scurrying lobsters. One of the divers surfaced by our canoe bleeding profusely from the side of his face after getting between a freshly speared lobster and a shark's mouth. That ended our lobster spearfishing for the night and thankfully with just a deep facial cut that just missed the lobster fisherman's eye.

The moral of the story are to not get in the way of a shark looking for a fresh lobster dinner, and it was the last time I went spearfishing for lobster in the dark! Still enjoying eating the barbecued lobsters on the cook house fires, I appreciated even more the lobster fisherman having to spear them in the dark ocean!

Ono Island was especially lucky to have its migrant workers from the other islands to add much needed manpower to build the dispensary. This island's shortage of manpower was critical and it was with dismay that the PATS carpenter informed me that he wasn't going to be coming down from Magur anymore to help because of a problem on Magur he was having with Red Sail, the Peace Corps Volunteer. And just a few days later, I received a letter from Red Sail delivered on a canoe requesting that I support him in an **undisclosed** complaint by Bastor. I was being asked to support Red Sail against an Ono Islander.

This was not why I joined the Peace Corps-not to take sides against the very people I was sent to help, especially when Red Sail didn't shed any light on anything about the complaint. Who did Bastor complain to and why was it important to involve me? Being the new guy on Ono, I saw no reason to take sides with either party, but especially with a **re-won**! It went against the idea, to paraphrase President Kennedy, to ask not what the people of the *Namonuito Atoll* can do for you, but what you can do for the people of the *Namonuito Atoll*. And to do that on the small Island, we needed every man and woman on the team to build the dispensary. Like in my small town of Silver Plume, Colorado mostly all on Ono were related, neighbors, and friends- where family stick together!

My hastily written response, given to the messenger who was anxious to get back to his canoe, was short and direct. "NO! I won't be taking your side in your dispute with Bastor; that's between the two of you. I was just told by the PATS carpenter that he had a problem with you, and he can't leave Magur and return to work on Ono Island. If what he told me is true, you need you consider what you are doing to him. He is needed on Ono. Just stop it!" Sincerely, Bob (*words to that effect.*)

Once again lady luck comes my way in the form of Marvin who shows up unannounced on Ono in a sailing canoe from Magur. He was taken out to Magur Island on the Peace Corps' sailboat sent there to assist Red Sail in building the school project. He looked very native in his loincloth. Of course a feast was held on his behalf to thank him for his invaluable contribution to the dispensary.

There were now new foundations completed on Piseras, Onari, and on Ono Islands and the cement block was available for all three dispensaries. Before Marvin's unexpected visit to Ono, it was the agreed plan by the three chiefs that I would return to Piseras to begin the final phase of constructing the dispensary where there were already trained workers thanks to Padre.

The next morning, Marvin looked over the foundation and began marking the foundations four corners outside edges. He then nailed vertically two straight two by fours on each of the building corners to the outside foundation walls, plumbed with a level and braced all around from which a string line could be stretched. Marvin marked the eight two by fours; two on each side of each corner, where string lines could be raised for each course of block. This aligned the placement of the blocks' outside edges. Following the string lines, the block walls would rise correctly straight and vertically plumb, row -by- row, all the way around the building to the top of all four walls. Next he had us mix a cement and sand mortar batch and conducted a class on how to properly lay the block.

SURPRISE! By the time he was finished with his carpentry class we had 3 courses of block and the vertical construction begun on Ono Island's dispensary; so much for my previous plan to move down to Piseras. But that was all right; I liked the new plan to now keep rolling on Ono Island until the dispensary there was completed. Thank you Marvin again for helping me!

Red Sail and his own wa (canoe) with its bright red sail cruised by Ono on its way to Onari on many occasions and never stopped by to pay Bastor or me a visit. Maybe Bastor didn't like his red sail! I know I didn't like his letter! And I'm sure he didn't like my brash reply! Whether his nose was out of joint because of me or Bastor, I wished he would have stopped on his way to Onari, so I could have gotten to know him better. I did admire the fact that Red Sail completed 2 years on a very small isolated Island the size of Ono and was a TESL teacher in Magur's school giving up two years of his life for young eager children wanting to learn English. Also he had secured a School to School Peace Corps Project which brought Marvin to my aid on Ono Island!

One thing for sure, Ono needed a well-stocked dispensary and a hospital trained health aid when a one year old baby toddler tumbled and fell into a fire spilling a large pot of scalding hot water on himself. When he was brought to my house hysterically crying, large sections of skin were already hanging in large slabs from both thighs, both of his little forearms, and his small belly and chest. My Loveland Ski Patrol training hadn't prepared me for this. The top skin layer appeared largely to have blistered and broken and exposing bright red flesh. And I knew it wasn't good to have such a large burn areas, but I remembered that pain was good and therefore the burns hadn't been so severe as to have destroyed his nerve tissue.

My Peace Corps first aid kit was stocked with a supply of antibiotic salve, thank goodness, but it didn't have any bandages large enough to cover such large burn areas. I asked someone to go and fill a plastic laundry tub with sea water and fetch it quickly. The mother and another woman then placed the small child into the cool water and gently washed off all the soot and ashes and grime from the burned areas. Rufina brought me my clean towels and gently dried the child off. I then applied the salve to the burn areas and swaddled him in the clean towels. After telling the women to keep the child from getting dirty and to frequently soak him in the cool sea water, they also needed to give him plenty of fluids. It was very gratifying to see the toddler recover without any visible signs of scarring.

There was an elderly lady who would have me bandage a sore on her foot for weeks and the sore never healed. Not knowing why it wouldn't heal. Later I talked to the Health Department representative onboard the Field Trip ship about her and asked him if he had any thoughts. He told me that she had **leprosy.**

The dispensary construction was progressing every day and exciting to see it daily take on new features like windows and door openings and a roof. Marvin's construction drawing told us where all the pieces would go so it truly wasn't a puzzle. This was a total island commitment and effort with all men and women on deck, especially, when we would have a big concrete pour. Months later we had a completed dispensary building with benches on the outside covered porch's waiting room to sit on and enjoy the ocean view. Now our next challenge was to build the water tank which was eight feet wide and tall with a cement roof and an access hatch on the top. The forms were a real challenge for me to come up with a design so the tank could be poured including the foundation floor and walls of the tank all at once. The interior wall forms were complicated so the concrete could flow under to the exterior wall and later be able to remove the forms. Cutting and bending and hanging the rebar was time consuming. But finding more needed laborers was a must since a concrete company refused to deliver to the site!

Chief Sak and I sailed over and met with Chief Paulus on Onari about the two islands mutually supplying the additional labor force when we poured the tank on each island. The mutual pooling of men from each island to help when the time came to hand mix the concrete, form a bucket brigade to lift the concrete to the top of the forms, and relieve exhausted laborers.

And what an event it was! The day came for the huge water tank to have the concrete pour. Tents for the mixing area and the stack of cement bags were hung up. We filled four fifty gallon drums full of fresh water to be replenished by the women when they ran low, huge piles of sand and aggregate collected and washed by the women, and the freshly stacked bags of cement moved out of the oot, food prepared to feed the large gathering of workers, and a large supply of coconuts for the thirsty workers to drink, and I had stocked up on several cartons of cigarettes to hand a pack out to everyone after the concrete pour. A loud shout signaled the sighting of sails and every outrigger sailing canoe on Onari was headed our way. Thinking back it was still one of the most beautiful sights I had ever seen! God hadn't forgotten His little Ono Island. I wished that District Administrator Jesse Quigley and Peace Corps Director Howard Seay could have witnessed our **Big Event**. Soon after the completion of the water tank, the Winter Park ski poster was taken down and stored with my pisek. With heartfelt thanks and "olela" said to my host family and friends, I walked back through the village with Adjubwah and Nargori, who were taking me back to Onari Island. We passed by the recently completed dispensary to our awaiting canoe, and I received heartfelt thanks from a line of men and women and children on Ono Island.

Young Ono Islander enjoys dancing and feast.

Bob with Bastor and his family on Ono Island

Josepio and his kids are on the same beach where I rested after
my encounter with a giant shark. The little boy, lying
on the beach, did the same thing as me when I reached shore.

My home on Ono Island with hosts Rufina, Santiago, their daughter, and my friend Lucio.

Marvin, the Peace Corps Carpenter and dispensary designer who was working on Magur Island's school, visited to inspect the dispensary progress and is enjoying a feast prepared for him on Ono Island. Chief Sak and his wife, welcome canoe with their daughter's family from Onari.

PATS certified carpenter

Chief Sak is dividing the catch of the day accordingly.

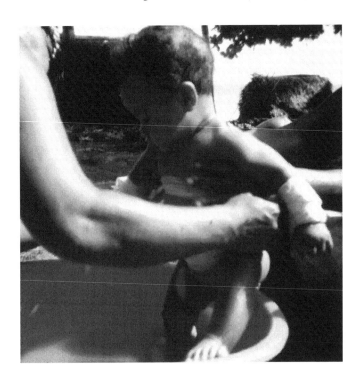

Bob and Piscenti inspected the earlier concrete pour.

Dispensary and water tank on Ono Island is ready if baby falls into cook fire again. Josepio mixed the concrete that went into the construction of the tank along with all the other men on the Island, as well as many of the women also took a turn with a shovel. Men from neighboring Onari Island sailed over to help on the day of the big pour for the big tank.

CHAPTER 12
Painted Footsteps

Arriving back on Onari I was surprised to find that John, the Peace Corps teacher, who I stayed with earlier, was not there! For some reason, not shared with me, Chief Paulus told me that he had met with the Peace Corps Director on Moen and requested that John be transferred off Onari Island. The Peace Corps Director listened to the chief and was responsive to his demand removing John quickly and quietly, I assume on the Peace Corps sailboat. The big news didn't make it over to Ono. But I was, selfishly, going to be alone in the small frame house.

After moving my belongings in, I unrolled my Colorado Ski Poster , and hung it on a wall with my friends wondering what snow was like. Adjubwah and his wife and small children were assigned by the chief to be my host family on Onari Island, and conveniently living next door. Usually after work Adjubwah and I would go spearfishing and bring home fresh fish for the fire or pot. And now I was much more capable to bring home the fish sometimes by myself while Adjubwah and his wife would harvest the breadfruit (mai- sounds like my) or pula (taro root). On some Saturdays, we would go trolling for big fish with large mono filament lines tied to the outrigger canoe and using a homemade lure made with coconut palms and colored weights with a small bait fish hooked on the end.

Adjubwah and his friends liked to listen to Trukese music from the Moen radio station on my shortwave Japanese radio. After a Saturday morning of fishing, the small house would be crowded with the local boys playing a three string guitar and singing Trukese folk songs with the chief's son leading the group. My tape recorder was kept busy! Trukese three string guitar music and folk songs weren't really my thing, although I did learn *Marian'ne* the Trukese love song of a very pretty wife of a friend of mine on Moen who worked for the Trust Territory government. *(Donna and I were staying at an Airport Hampton Inn overnight in Spokane, Washington a few years back with an early flight out in the morning. We were having a late dinner when the waitress served us and I recognized that she might be from Chuuk. So in Trukese I softly began singing Marian'ne, and her eyes about popped out of her head and she began to wipe away her tears! She said she was from Tol, but I suspected that was just how wretched was my singing of one of her favorite songs!)*

On one occasion that I was accompanying the deep sea fishermen on an outrigger sailing canoe, we hooked onto a giant fish which two men were hauling in hand over hand as fast as they could pull, which wasn't very fast! The fish was a real fighter jumping high out of the water while the men frantically were pulling it towards the canoe. Their fear was of a shark attacking the fish before it was gaffed and pulled aboard. The struggle between the big fish and the tiring men was finally lost by the fish, as it was finally pulled exhausted alongside the big outrigger canoe and the enormous fish was hauled aboard the sailing canoe.

But by no means was the fight over with the huge fish thrashing about in the hull finally dying from repeated blows from the machete. This one fish could feed the entire island of Onari. Too bad that the oot didn't have a hook and scale to measure the length and weight, but it required the four man crew to carry it into the oot. The sharp teeth could easily have seriously injured any one of us.

Fishing in the Caroline Islands was a very dangerous balancing act between risk and reward and sometimes the fish won the battle, but this time the reward made the feast more meaningful knowing first hand we didn't walk the aisles of Safeways filling up the cart. No wonder the 20 year expected life span is so short. There are many ways to die in the outer islands. These were a fiercely proud and powerfully built people, like the Ute buffalo hunters escorting young Dan and Ellen Griffin's covered wagon.

Early one morning I was surprised to see the Peace Corps sailboat arrive offshore and the Truk District Director, Howard Seay paddle ashore. It was what I thought would be a visit to inspect my progress on the dispensary on Onari, but it was just a short stop to see how I was doing. He also wanted to tell me that his tour with the Peace Corps had ended and personally wanted to thank me for my service. He was eager to press on sailing to the other Western and Namonuito Islands with other Peace Corps Volunteers to thank and give them his personal farewell. Howard was a casualty of the past presidential election and the prerogatives of President Nixon to replace the Peace Corps Directors with his own choices.

He didn't have to show me that courtesy, but I shall always remember it. He was a great director and I will always appreciate the opportunity he gave me with his choosing me for this assignment. It was a privilege and honor being one of his Peace Corps Volunteers and after he gave me a parting hug and a pat on the back on the beach, he sailed off never for us to meet again. I will always be thankful to him and remember him as a good man with a tough job who gave me the opportunity to live and work with such remarkable people.

Working diligently on the dispensary by the time the next Truk Islander field trip ship arrived off the coral beach of Onari Island, all of the block work was completed with door and window openings in place. The next order of construction was the attaching of forms to the top of the completed block walls to pour the horizontal concrete and steel band which ties and reinforces all the walls together with the roof. I was looking forward to receiving letters from home and restocking my food supplies from the ship and giving a tour to the Peace Corps Volunteer in charge of delivering our supplies and mail. The Volunteer was a friend of mine from training and brought me the shocking news that I was drafted months before by my draft board back in Colorado. The Peace Corps Office in Washington had unsuccessfully appealed my draft notice.

I had been ordered to report to the nearest Induction Center for a physical and immediate induction into the Armed Forces of the United States. Further I was considered delinquent for the draft and could be arrested.

The nearest Draft Center was on Guam, and I had to accompany my friend back to Truk where I would be flown up to Guam. We met with Chief Paulus and informed him of the situation and he was visibly upset, but I assured him that another Peace Corps volunteer would eventually be sent out to complete the construction of the dispensary in my place. The provost marshal of Colorado had reached out once again, but this time to the great- grandson of Dan Griffin. Again the mountain seemed too big to climb, but I didn't panic! I could climb any mountain or meet any challenge because my God was **bigger!**

The trip back to Moen was uneventful although the ocean was very rough. It made me think about stories I heard on the Namonuito Atoll of Islanders who ran out of cigarettes making the hazardous journey to Moen during the strong trade wind season. After the Truk Islander was being tossed around like a cork on the turbulent seas and burying its bow in the huge waves, I thought that being out of cigarettes wasn't worth their torture or the risk. They described their craving as really being (fokun asupang) hard up! Finally arriving in one piece and learning that I wasn't immune to seasickness, the Truk Islander arrived on Moen. I wobbled across the dirt main road to the Peace Corps offices opposite the Truk Trading Company and reported to Nancy, the Peace Corps office manager, to get my instructions.

She already had me scheduled to fly out of Moen in two days to report to the Naval Hospital on Guam to take my induction physical. I was not yet giving up hope that there might be a miracle that I knew the people on Onari were praying for as well as me.

I was picked up at the airport on Guam by two uniformed military policemen and driven in a military jeep directly to the Agana Naval

Hospital where the induction physical was to be taken. I wasn't alone at the Induction Center where there were **eager** Chamorro inductees from Guam. Because the spoken language was Chamorro on Guam, footsteps were painted on the floor which the inductees were instructed to follow after stripping off all their clothes. Being the only Caucasian present among the inductees, I thought the footsteps led directly to Vietnam. The footsteps actually led you around a room with Naval uniformed doctors checking on your suitability to be drafted.

When approaching the first doctor, he looked me over from head to toe asking, "Where did you get your full body dark brown tan and sun bleached blond hair?" Responding very politely to him, "I was a Peace Corps Volunteer working in the Truk District building medical dispensaries to fight a **cholera epidemic** wearing a loin cloth. I should be on Onari Island now finishing the second of three dispensaries to be buil down there, instead of here in Guam's Induction Center. In another year my Peace Corps deferment will expire."

Surprisingly, he agreed and asked what Islands I was working on? I replied "The islands in the Namonuito Atoll." He said: "I've been there on a Navy medical ship and know about cholera there! What are you doing **here?** You are needed down **there!** Come back here when you are finished at the rest of the stations. I've seen the tragedy of the Vietnam War here in this hospital." Ironically, I would soon see it myself.

With hope in my heart, I returned to the first Naval doctor's station after following the painted footprints around to all the other medical stations. The doctor asked me to step into a private exam room where he had my Peace Corps papers which I brought with me from Truk. This time he didn't ask me about my dark tan, but he did ask for my recent medical history. Definitely carrying cement bagsbothered my knee. The doctor had me climb up onto an examining table and examined my knee. It was unstable and loose.

My doctor back in Colorado wanted to try physical rehab of the knee first, before scheduling a surgical repair. That worked for me, as I was also on Regis's ski team and had hopes to ski in the upcoming ski racing season. And I knew that I didn't stand a chance with a long surgical operation rehab. The Naval doctor said, "I am going to recommend a reclassification of your 1-A draft status to 1-Y which means that you would be called up again only in the case of an invasion of the United States Homeland. And I will request the medical files from your doctor back in Colorado who treated your knee last year as back-up. **Go back and build those dispensaries!**"

What were the odds! Colorado's provost marshal may have killed Dan Griffin in Central City, but Dan wasn't going to let them get his great-grandson!

That wasn't the only MIRACLE but just a couple of weeks later I was back flying Air Micronesia from Truk to Guam with appendicitis diagnosed by the Peace Corps Doctor on Moen. **I could have been on Onari!** Again I was met by Navy MP's who took me this time to a Navy surgeon's office upstairs at the Agana Naval Hospital who after examining me; he immediately rushed me into surgery.

Remembering the masked and gowned anesthesiologist asking me, "Would I approve of a Micronesian doctor giving me a **spinal tap** just for practice?" The Naval anesthesiologist said that he would supervise. I said, "Go ahead," thinking I couldn't feel any worse. **Wrong!** My right leg began uncontrollably kicking, which believe me was not a good sign. So the anesthesiologist had the Micronesian student re-direct the needle. Now my left leg began jerking even worse. The surgeon declared, "Stop.........around. I have a............ hot appendix here," Navy jargon deleted. The gas mask was immediately placed over my nose and mouth and goodnight Irene and sweet dreams.

My first night after the appendectomy was difficult since I was very nauseous with nonstop dry heaves which caused lots of bleeding. The post-surgery ward at the hospital was filled with Marine combatants, who recently were airlifted freshly wounded off the Vietnam battlefields, and

and whose cries for their mothers was very poignant. Loud groans begging for pain killing shots and occasional screams punctuated the painful night's living hell. I was so impressed with the young male and female nurses who so professionally and tenderly administered to the wounded; they were just amazing!

Being in a lot of pain, I received a shot of Demerol allowing me to escape my pain and the profound sorrow I felt for the seriously wounded and for the two marines who died during that night! I stayed only a short time in the post-op ward and moved to another ward just around the corner filled with patients like me. I was placed near a young 18 year-old Boston Irish marine who had been shot in the back leaving him paralyzed below his belly button. The Navy man on my other side had also been wounded and was worrying what he would tell his young wife back home about losing his manliness. The marine next to him was swathed in facial bandages and had lost all of his facial features, including his eyes. I didn't talk much at first not wanting my hospital bed neighbors to know I was a Peace Corps Volunteer who only lost his appendix! Every morning the doctors made their rounds and put fresh bandages on their screaming patients who experienced excruciating pain when the old bandages were ripped off, not too gently!

While staying on this ward an injured Navy patient, who I had known in Truk before I took my assignment in the outer islands, ended up just a couple of beds down from my own. He was with a Navy Seabees Unit which had been sent to Moen to help fix the roads and repair the runway at the airport. He had been thrown out of one of the pickup taxis when it rolled over throwing out two of the Seabees. He was one of them and had required surgery and the other was up on the top floor of the hospital with other patients in comas. I was told the entire top floor of this massive hospital was filled with unconscious patients, mainly from Vietnam.

It's a shame that the painted footsteps downstairs in the induction center didn't lead to an elevator stopping at a station up on this floor or the top floor, and for some of those excited Chamorro Guamanian kids the footsteps did eventually lead back to a station here! *War* is the most contagious scourge of all human disease which we seem unable to cure but so eager to catch and spread! There was no glory in war known by the marines in Agana Naval Hospital!

My cover was blown when a very big Marine in full uniform was walking by the bedsides of the wounded and talking to each man. When by my bedside, he took a very long look at me and said, "Isn't it time you get a haircut?" Taking his question as an order and replying, "**No sir,** not meaning any disrespect, **I'm not a marine.**" Now he walked around to the foot of my bed to read my name, and underneath my name was <u>Peace Corps Volunteer</u>. "PEACE CORPS." He loudly began asking questions about why I was in the Naval Hospital on Guam. He quietly switched his demeanor, scaring me one moment, and being genuinely concerned about me the next. I appreciated his quietly saying to me, "Only officers were called, "Sir" and not sergeants-breaking the ice for me with my nearby fellow patients.

Approaching every bed and keeping with Marine Corps discipline, he was "sergeant" here, but he was also father and mother and showed a very comforting side with the suffering boys reminding them that they were also members of the marine family. He came by every morning, and I now knew to address him with the respect he earned and deserved for his service to our country. "Good morning, SARGE!"

Now that the word was out that lying among these gravely wounded marines was a Peace Corps Volunteer, I thought that there would be a very negative reaction. But just to the contrary, Marines from all over the ward, sought me out with genuine friendliness and was asked many questions about the Peace Corps. The Marines who were able to walk would come over to my bed and shake my hand and say, almost to a person, that they wished that they could be doing what I was doing. These were mostly young enlisted men between 18 and 20 years old who had been fighting a war thousands of miles away from home. The less severely wounded feared that they would be sent back to Vietnam. When I was disconnected from my IV's, I was encouraged to walk around. And visiting with my neighboring patients, I was struck with the fact the walking wounded were put to work every morning either mopping the floor, cleaning the bathrooms, straightening the lounge, and dumping the ash trays- all at double time.

The only officers on this ward were the doctors and nurses; wounded officers were in a different part of the hospital in keeping with a caste system that totally separates officers from the enlisted men and 18 year old wounded draftees. I would accompany some of the ambulatory patients to a movie theater on the same floor, only for the enlisted men, showing new movies from home. The black Marines sat on the left and the white Marines sat on the right. Don't get too comfortable sitting in the middle. If they could only harmonize, maybe they could sing like the men on one side and the women on the other on Ono, Onari, and Piseras.

I did walk over to the bedside of the young marine from Boston who had been shot in the back paralyzing him below the waist. I asked him how he was wounded. He explained to me that he had been with his squad of marines walking slowly up a very steep hill in heavily overgrown jungle, and was on point when he was shot in the back by a "Gook" who popped up from a concealed underground hole. He hadn't seen it when he passed it but remembering tumbling uncontrollably down the steep hill and being stopped down below by his buddies. And as an afterthought he said, "**He was going to miss squeezing Gooks!**"

I looked into his deep blue eyes and thought this must be the mentality of a young IRA gunman; kids at this young testosterone amped age actually **enjoyed war** and **killing**- all the while thinking they were invincible. It's a violent game which leaves real dead and real wounded people. The "**Gook**" had a mother, and a father, and probably brothers and sisters, and maybe a wife and kids likely in a nearby village, and was also likely just a teen, and likely also enjoyed **squeezing marines** who were in **his** country. The handsome blue-eyed Boston-Irish marine had been just a trusting patriotic eighteen year-old, a young Jack Nicholson look alike. He was **8,795.1 miles** from his home in Boston, just a boy by any measure, paralyzed for life fighting in Vietnam. And for what? Perhaps as this handsome paralyzed young Marine grew into maturity, he lost his teenage innocence and his thinking probably changed! Marine recruiters focused on the young impressionable high school candidates who lacked much knowledge of the real future consequences of a deeply flawed national policy. This marine was heading back home to a divided country where some might not appreciate his sacrifice .

After three weeks at the Agana Naval Hospital, I was finally winging my way back to Truk having survived! I gingerly walked into the Peace Corps Office and received *gentle* hugs from Nancy and the rest of the staff who were relieved and were genuinely happy that I was alive and in their office! If they hadn't pulled me off Onari the odds were not in my favor surviving appendicitis on remote Onari Island. Nancy, a PCV from Micro 7 and office manager, asked me, "Do you know how lucky you are?" Yes, I could have died on remote Onari Island! The apparent bad news delivered to me by the Peace Corps representative on the field trip ship was just another example of God saying to me, "I am in control. Keep the Faith and I will turn all things in your favor. I am on the Throne and this is My World!" (Joel Osteen)

But now what do I do on Moen while I await the next field trip ship not departing for the Namonuito Atoll in months? The answer came when I reported back into the Community Development Office. There was a short term landscaping project around the Peace Corps Office and the Truk Trading Company. Using a Motor Pool truck, I would stop by the District Jail and pick up a prisoner labor force and drive to the southern end of the island to dig up coconut tree saplings to plant along the walkway. On one of our frequent road trips to dig up trees, I would drive past a woman and her small children waving at us from the side of the road. After passing them several times, I asked one of the convicts the reason for their continued greetings? It turns out the friendly greeters were the wife and children of one of the convicts riding in the back of the truck. So the next time driving by them, I stopped the truck and let the convict out and told him that I would pick him up on the way back from digging up the trees in a couple of hours. His house was just uphill from the road and we would be making at least two trips back and forth. When I returned back, I honked the horn and a smiling convict walked down the path waving back to his family standing in the doorway. It was certainly his **lucky day,** and mine that he was there! Unfortunately for him this was just a very short term project.

This was June and most of the outer island Peace Corps TESL teachers were traveling back to Moen and going on vacation. Some of the Micro 7 volunteers had planned a trip to Japan for their Peace Corps vacation. My friend Lewie from Ulul and I decided we would take a week and go to Saipan in the Marianas staying in the new Continental Hotel, built by Air Micronesia (Continental Airlines) and eat like kings and be tourists for a week- just laying back! I was still recovering from my recent vacation at government expense on Guam in the Naval Hospital.

Gazing out from our ocean front room, I saw a barrier reef with scuttled tanks and LST's on them from the American invasion of Saipan during World War II. Lewie was interested in ordering bacon and eggs for breakfast and eating a hamburger and finding a bar on Saipan to savor his first cold beer in over a year. I enjoyed those pleasures just a few weeks before thanks to the U.S. Navy Hospital which lived up to its reputation of having good chow. Unfortunately I still couldn't enjoy the hotel swimming pool just yet with my incision still not completely healed but enjoyed sitting around the pool and talking to pretty Air Micronesia stewardesses- and drinking cold beer!

Lewie and I hit the hot spot on Saipan for young employees of The Trust Territory Government on Saipan. Many beautiful young girls of Saipan were dancing to Creedence Clearwater Rival's *Proud Mary, Lookin' Out My Back Door, Green River,* and *Have You Ever Seen the Rain* on a crowded dance floor. Using my recent operation as an excuse not to dance, I sat watching Lewie dancing the night away while enjoying listening to John Fogarty. I can't hear Proud Mary without thinking about that great little bar on Saipan and the cute Chamorro girls!

We met a Peace Corps volunteer at the Peace Corps office on Saipan who was planning a hike up to the north end of the island along the coast. The Army Corps of Engineers was still cleaning up the unexploded ordinance from the war on the Northern part of Saipan which was still closed to the public for safety reasons. He had cleared the hike with an army friend, so Lewie and I were invited along. We hiked North up the ocean front of beaches and rocks seeing many unexploded naval artillery shells and making a wide path around them. After walking for over an hour, we spotted a cave high above us and decided to climb up and to take a look inside.

We climbed cautiously up to the cave and upon entering saw lots of broken cutlery, human bones, tattered uniforms, hand grenades, and shattered rifles. Obviously the Corps of Engineers hadn't yet cleared this cave and, careful not to touch anything, backed out not wanting to disturb the site. This was not too far from the Banzai cliffs where thousands of Japanese civilians jumped off in mass suicidal fanaticism. Later that week, Lewie and I toured the last Japanese Army Command Post in the bloody battle for Saipan. A tour bus, at the same time, unloaded a large group of Japanese tourists who somberly joined the two young American Peace Corps Volunteers walking through the site of battle carnage- when it started to rain.

Still the rain kept pouring
Fallin' on my ears
And I wonder
Still I wonder
WHO'LL STOP THE RAIN?"
(John Fogarty)

Let it rain. Let it rain
Open the floodgates of Heaven.
Let it rain. Let it rain
MY SOUL LONGS FOR YOU
LET IT RAIN
(Song by: Jesus Culture)

Bob in the rain on Onari

CHAPTER 13
Sail Away

Being drafted by the Gilpin County draft board when I was so close to finishing the dispensary appeared to be a capricious twist of fortune and a setback for Onari Island, but it was actually lifesaving for me and part of God's plan. Now with my appendix removed on Guam and back from a week's vacation on Saipan, I was watering the freshly planted coconut trees in front of the Peace Corps Office when I heard a loud commotion across the road at the main dock on Moen and saw a large white sailboat entering the harbor.

This wasn't an everyday occurrence and I, along with a small crowd of Islanders, rushed to the waterfront to see it tie up at the dock. The captain saw me in the crowd and asked if I can speak English? "I speak a little. Can I help you?" After tying his sailboat up and leaving his teenage son to watch the boat, he and his pretty blonde wife came ashore. He explained that he needed to resupply quickly and continue onto Saipan where he was to begin a new job. He had left Australia where he had been working as an engineer for the past five years.

Without hesitation I asked him if he would drop me off on his way to an Island that I was working on for the Peace Corps almost directly in a straight line to Saipan. I had seen it from the air on my recent Air Micronesia flight. We walked across the road over to the Peace Corps

Office and made all the appropriate arrangements with the Peace Corps Assistant Director who paid the two Americans for my trip back on their sailboat to Onari.

While he was across the parking lot shopping at the Truk Trading Company, I retrieved my few belongings and returned to the sailboat in less than an hour. And in just over six weeks after leaving Onari I was on beautiful white sailboat headed back to finish the dispensary on Onari Island! What a miracle!

This wasn't just any big sailboat! It was hand built in the engineer's backyard in Australia and built out of ferrous cement and chicken wire. I had never heard of a cement boat and was wondering how long it would stay afloat in seawater. I couldn't see the difference between this cement boat and a fiberglass boat, and it had already sailed from Australia to Truk so it looked plenty sturdy to me. But what do I know about boats!

The captain's pretty blonde wife was the 1st mate on the sailboat, and their 15 year-old son was the navigator who allowed me to take shots with a sextant and helped his plotting of the course to Onari. And they were all very interested in what I was doing there and what to expect on the island.

When I described the customs of the people of the outer Caroline Islands to them, I delicately approached the topic of the women going topless- not knowing if she would be offended by what she would see on Onari! And I told the captain, that the men wore loin cloths. This didn't faze them coming from topless beaches in Australia.

At night the captain kept the North Star off to the starboard bow and the Southern Cross port side of the stern on that beautiful South Pacific star filled night. *"When you see the Southern Cross for the first time you understand why you came this way."*(*Southern Cross* by:Crosby, Stills, and Nash)

We finally dropped anchor off Onari Island and were soon met by paddle canoes. You could hear the loud whoop, "Wi-yo..ooo" when they saw me! Someone began banging the church bell to signal a sail canoe and the return of their lost Peace Corps Volunteer. A pig was slaughtered and the celebration began for the return of their prodigal son. To say it was a total surprise to see me was not doing the word *surprise* justice! And for the next two days the Island of Onari danced and sang and feasted celebrating and entertaining their unexpected guests on the white sailboat which arrived unexpectedly from the South carrying their lost (sheep) Volunteer!

The captain proudly toured the curious men and women of Onari on his sailboat displaying all the features on a state of the art open ocean *re-wan* boat which very much interested the island's outrigger canoe sailors and navigators, especially the modern compass. I know the American couple and their son enjoyed the festivities and the opportunity to learn about the way of life on a South Pacific Island. And I am deeply thankful to them for taking me back to Onari and allowing me to enjoy the beautiful star filled night on their sailboat.

But something happened to me since two apparent unlucky bad breaks proved to be the luckiest breaks in my young life. "Do you know how lucky you are?" to see both the Southern Cross and the North Star that first night sailing back to Onari after having my appendix removed courtesy of the United States Navy. I was deeply grateful for the excellent care given to me by the doctors and nurses at Agana Naval Hospital and a hamburger, fries, and Coca Cola with ice!

And I will never forget the screams and the pain filled groans of the wounded marines crying for their mothers in the middle of the night, or the wheeling out of dead marines on gurneys in the morning, or Banzai Cliff on Saipan, or still *rolling rolling* in my mind- Creedence Clearwater Rival's *"Have You Ever Seen the Rain"* while walking through the last Japanese Command Post on Saipan. Or hear *Sailing* by Christopher Cross, **"Oooh the canvas can do miracles... Just you wait... and see... Believe in me!"**

Bong.....Bong......Bong. I walked into the church and took my place at the far back of the little thatched Church and prayed the Rosario with the women of Onari. Looking around the small church, I noticed the daughter of one of my good friends and a faithful worker nursing her newly born

white baby while she was praying the rosary. I know I was supposed to be praying and not looking around! But I was thinking that the father must be John, or maybe … …..!

The family was very discreet and there was no talk of who the father was, but there was no doubt the baby would be well cared for and loved. About twenty years later by accident I met up with John the former PCV on Onari at a Lahaina, Hawaii's Safeway Store. He was sacking groceries to earn money to provision his sailboat which was anchored in the Lahaina Harbor. He had been sailing around the world and Lahaina was his home base. So Donna and I invited John to dinner that night and for years I had unsuccessfully attempted to contact him not knowing he was sailing around the Pacific aboard his sailboat anchored now in Lahaina.

After enjoying a couple of Pina Coladas and Mai Tais, I discreetly told him that he had a child on Onari. He immediately replied that he wasn't the father and after all the years thinking that was the reason for my having his cozy little house on Onari. I did know that the beautiful child was another treasured surprise gift from God for Onari Island! **The best gift of life!**

One night, listening to my Japanese short wave radio to Armed Forces Radio, I was thrilled hearing Neil Armstrong's words, "THAT'S ONE SMALL STEP FOR MAN, ONE GIANT LEAP FOR MANKIND" after becoming the first man to land on the moon. The stars and moon were so bright from the pollution free South Pacific Island you could almost see him walking on the same moon!

The dispensary construction was just as I left it and we picked up working as if I hadn't been gone. One of the important features of the building was that the holes in the block were filled with steel reinforcing bars and concrete making the block building essentially a solid concrete structure with rebar attached to the roof rafters. This proved to make the dispensary also a small typhoon shelter- and none too soon. A couple of months later the Truk District of Micronesia was slammed by a glancing blow from a Pacific typhoon, and Onari was not spared. The wind and rain blew through my screen windows so hard that I had to take my Winter

Park Poster down before it blew off the wall. When rain is being driven by howling winds, it is actually very cold in the tropics- especially when it was blowing right through my house.

Thinking the dispensary might be safer than getting soaked by the rain, I pushed against the wind and driving rain to the safety of the little concrete building. Opening the door, I was surprised to see that it was already packed with the island's nursing mothers, young children, and a couple of parents calming them all. Making my way back to a thatched house, I found two of my friends drinking yeast. **The typhoon was blowing down trees with loud smashing noises** in the forest. The deafening sound of the wind and the crashing waves seemed to get louder by the minute as you wait expecting them to wash over Onari. Hunkered down low on the floor next to the thatched wall, the house was disintegrating above my head. Strange as it sounds, I fell asleep listening to the fury of the storm and the shouting of my two **yeast** fueled friends having an argument.

I awoke early the next morning hearing the bong...bong...bong of the church bell, but not the roosters that were probably blown across the sea to Vietnam. In the daylight you could see debris was strewn everywhere along with fallen coconuts, palm branches everywhere, and fallen coconut trees. The island village suffered major devastation to thatched homes and boat houses which were no match for the violent winds. The island's food supply also took a direct hit with most of the breadfruit harvest blown down along with many of the giant trees.

I think I might have been the only one sleeping blissfully ignorant of what the consequences could have been for the low lying island. The small framed house I was living in was still standing and incredibly the tin roofing was still attached. It would take the island some time to repair the damaged thatch homes and go back to working on the dispensary. Walking over and inspect the dispensary, I was grateful that the roof was still attached and proud that the dispensary was a refuge for many of the island's children. I spent the rest of the morning walking around the storm ravaged island taking pictures of the limited damage for the chief, including taking many photos in the forest of the fallen breadfruit trees. Chief Paulus thought at some point he might have to sail into the Truk Lagoon and petition the government for emergency food supplies for his beleaguered island. Later that day an American Air Force recon aircraft flew slowly over both Ono and Onari Islands and probably the rest of the islands in the Namonuito Atoll, as well as the entire storm damaged outer islands. My guess was that Jesse Quigley, the District Administrator for all the Islands in the Truk District, already had relief efforts underway.

Less than one week later a huge U.S. Air Force transport plane loudly flew low over the island appearing suddenly from out of nowhere. As it circled back, large containers were pushed out of the rear of the cargo bay and parachuted down to the beach and the open ground of the village below. Everyone on the Island was waving to the men that were waving back from the cargo hold. Huge pallets of rice, flour, baby food, and tins of spam and evaporated milk all landed softly and safely. At that moment I couldn't have been more proud of being an American! Thank you United States of America, Jesse Quigley, and thank God!

Living on a small island in the middle of the Pacific Ocean you wonder if anyone knows you are there or cares what happens to you. After the island repaired the oot and houses and starvation had been averted, the construction began again in earnest on the dispensary. The workers from the Island of Ono came over to Onari, and with their help shoveling and mixing the concrete, we finally finished the water tank just in time for Christmas.

A group of men, including me and our new health aid, paddled out to spear fish in the deeper waters of Onari's lagoon. The health aid had been beneath the surface and came up suddenly, vomiting violently after being stung across his neck by a blue bottle jellyfish. We helped him back on the canoe where he continued retching. It was a good enough reason for me not to go spearfishing that day. I had already had an experience with a blue bottle in the shallow water at night when a wave brought one in with the tide and whose tentacle stung my ankle. The burning pain was just excruciating, and I knew what our new health aid was feeling. Luckily there were no other incidences of blue bottle stings that Christmas Eve.

Christmas arrived with a visit from Santa Claus, not in a sleigh drawn by eight reindeer, but in an Air Force cargo plane, because Rudolfo had been stung by a blue bottle the day before and couldn't fly. The cargo plane parachuted large containers of more food and a full container of wrapped Christmas presents for the island children donated by the children of Guam. But this time one of the chutes failed to open crashing through the newly repaired roof of the oot which would be repaired again, and didn't diminish from the Christmas Joy. Merry Christmas to all.

Chief Paulus played Santa passing out the presents to the happy children. The Christmas feast celebrated the birth of Jesus of Nazareth and the many presents He bestowed on all of us in 1969. It was time for me to move back to Piseras where this all began and with a very tight time schedule to finish the dispensary there. But this was a very special Christmas on Onari Island, one I will never forget! Nor will I ever forget Onari Island and all the wonderful people and friends who were so generous to me. Nor will I forget close calls with blue sharks, the draft board, an emergency appendectomy, and a typhoon making me realize, "**There is power in the name of Jesus! Break every chain.**" *BREAK EVERY CHAIN* (Song by:Jesus Culture)

I will miss Onari Island and am grateful to Chief Paulus and my hosts, Adjubwah and his wife, who were much more than caring hosts, but became true friends who enriched my life with song, laughter, shared danger, and love!

My friend Adjubwah and his wife outside their thatched house on Onari Island

Onari Island block making with child labor

There was a good time to be drafted!

A Good fishing day for Chief Paulus and Onari Island!

Surprise emergency food parachuted down by a huge U.S. Air Force cargo plane flying low over Onari Island which had lost many breadfruit trees in a typhoon- one seen in picture below.

Air Force surprise Christmas presents from the people of Guam parachuted down by a huge U.S. Air Force cargo plane flying low. One box hit the roof of the canoe house (oot)! No problem!

CHAPTER 14
Feet To The Fire

The outrigger sailing canoe ride from Onari Island to Piseras Island was rough and wet with the full trade winds blowing. I was soaked, cold, and happy to be back on solid land when our canoe landed on the beach. I helped to push the big sailing canoe up on the coconut staves to the oot. N-a- **Hoy!** N-a-**Hoy**! When I arrived I was told by my friend Chief Santiago that Emere' needed his little thatched house, but I was going to live in Lucia and Buus's (B-use) small frame house by the church. Lucia was the sister of my friend Samuel, the principal of the school on Onari, and her husband Buus was another (traditional navigator) who I would discover had some very interesting stories especially about his crippled father-in-law and his marathon fifty mile open ocean swim to freedom.

The time was getting short now with only five months left with my Peace Corps two year enrollment period. I remembered the day I first stood on the beach on Piseras, almost two years before and thinking that two years was sure a long time. A lot had happened since then! I really liked my new housing and, you guessed it, I hung the ski poster of my friend Johnny Kruger who kept me company for nearly two years during lonely times. I would carry on long conversations with Johnny, who was the silent type!

I walked from my new house down the main Island path and turned right just before the big boathouse (oot) to a small compound of thatched houses belonging to my new extended host family including, Lucia's elderly mother, crippled father, and younger brothers Leon and Kevin. At the family compound by the oot, I was given four coconut trees to harvest ari (coconut wine) and the children's drink ari-mum. These weren't fifteen foot coconut trees, but tall trees standing 30-50 feet above their family compound. These four trees had notches for your feet chopped into the trunk of the tree making it much easier to climb to the top. Harvesting the ari and ari- mum every morning and evening, once in a steady rain I slipped at the top and bear hugged the trunk all the way to the ground with the insides of both arms and legs scraped to a red rash.

Piseras had a new Peace Corps Volunteer from Truk where things just hadn't work out for him. The school needed another teacher to replace the previous Peace Corps living legend, a really dedicated teacher who built the Piseras School building and was a world champion spear fisherman. "You are good at spearfishing, but you're not as good as Joe!" It was hard following in the footsteps of a living legend, but I am lucky I didn't have to compete as a teacher. But Alan did and I am sure he heard all about Joe!

Both Joe and Alan were from New York City and the kids were all going to sound like Padre and James Cagney! Or maybe Padre had shown a James Cagney gangster movie so many times that the young children memorized the script. A Field Trip ship brought Piseras another teacher named Nancy who wasn't happy teaching in the Truk Lagoon. Both Alan and Nancy were energetic and enthusiastic teachers who I could hear while I was working next door on the dispensary. Piseras was a big Island and I was always friendly to both, but I really didn't see either of them all that much. We all were so busy that we kept mostly to ourselves.

The Peace Corps TESL teachers worked all day in school and at night. I admired them greatly! When I finished the day working on the dispensary project the time was mine and after having dinner down with my family and enjoying a couple of cups of ari with Buus, his brother-in-law Leon, and Lucia. I would walk back to my home and go to bed. Some weekend nights though I walked past a group of stick dancers which usually included Alan and Nancy, but like on Saipan, I chose to sit the dance out. Things were working out on Piseras nicely for both Alan and Nancy.

The Field Trip ship which brought out Nancy had also delivered glass louvered windows for the third dispensary on Piseras. The chief and health aid looked at the wooden shutters on Ono and Onari, and because Piseras had the luxury of being last, I could order these fancier windows in advance.

I really enjoyed working daily with Santiago and Bogey who were consistently stalwart and faithful workers. Santiago was one of the people I most admired on Piseras. He was probably in his fifties and just beginning to grey, tall and very handsome and dignified as both a chief and a palu (navigator). Bogey was young and handsome, and a bit of a lady's man, and very interested in hearing about America from me while we were laying block. I sensed that he might have a hidden tragedy in his life. One day Bogey surprisingly didn't show up to work with Santiago and myself when we heard a loud "Wi-yo…ooo!" coming from the forest. Santiago instantly had me drop what I was doing and took me by the arm leading me into the school and hiding me behind a bookcase and told me not to leave.

After more than an hour Santiago finally returned and retrieved me and we went back to work. While working with Santiago that day he told me that Bogey had been drinking yeast by himself in the forest and was very dangerous! He was now sleeping it off. I had heard the story of one of the islanders who had chopped off the head of a German radio operator with his machete during the war while they were drinking yeast together; I didn't argue with the chief, but Bogey was my friend! He wouldn't hurt me. Santiago thought otherwise.

On another day. Bogey told me to join him and Santiago that night. They had something they wanted to show me. We three walked across the island through the forest to a big beach on the backside of Piseras to where a huge female green sea turtle was laying her eggs. Santiago and

Bogey flipped the turtle over on her back where she was helpless and couldn't escape.

The next morning we met after Rosario and immediately returned to the turtle and dug up the eggs placing them in a palm woven bag. The two of them then tied ropes to the flippers of the turtle and pulled it along the shallow water back to the oot while I carried her eggs in the basket. While we brought the turtle around to the oot, Leon, Buus, and Emere had dug a pit in the sand and built a fire in the bottom of the pit and threw coral rocks on top of the fire.

When the turtle was dragged ashore Bogey killed her with sharp hard blows to the back of the neck and head with a piece of dry driftwood.

Flipped over on shell is one unhappy sea turtle

Santiago and Bogey

Then the dead turtle was slowly lowered down in its shell on its back on top of the hot rocks and covered with leaves to the top of the pit and the leaves had sand shoveled on top. Slowly the turtle baked in the ground oven (oom) while her eggs were distributed to the happy families. Turtle was a rare treat and the most appreciated meat on these outer islands. Sometimes the men would sail to other uninhabited islands, and return bearing turtles and welcomed home as heroes. I truly enjoyed the impromptu feast of turtle.

The men of Piseras went spearfishing and I was again impressed how the open ocean side of the reef on Piseras was a sheer cliff dropping straight down like a wall into a bottomless depth. Swimming over the cliff,

I saw some very large sharks deep below and quickly retreated back to the relative safety of the interior reef. The other spear fishermen didn't seem very concerned when I was pointing out these sharks of the deep. The waves were breaking over the reef and a wind was blowing our canoe, with the one paddler, back in the direction of the island. I had enough thrills for the day and was getting chilled and waved for the paddler to pick me up as I was actually cold and shivering. I thought it was from being half scared out of my wits but a couple of days later I developed a very painful earache. I had to put cotton in my ear and tape over the opening to keep the wind out of my ear. I had a green colored fluid which was draining from my ear and sadly kept me out of the water for my remaining months on Piseras. Lucia warmed some coconut oil (deeka) and poured it into the ear washing out some sand and more green liquid. When working on the dispensary I kept the ear covered and I interpreted my earache as God telling me to stay away from spearfishing and focus on finishing the construction on Piseras. I didn't know how many more warnings I was going to have with sharks!

Lucia and Buus would catch needle fish outside of their thatch hut like fly fishing in the clear waters of the South Platte in Colorado. Buus had a long pole with a heavy monofilament line and at the end was attached a single string of puffer fish intestine. The sea current next to their beach was very swift and he would cast the line into the riffles and a foot long needle fish would take the bait. With a quick backward jerk on the pole by Buus the fish would fly backwards out of the water and off the line to be quickly gathered up by Lucia. They would clean a dozen fish and place salt in their bellies and then lay the salted fish on the hot coals of their cookhouse fire. Talk about a tasty treat! One evening after enjoying our roasted needle fish and breadfruit, we relaxed around the fire telling stories and enjoying a few cups of ari. On this occasion I heard about a very young Buus escaping captivity from a Japanese ship returning back to the Truk Lagoon. He was a native palu (navigator) and knew that the ship was passing about fifty miles away from Piseras and in line with the stars and sea current and he escaped by jumping overboard in the open ocean and swimming home in the same fast current we were catching our needle fish dinner. He also was a very strong swimmer!

Back during the war the Japanese would sporadically anchor their ships offshore Piseras and armed landing parties would come ashore and forcibly take young men and women off the island to be slaves for them on their ships. The people of Piseras, to defend their remaining children, had built underground hiding places in the forest for their young sons and daughters and a conch shell alarm would be sounded warning the island of a Japanese approaching ship. Having been alerted the young men and women hastily sought refuge in their hiding places. Lucia's father who was chief greeted the armed Japanese who began a search through the village for young potential slaves. You know what the Japanese were looking for with the young girls.

When not finding any they grabbed the chief and tied his hands **behind his back**, threw a rope up and over the main beam in the oot, and tied one end to the rope holding Lucia's father's tied hands. They asked the chief where the young people were and he answered that another Japanese ship had earlier removed them. Angrily the Japanese jerked the rope hauling the chief off the ground and dislocating both shoulders until he was hanging straight up and down. "Tell us where your young people are hiding!" The chief answered the same, "They were already taken earlier by another ship." The Japanese sailors went ballistic and built a fire under the hanging man and slowly lowered him down by the rope until his feet and legs dangled in the fire, literally putting his **feet to the fire**. Buus said he didn't break and defiantly refused to tell his tormentors where the youth of the island were hiding. Frustrated! The Japanese finally gave up and boarded their ship empty handed leaving Piseras and the chief crippled for life, but the children of Piseras were saved from becoming forced slaves to the cruelty of the Japanese. This brave man stood up to his tormentors knowing, like Jesus, he would pay a price for saving them.

Brave handicapped chief with wife and grandchildren was the patriarch of my host family who saved young teenagers from being forced into Japanese slavery. A story told to me by Buus while swapping stories sitting around the cook fire and enjoying just one cup of falluba- maybe more than just one judging from my trying to prove I could ride a turtle bareback.

Buus jumped from a Japanese warship in the middle of the Pacific.
He and Lucia were my host family on Piseras.

Samuel is the oldest son of the chief and Lucia's brother,
as well as the Principal of Onari's school.

Lucia my host mother

Kevin, youngest son of brave chief, with Bob outside of Lucia's cookhouse

The children of Piseras were saved from the torment of enslavement on a Japanese ship that drove Buus to jump off a ship in the open ocean. The chief still fathered a wonderful family and one of his children, Lucia, and her husband were caring for me while I worked on the dispensary on Piseras, feeling privileged to be a part of this very special family and extremely thankful for their generous care. Especially allowing me to harvest falluba (coconut wine) and ari mum (sweet children drink) on four of their coconut trees. After dinner with Buus and Lucia, I enjoyed listening to Buus's stories around the cook fire and sharing falluba. After living on the three islands of the Namonuito Atoll for two years in the Peace Corps, like Dan and Ellen, I was sitting around a campfire swapping stories. It must have been in my DNA.

One day a Japanese fishing trawler entered the Piseras lagoon and a group of the dispensary workers and I headed out to the trawler and climbed aboard. One of our crew who was hard up (asupang) for smokes and spoke a little Japanese conversed with the captain about trading coconuts for cigarettes.

The Japanese captain was highly upset that a white person was among the natives and began shouting and waving a pistol at me which at this point we all made a hasty retreat. It was explained to me later that the captain thought I might have a radio and report the trawler to the United States Navy in charge of keeping the Japanese fishing fleet out of Micronesian waters. The Japanese fisherman's maniacal temper brought the brave handicapped chief's story to mind sitting around the cook fire with Buus and Lucia- wondering if I would have been so courageous!

One Friday morning Santiago asked me if I would like to sail with him and three others to Ulul after work. The dispensary project would be on hold anyway over the weekend. With my ear infection keeping me from spearfishing, I wanted to get back in the ocean if only on an outrigger sailing canoe with my friend Santiago. I looked forward to seeing my friends on Ulul. Santiago was an experienced palu and this would be a trip of a lifetime. The three others were young men courting sweethearts on Ulul and pining to see their girlfriends. Most potential unrelated marriage partners are sought from other islands. All three of the young men were already preparing the big outrigger canoe to be pushed out into the lagoon. You might call this the *Love Boat* nervously awaiting for their navigator, Santiago, and me.

When final preparations were complete along with everyone on the canoe, with the mast, the sail, boom, and the food and coconuts stored aboard we paddled out into the deeper water of the lagoon and raised the sail. As we sailed out of the Piseras pass, Santiago aligned the canoe on a course for Ulul using the southern opening of the pass as a point on line with a back sight on the island (*As a Vail surveyor, our crew did the same with an established back sight, a transit, or compass*). Santiago was definitely in charge of the wa and most serious about his role as navigator. I was placed on the lee platform opposite the outrigger, where I wasn't in the way. After we let out fishing lines, it wasn't long before we began pulling in fresh tuna for our dinner.

I sat on the opposite side of the outrigger on the lee platform where women and children ride and enjoyed the broiled fish hot from the coals of a special pan holding the small fire. I had not seen Santiago in his role as a palu and was so impressed with his quiet and natural confidence sitting in the middle on a center platform where he held the rope controlling the sail and quietly commanding the sailboat. He trusted me to man the hand carved sea water bailer (noom) from the bottom of the hull to fling out the sea water which leaked into the canoe from the seams of the hull and wave splash.

Santiago was totally focused while the young men were enjoying themselves telling stories and excitedly pulling in small tuna. Always someone was sitting holding on the rear tiller and another would occasionally fling sea water with the hand carved noom. When Santiago ordered a tack in a new direction the entire sail rig was moved from one end to the other making the stern now the bow and off we would go. The ancient design of this durable and efficient wooden craft was just amazing and no wonder these were strong and proud mariners. Similar designed wa (canoes) were used to populate all of the South Pacific including Tahiti and the Hawaiian Islands.

In 1976 as part of the bicentennial of the United States, Hawaii's Polynesian Voyaging Society built a full scale double hull *wa' a kauhua* sailing canoe called the Hokule'a. The wa sailed almost 3000 miles to Tahiti using the traditional navigational method, but no one in Hawaii still retained this special navigational knowledge. The Polynesian Voyaging Society recruited Mau Pialug from Satawal Island in the Western Islands and a relative of my Peace Corps friend Mike and his Satawal wife.

Using ocean swells, the stars, moon, sun, and birds flight patterns, and the recorded chants of past Hawaiian navigators in the language of old (Lamalam) only understood by the navigators, Mau navigated the Hokule'a on the 3000 mile long-distance voyage to Tahiti. (The wagon train journey of my great-grand parents across the prairie to Colorado was much shorter and they had the Platte River and wagon ruts to guide them.) The Pacific Ocean looked like a never ending desert without reference points; Mau could follow the ocean currents and the sun, the moon, and stars, and birds guiding him just as sure as the South Platte River.

Mau would later live with Mike and his family on the Big Island and teach eager University of Hawaii students the traditions of their Hawaiian ancestors keeping the old ways alive in Hawaii. Too bad Mau wasn't available to the captain of the large modern cargo ship that grounded on East Fayu Island when I first went out to the outer Islands.

I fell asleep at night on the passenger lee platform of the large outrigger canoe as I was exhausted from earlier working on the dispensary. But sometime in the middle of the night I awoke to see Santiago still sitting in the captain's seat and holding the sail's rigging rope along with one of his young apprentice palu learning the navigational way from Piseras to Ulul. Santiago was keeping his eyes on the stars and occasionally would let the canvas fall slack to stick his arm down into the swells and feel for the ocean current or look intently at the sea's surface for riffles.

Being an adaptable navigator he was also aided by his valued large compass secured safely in a wooden box and brought out for just such voyages and he would shine his flashlight on it sparingly to save his batteries. It wasn't the South Platte, but it was for Santiago who knew just where he was on the vast open ocean. I fell back asleep again and was awakened later when the wa was drifting and the sails no longer straining but flapping in the wind and the canoe's creaking ceased with the wa's struggle against the wind and sea coming to an end!

All hands were pointing in the dark at the Island of Ulul which was still out of sight for me. I couldn't see the island until the sun lit the sky at first daylight. Santiago pointed to the white terns (birds) leaving the island at dawn and tightened the rope on the sail rigging and we were sailing again with the wind and it wasn't long before we pulled up in the shallower water just offshore on the eastern side of Ulul. Waiting for the people of Ulul to be alerted to our presence, we enjoyed a breakfast of pounded breadfruit and raw tuna sashimi before paddling to the beach and an increasing crowd of excited villagers. Santiago handed many tuna caught on our trip to friends to carry up to the oot to be distributed to the people by the chief of Ulul. We then pushed the canoe up onto the beach as the other outrigger canoe mates carried the sail and rigging up to the oot to be stored for the night.

The three young sailors of Piseras strolled together slowly down the beach with their happy girlfriends. I asked Santiago where they were going and he gave me a wink and a wide grin and said this was the custom of these Islands with courting couples. The couples would separate and go their own way into the forest drinking an island drink prepared only by the women for their suitors called "**api all**" (sounds like *happy all* and means just that). He only gave another grin which basically was telling me in friendly gesture to figure this out for myself.

Santiago was heading towards the village to visit with his family members living on Ulul and was to catch up on lost sleep. He carried a fresh tuna with him to gift his family with for breakfast. I wandered over to my friend Lewie's house and surprised him with a fresh tuna and my unexpected presence so early in the morning. This was Louie's day off so he had the time to fill me in on his news. Later that day Louie showed me a Japanese Zero in the forest that had crashed landed on Ulul on its way back to the Truk Lagoon.

Early the next morning Santiago and the young *Romeos'* and I departed back for Piseras. Our navigator was fully recovered from his all night sailing and I came away from Ulul still thinking it was an incredibly beautiful Island with beautiful people. I was happy though to be heading back to the unfinished job with time speeding by and still so much left on the construction of the dispensary.

But Piseras with its abundance of trained workers and of eager laborers to continue with the gathering of food for the island, the prospects looked very promising that the dispensary would be completed by the June Field Trip ship. Our canoe was swift on the return and I was happy to be home on Piseras and my wistful young friends already missed their future wives left back on Ulul Island.

The construction on the dispensary and the water tank went well and the final touches of cutting the glass louvers to fit our window openings came down to my very last day on Piseras. It was an all-night push for me cutting the glass alone, as with all Field Trip Ships there was a lot that the island workmen had to do to finish their gathering and trading their copra and buying their necessary ship store goods, especially cigarettes. Just before dawn I fitted in the last louvre.

I said my thankful farewell to Lucia and Buus at the house and left all of my household belongings (pisek) with them, including my ski poster still hanging on the wall! When I was recovering from my appendicitis in the Truk Lagoon, I was honored to meet Phillipe Cousteau who, with his famous father, Jacques, was filming the sunken Japanese wrecks in the *Lagoon of Lost Ships* for the *Undersea World of Jacques Cousteau*. We shared a cup of coffee in the Bayview Restaurant on Moen, and I related my shark encounters out on the Namonuito Atoll. He said to me, "Do you know how lucky you are? Even the reef sharks are dangerous. And they could have easily attacked you causing a deadly shark frenzy."

Feeling such a sense of gratitude for all the people who made this experience possible for me. my parents deserved more than just thanks but also my undying love and appreciation for what I put them through. They were understandably very worried and praying for my safety all those days and months for two years when I was to out of communication. With a small Japanese battery operated tape recorder, I was able to record the song *Happy Birthday* **off key** for my father's birthday and months earlier put it in The Truk Islander's Field Trip Ship mail, and remarkably the tape arrived for my dad's birthday celebration. Growing up my family would attend Lenten Novenas and I could always get my younger sister, Sheila, to crack up with her huge laugh by singing **off key.** This distracted all those near us in the church, much to my parents' embarrassment. My mother later told me my dad cried and laughed at the same time through the entire painful rendition.

Back on the Truk Islander off Piseras Island sitting alone on my mat, I relaxed for the first time in 24 hours and marveled at the beautiful turquoise waters and the small children happily splashing in the shallow water. Thanking God for allowing me to have been so blessed to help build the three dispensaries. I was tired-and happy to be going home!

Dark green Piseras Island and turquoise Lagoon surrounded by the reef seen from my window on Air Micronesia flight.

Santiago was carrying the cement blocks for Bogey
and cleaning up the mortar joints on the outside wall.

Bogey and Bob laying block on Piseras

The Island magistrate mixing mortar

Bogey leaving the Piseras Lagoon

It was a fun day on the open sea and a welcome outing
for Alan who had fresh fish for dinner.

Piseras men's bathing pond in forest

Completed Piseras dispensary and concrete water tank

Alan Knuer, a Peace Corps Volunteer teacher on Piseras, riding
on the lee platform where safely out of the way of the islanders.

I said olela (goodby) to Piseras after two years in the Peace Corps. The elected
magistrate also boarded the ship to attend a meeting on the future of Chuuk.
Surprise! The baby sprung a leak just after handing the child over to him
while I accepted a flower maramar headband given to me by the children of
Piseras.

BOOK THREE: IT RUNS IN THE FAMILY

10 YEAR-OLD BRIAN BUCKLEY
AND FRIENDS ON PUNLAP ISLAND

CHAPTER 15
Colorado Family Buckley

When I arrived in the Denver Airport both my mother and father greeted me and we gave each other a long hug. I surprised them by bringing along my Peace Corps friend Lewie who was traveling back to Boston through Denver, and I talked him into staying and seeing Colorado for a few days. My parents had a celebration dinner awaiting us up in Black Hawk. The German owner greeted us at the Bavarian Restaurant famous in the Central City area for the pretty dirndl wearing waitresses and a great offering of authentic German food. Both Lewie and I were most interested in talking to our waitress and ordered an ordinary fish dinner. It would take time for us to acclimate back into American culture.

Not only had I returned to Colorado, but also I returned to an entirely different culture and economy from that I had come to know on Ono, Onari, and Piseras Islands. At first, I must admit, I suffered from culture shock! No more living off the land and the sea, but now I was in the money economy which I left two years earlier.

At first I began giving tours of the Belford House to the Colorado summer tourists many who came to see the historic mining town, but also to many who came to go to the opera in the Historic Central City Opera House. The Belford House was literally up a staircase across the street from the Opera House and the Teller House Hotel and half a block down the road. Most interesting to me was making some immediate cash flow, and my parents were very supportive. Mainly, business was slow. My newly retired father and I would sit out on the front stone deck swapping stories of his early years growing up in Silver Plume and my recent adventures in the Peace Corps. It was an occasion for me to hear these stories of his early life which now were very important to me. This was very special just having this time with my dad.

But having been separated for two years from both my mom and dad and wishing I knew more about their lives, I now had that opportunity. And the stories he told! When we went to Mass on Sundays without fail he would say to remember his grandfather who was about my age when he was shot and killed by the provost marshal and buried under St. Mary's Catholic Church. It was a little too close to home to tell my dad about the Japanese fisherman pointing a gun at his son!

While still out on Piseras, I had been thinking about what I would do after Peace Corps. Should I go back and apply to graduate school or return to the ski business? After only a few weeks at home and giving tours at the Belford House, I decided upon the ski business. Dropping my resume off at the Loveland Basin Ski Resort was a start. The manager, Otto Werlin, was a friend and a Regis University graduate. Next I met with the construction manager of the Keystone Ski Resort. And because my family knew Pete Seibert, I also gave my resume to his executive assistant, Sara Newsom in his Vail office.

My Uncle Ron, a friend of Pete's, wanted me to open a can of beer and spray him with it in his office, a trick that Pete played on him after Uncle Ron cut off Pete's tie in the Buckley Store in Silver Plume. Otto offered me a management job in the ticket office at Loveland. Keystone offered me a job on the Ski Patrol provided I started immediately as a carpenter. And Joe Macy, Assistant Ski Patrol Director of the Vail Ski Patrol, invited me back for an interview.

Joe and I were friends from the Loveland Ski Patrol, and I accepted his offer to meet with him the next day in Vail. Meeting over a beer at the Ore House, a favorite watering hole in Vail, I mentioned to Joe that I had thought I would be taking the management position at Loveland Basin. Joe and I had both worked for Otto and knew him to be a good friend.

While Joe and I were meeting at the bar, he told me another story about a sergeant being heard saying out loud, "PEACE CORPS!" But instead of wounded marines who overheard the sergeant, Joe overheard the Manager of Slopes and Trails, Sarge Brown who was tossing my application into the waste basket. Joe walked next door into Bill Brown's office and fished my application from the round file. Once again I had plan 'A' and God had another plan for my life, thanks to Joe Macy who offered me a job on the Vail Ski Patrol which I accepted on the spot.

At that time accepting Joe's offer to be a Vail Ski Patrolman, I had no idea that I would live and work in Vail for the next 30 years, marry the love of my life, and raise three children in Vail. All because my friend overheard a loud dismissive remark by former 10th Mountain Army Division Sergeant Major William Brown, a highly decorated veteran of both World War II and Korea. I'm honored to call both Joe Macy and Bill Brown my friends.

After 13 years in Vail and inquiring in a letter to Padre if he needed any help with a construction project on the Namonuito Atoll, he wrote back that he was no longer the pastor there. He thought that Fr. Morrison didn't have any needs, besides he was quite senile. Padre did need help building a church on **Punlap Island** in the Western Islands of Truk. He had been working at this particular construction job more than four years. The walls were just a quarter complete. His parish headquarters was on Puluwat Island, and he just didn't have the time to work on Punlap's church full time. Padre repeated his desire for me to help him out on Punlap Island and was sure there wasn't any need for me on the Namonuito Atoll.

Donna and I discussed this opportunity and felt it would be a wonderful life experience for our children to learn about another culture and simpler life style. We wrote back to Padre that, "Let's see if we can make it work. We would like to help you on Punlap Island."

When I first started working for Vail Associates, soon after returning from the Peace Corps, I was a surveyor in the summer and a ski patrolman in the winter- just an ideal working situation for me. I met Donna the following summer, and we married February 19, 1972. My journey through life would not have been as complete, exciting, fun or even as long without Donna by my side. If I were to list the miracles in my life, meeting and marrying her would be at the top of my list! Donna Balecia grew up on the east coast, became a teacher and was never well suited to the gray skies of upstate New York winters. Seeking sun and a master's degree, she packed up her life, put it in a white Corvair and did her own version of a Pioneer heading west. Being in her early twenties and fearless, she made the trip alone not knowing what the future would hold. After spending a short time in Denver with a friend that she taught with in Rochester, she saw an ad in the Denver Post for a governess for a family that owned a Lodge in Vail.

That ad changed her life, got the job, and moved into the penthouse of the Tivoli Lodge, and put grad school on hold for what she thought would be just a few short months. But alas, God had different plans! The few months turned into many years and thanks to a blind date, we met and were married just a few months later.

Our first child, Brian, was born July 5, 1973. John followed on May 18, 1976 and Amanda on June 1ˢᵗ the following year in 1977. I had been offered the opportunity to join the real estate sales arm of the Ski Company in 1973 but still ski patrolled in the winter.

I also was asked to join the Hospital Board of the Vail Valley Medical Center when Dr. Jack Eck, my friend and special medical advisor to the ski patrol, recommended me to the board. The Vail Ski Patrol in those days were trained as Emergency Medical Technicians and trained to administer IV's as a lifesaving measure to seriously injured skiers and potential heart attack victims on the slopes. On one successful heart resuscitation of a 43 year-old skier, our ski patrol team was aided by another passerby skier who was a Cardiologist back in his home town. While we were awaiting a snow cat to transport the successfully resuscitated heart attack victim down off of the mountain, the Cardiologist turned to me and asked, "**Who are you guys?**

One of my acquaintances from the Vail Hospital, Dr. Doug Canham, was the head of the Emergency Room Group in Vail. Telling him about going back to Micronesia and my real medical concerns taking my family to such a remote part of the world with a cholera problem, he offered to put together an emergency kit for me and my family which should be helpful in any situation. What I was expecting was a small backpack size emergency kit. What the doctor gave me instead was a very large canvas duffel bag full of IV fluids and set-up equipment, medicines for everything that one might encounter in the tropics, heart medications, antibiotics, preloaded syringes of emergency medications to be injected into an IV line, bottles of aspirin, ibuprofen, sleep aids, cough medicine, sterile bandages of all sizes and purposes needed in an emergency room. He carefully labeled every medication and wrote a very detailed explanation for the reasons and the indications for giving certain medications and the dosages- spending well over a month carefully putting all of this together for us.

A year is a long time to be away from home and the good medical care provided back home in America. I couldn't ever imagine needing this much medicine for my family that was in this large stuffed heavy canvas duffel bag! But I couldn't be too careful taking 10 year-old Brian, 7 year-old John, and six year-old Amanda to such a remote area of the Pacific. This was an overwhelming and daunting challenge taking Donna, our children who were taken out of school, and preparing our entire family to live safely out on a remote island in the Pacific.

Padre wrote to us and said that he had made arrangements for a small house on a beach of Punlap Island which belonged to a man that Padre had helped to be accepted at Xavier High School and worked and lived on Moen Island. The owner of the house was delighted we were willing to sacrifice the time and financial commitment to go to work on his Island of Punlap. Padre would make arrangements to meet us on Moen in August of 1983, and we could stay at Xavier High School while we awaited the Field Trip Ship to take us out to Punlap.

Donna and I now faced an enormous organizational task for moving to Punlap Island. Vail Associates gave me a leave of absence allowing me to keep my company insurance and retaining my seniority. I worked out a co-broker agreement with close friend, Craig Denton, at Vail Associates Real Estate to handle my real estate clients and pending contracts. Craig and I had worked together for many years and had developed a close working relationship and mutual trust. Craig allowed me to follow my heart..

There were many other arrangements facing us including, but not limited to, obtaining U.S. passports for the children, getting the children vaccinated for many childhood diseases, as well as cholera, packing for five people, renting our Vail home, making the proper arrangements for taking care of our on-going bills, medical and dental examinations for all of us, and booking the flight tickets for a family of five. Donna was an elementary school teacher, and she, along with the local schools, help planned the home school curriculum for each of our children's upcoming year obtaining their individual lesson plans and books for three grades. This was just the beginning!

We were lucky to have found a local attorney and his family who wanted to rent our house. We rented our single family home to them at a very favorable Vail market rental rate to have people who would take good care of our home. We also charged their rent in advance for the whole year to help finance some of our upfront expenses. The Buckley Family Journey to Punlap Island was coming together.

The Catholic Mission in Truk was not contributing anything to the expenses to be paid by us. My mother thought we were crazy! I thought she just might be right! She had a sixth sense that something was wrong! The day came in early August for our departure with a suitcase for each of us, our medical duffel bag, and two heavy steamer trunks packed with school books and supplies. And I had a nagging sense that I should have listened to my mother and also should have ,at least, written to the priest on Ulul.

Handling the heavy luggage, it was very lucky we didn't hurt our backs. This was much different than when I left fifteen years earlier leaving by myself for Peace Corps Training. Donna and I had to pack for all five of us. We packed two cars with all of our luggage and trunks, and my mother's car was also carrying an exhausted Donna and our three excited young children as well as our suitcases. Our Jeep Wagoneer which I was driving carried our two steamer trunks packed with dried food, school books, and other items we felt were necessary. Walt Olsen, a Vail Ski Patrolman, was helping with everything. He and I were nearly run off the road by a semi-trailer truck that moved into our lane almost ending the Buckley Family Journey before it reached Denver.

Our time came to take our seats on the plane. It was incredibly hard for all of to say our goodbyes to my mother at the airline gate leaving her in tears. Remembering how difficult it was for her when I departed for two years in the Peace Corps, she at least had my father then to worry and pray with her. This was again a sacrifice for my mother who was through this before with me. She was wondering, understandably, what was the reason that I would be taking such a risk with my wife and children. Helping Padre, sharing with my family the specialness of the Outer Islanders of Chuuk, and gratitude to our Lord were important ones.

We had a three day lay over in Honolulu awaiting our Air Micronesia flight to Moen in Truk. The first morning awakening in Honolulu, Donna was so exhausted after the big push to leave Vail, she was suffering from almost a complete physical breakdown unable to get out of bed the next morning. The three kids, on the other hand, were so excited to do something at the beach that I left Donna to sleep, and the children and I went down and enjoyed playing in the waves and walking on the beach of Waikiki.

After swimming, and Donna still sleeping, we took a city bus to Pearl Harbor to visit the Arizona War Memorial with its 1102 American sailors and marines entombed barely below the sea in the Battleship Arizona. Their names were endlessly inscribed on the wall. When I was on the Namonuito Atoll and relieving myself from a benjo latrine hanging over the lagoon, sometimes I would say, "Bombs away! Remember Pearl Harbor!" And hoping my message would float all the way to Japan for their sneak attack on that fateful December 7, 1941. My children were too young to understand the full dimensions of the Pearl Harbor tragedy. But soon they would see Japanese ships that were hit and sunk by American torpedoes and bombs on February 16 and 17, 1944 in Operation Hailstone- one of many thousands of hitting back when attacking the Japanese equivalent of Pearl Harbor. We were scheduled to fly to the Truk Lagoon in just two days and would fly over some of the sunken ships and scuttled wrecks where some families in Japan learned what it was like having their own sons entombed in a war memorial.

The Truk Lagoon was a huge Japanese Naval Base in the Western Pacific. Like at Pearl Harbor, Japanese tourists can take pictures and read the names of those who lost their lives there. Franciscan Fr. Richard Rohr defined the history of war as, "Who killed Who;" the "Who" killing were American pilots and the "Who" killed were Japanese sailors.

When we returned back to our hotel, Donna was still sleeping in bed, so the kids and I went to dinner and back to the room and to bed ourselves. Scared that Donna might be suffering a total physical breakdown, the next morning after so much sleep, she was eager to get back on her feet. After breakfast the five of us caught a bus from sunny downtown Honolulu up the hill to the University of Hawaii which was sitting in the clouds with pouring rain.

Contemplating which college to attend in her senior year in high school, the University of Hawaii was her dream choice thinking to get out of the gloom and wet gray skies of upstate New York. We were going to the School of Horticulture at the University to acquire seeds for vegetables that would grow on Punlap. We were not dressed for pouring rain walking around the campus, and soon we were soaked to our skins and cold. So much for Donna's dream school! The next day finally arrived for us to catch our flight to Truk and to our missionary adventure of a lifetime, **Swiss Family Robinson** style only the **Colorado Family Buckley** version.

When our Air Micronesia flight landed it wasn't the scary experience of my Peace Corps years. Some things do change in life. And besides a paved runway and smooth landing, I hardly recognized the stern faced Padre when he met us at the airport on Moen. There was a big difference from the fifty-eight year old friendly Padre I last saw last on Piseras Island and the now 71 frowning priest.

Donna was expecting a friendlier greeting after all of her sacrifice and hard work, and instinctively was worried about the children while she was still recovering from her physical collapse on Hawaii. Though her first impression was not indicative of her trust in God that everything was going to work out for the good! On the other hand, I was expecting more of the type of friendly welcome to Truk at the same airport that Howard Seay offered to his newly arrived Peace Corps Trainees.

A short drive from a newly built terminal up to the former Japanese Pacific Communication Center, now Xavier High School, would be our temporary living arrangement on Moen Island while awaiting the Field

Trip Ship to take us out with Padre to Punlap Island. The massive concrete and steel reinforced structure had withstood direct bomb strikes during Operation Hailstone and reminded me of my alma mater Regis High School-known as *The Rock* back then.

The Main Hall of Regis College Campus housed my high school (it has now been moved out to the Denver suburbs and is coed). Regis's iconic solid stone building was constructed in 1887 of rustic rhyolite volcanic granite which looked like it could stand for another 1000 years. More important than *The Rock's* solid construction was the solid education I received both in the rigorous four year high school and four more years at the Jesuit University. This Jesuit education and my Peace Corps experience **uniquely** prepared me for the challenge on Punlap Island.

The five of us were housed in a small empty house on the campus at Xavier which was used by a married teacher's family when school was in attendance. The only people at Xavier in the summer were the Jesuit teachers who were living there and who treated the five of us with exceptional kindness and generosity, and curiosity as why we were working with Padre. One warned me of the challenge facing us with Padre and some of his peculiar behavior and views. But I was just helping Padre build a church, so I wasn't too concerned!

The windows and doors at Xavier had solid steel shutters which were closed during the American pilots' bombing and machine gun attacks in 1944. The roof was six feet thick reinforced- concrete which withstood direct bomb hits failing to penetrate through to the interior. The main cafeteria and some school class rooms and staff offices were in this building. The large main staircase featured photographs on the wall of wartime Truk, including the beheading of a captured pilot. We enjoyed some wonderful meals with the young priests and watched recent new movies shown almost nightly. Most of the political leaders in Micronesia had attended the prestigious Xavier High, including a future leader in Truk who married the beautiful young Marianne from Tol, an Island on the far side of the Truk Lagoon. The same *Marian'ne* in a popular folk song, I learned from Adjubwah on Onari Island. .

The Rock withstood a direct cherry bomb hit when one of my classmates dropped one down the toilet, and after the explosion a torrent of water cascaded down the stairs and past my locker. The Prefect of Discipline came running down the stairs past my locker looking for the likely bomber who was just ahead of him. "Did you see who did this?" I wasn't given an opportunity to answer him as he flew past me in his flapping black cassock. No doubt the cherry bomber would have gone to **jug** for many a month after regular school hours and forced to write an exposition on Father Davis's *Moral Theology*, an earlier assignment of mine in freshman year. He had melted into the crowded lower hallway and escaped the clutches of the most feared Jesuit at Regis High who would have enjoyed administering infamous Jesuit discipline.

Donna and I and the three children went shopping at The Truk Trading Company (TTC) for the household supplies and food that we would need out on Punlap. Knowing from my Peace Corps experience, our children would need to ease into the diet of breadfruit, taro, and fish. Donna couldn't believe that we would ever eat all of a fifty pound bag of rice in our lifetime. We also bought cases of canned mackerel, peaches, pears, and large tins of hardtack navy biscuits, peanut butter, and large bags of salt, sugar, and coffee. Not too unlike Dan and Ellen Griffins' supplies crossing the prairie.

Donna did know that we would need mosquito nets for all five of us, pots, and pans, kerosene stove, and kerosene lamps, woven pandanus mats, and the luxury of futon foam pads for us soft Americans to sleep on at night. The futons could be used to sit on during the day, a concession a husband makes to a wife who just barely went along with my inner voice to return to Truk. The TTC would box everything up for us in a wooden crate and deliver it to the ship. By the time we were done shopping, I knew I was truly the *Ugly American-* a book in my Peace Corps book locker by William Lederer and Eugene Burdick.

The five of us went to Mass that first Sunday down at the Catholic Church in Tunuk Village where Padre was staying. After Mass and just leaving the church was a crowd of men and women expectantly waiting for me outside of the church. They had recognized me during Mass and all came to give me bear hugs and handshakes. One woman literally picked me up off the ground and squeezed and shook me like I was a rag doll. One woman in the group was Rufina my host mother who was crying and smiling at the same time finding her prodigal son of Ono Island!

The Ono Islanders were on Moen because Rufina's brother, Chief Sak, was dying of cancer and in the hospital. I learned from her that her husband Santiago had already passed on, and she asked me if I would go and visit my old friend who would be really happy to see me. I made arrangements to meet Rufina at the hospital the next morning. Donna and I asked the house keeper at Xavier to watch the three children for a short time while we went up to the hospital to meet with Rufina and go in and see Chief Sak. Amazing the timing to have made the long journey back to Chuuk and able say a final farewell to my dear friend. What were the odds?

While at the Truk Hospital, I also wanted to meet with some of the doctors and show them my huge duffel bag of medical equipment and medicine. Donna and I made our way to the Hospital Administration desk and asked to meet with a doctor. Much to our delight and surprise, we met two young, energetic American doctors recently graduated from Stanford Medical School. The Stanford doctors were paying off their college loans working for the U.S. Public Health Service in this small hospital on Moen. When I opened my duffel bag for them and they looked at the inventory of drugs and medical equipment, their eyes opened wide in astonishment! One of the doctors asked if he could take one of the heart drugs for a patient he had in the hospital but didn't have the proper medicine to treat his patient. Until it just then magically appeared. "Of course, help yourself!"

Padre wrote in one of his letter that nothing had significantly changed from when I left Truk thirteen years earlier, but the two Stanford doctors explained to me that now there were solar powered radios on most of the outer islands connecting the health aids directly to the hospital. Now I could radio back to them at the hospital anytime there was a medical emergency. I didn't know then how important that would be! But it gave me a great deal more relief knowing if Donna or the kids really got sick, I could call these guys for help. I am sure that the medicine that they helped themselves to in the duffel bag would be put to good use in the Hospital- a soft bribe that might be useful in the future.

The morning arrived for us to board the ship and leave for Punlap Island. Everyone was ready to depart from Moen on our family journey to a remote Pacific Island. This was not just me heading into an unknown destiny as a Peace Corps Volunteer, but this was my wife and children. Thinking the outer islands were hard on young Peace Corps Volunteers, it was too late now to worry about Donna and our young children. Padre and the other elderly priests were another matter remembering the elderly engineer on Uman during training. Learning that there were only elderly priests assigned to the outer islands, and meeting the priests at Xavier who were by and large young men, I asked myself "Why were there only old priest sent out to the outer islands?" It seemed backwards to me knowing the challenges I faced in the Peace Corps. Unless it was an elephant burial ground for old priests, not exactly a retirement home with health care!

The ship traveled smoothly through the Truk Lagoon leaving behind the modern world for an unknown life on the remote Punlap Island. Donna and the kids made themselves at home in the cabin once we entered into the open ocean. The ship began to toss and Donna and the three children started to experience classic sea sickness with gusto. All four were vomiting, almost at once, on the floor of the small cabin. Donna wasn't in any shape lying down in her bunk, so I cleaned up the mess. Eventually the kids went to sleep in their bunks, and I went outside and stood by the rail of the ship to get some fresh air when a man from Punlap, Seles, introduced himself and said in Weito that Lambert's house was not available. Years ago Padre said, "We may be chagrined, but never surprised!" **Surprise!** Don't get too comfortable, you don't know what's going to happen next!

Lambert was a very successful man from Punlap who ran the Transportation Department for the Truk District and in charge of the ships going out to the outer islands. Lambert was the man Padre had made house arrangements with for us on Punlap. Earlier while I was on Moen, I had gone to his office down at the dock and introduced myself and thanking him personally for allowing my family to use his house. He said he was happy for us to stay there.

Seles now was saying that there was a change of plans with Lambert's house. He was moving us upstairs in his house because, he and Lambert's mother were currently living in Lambert's house. This was not good news! I sought out Padre on the back deck and told him what Seles had said, that I was hoping he could fix this before we arrived on Punlap. I returned to the cabin full of my sick family, including me.

I slept on the back deck on a mat, but I was getting up often to check on Donna and the children. The next morning everyone but Donna seemed to be doing a little better and joined me in the galley for a very light breakfast. concerned that they were getting dehydrated, I wanted to make sure they were getting fluids into them replacing what was lost the day and night before. John seemed to be rebounding and stayed out on deck with me when the ship approached Pulusuk Island and anchored off shore. Soon there were young teenage girls who paddled out waving to all those on board. What was my seven year old son's reaction seeing the topless girls from Pulusuk in their canoes.?

He was seven! All he said was that he wanted to go for a ride in the outrigger canoes. Donna did get up to see this colorful scene and quickly retreated back to her bed. The next day we came to Puluwat Island which was where most of the large sailing canoes were still being built the traditional way by skilled craftsmen. Puluwat was also famous for superior traditional navigators. John and I went ashore and walked around Puluwat coming upon the Catholic Church which Padre had built not that long ago in concrete age. Just shocking to me, I saw damage to a building that you shouldn't be seeing for at least 100 years. Walls around the entry and some of the windows literally disintegrating with rusting steel reinforcing bars hanging out of holes where chunks of cement block had simply fallen out of the walls. More disturbing, I could actually see big coral rocks ready to drop out of the walls.

Something was really wrong with his cement to sand to aggregate ratios, and I wondered if all the rest of his churches were falling apart. Padre's second floor of his house was beginning to show similiar signs of crumbling concrete. Later asking Padre about this, he replied, "It was no problem!" As I saw it, the church's concrete problem went to the very structural integrity of the building!

Afraid it was an expensive problem without an easy solution, a cosmetic solution just wasn't going to fix why the concrete and cement block were so obviously failing in multiple locations. Padre remarked to me, "No problem." He was either delusional or embarrassed! I was beginning to really worry about what was next from the man who knew it all about construction. Marvin specified the ratio on his plans for the dispensary. Fortunately, I didn't take Padre's advice for his ratio of sand, cement, aggregate, and water when mixing concrete when in the Peace Corps. But when I was building my house in Booth Creek, it was so much easier for me to just order my concrete from Mountain Mobile Mix- delivered to the site ready to pour.

My brother-in-law, Bill Kaiser, is known in Rochester, N.Y. as a successful builder, and would know why the church on Puluwat Island was having concrete issues. He not only built excellent buildings, but Bill and his wife June, Donna's sister, helped to build a future for Donna by having her come to spend summers in Rochester and introduced her to city life, sailing, and jazz music Donna and June's actual father died when Donna was just a few days old and June was 8 years-old. Their mother moved back in with her loving parents until she remarried when Donna was 12-years old. The father figure that Donna knew as a young child was her kindly grandfather, who was a devout member of St. Paul's Lutheran Church in Ellicottville, N.Y. and manager of the local timber company that manufactured Little League Louisville Slugger baseball bats, and also a wonderful gardener who with Donna's grandmother instilled in Donna a love of God, plants, and flowers.

From Left are Donna, her niece Nancy Kaiser Britton, Nancy's daughter Carly, and Donna's sister June in the Thousand Islands of Upstate N.Y.

CHAPTER 16
Punlap Island

It wasn't until late in the afternoon that the ship dropped anchor off of Punlap Island. Donna, the three Buckley children, and I were very anxious to finally arrive after so much dreaming, planning, packing, and travelling. The island was beautiful with the setting sun lighting the green background and waves breaking on a wide white beach. It was as romantic as our dreams! The ship was unloading only passengers and in the morning it would begin offloading the cargo..

Not ready for adopting the traditional native style of women and young girls going topless and men and boys in loin clothes, Donna dressed in a pretty strapless pull up dress with a large wide brim hat, and the boys and I wore shorts and t-shirts. Only six year old Amanda jumped right in and arrived wearing only a little blue skirt. I knew she would do great here! All five of us jumped aboard the ship's runabout headed to the island which was beautiful with its white sand beach sparkling in the late sunset. Suppressing the urge to laugh, I heard two women laughing about Donna when one said, **"I wonder where this lady thinks she's going?"**

The ships runabout was not only full of people offloading the ship, but it also carried two large squealing pigs. When the runabout came up to the beach, we jumped out in the shallow surf soaking us all. It was truly amazing how quickly darkness fell here when the sun dropped below the horizon. It was light when we left the ship and only a few minutes later, when we finally arrived on the beach of Punlap filled with excitement and some trepidation, it was pitch black like a black hole sucking us into darkness.

There was no electricity on these islands and consequently no lights. The eyes of the islanders are accustomed to this, and they could see us while we were stumbling around wondering where we were going, what we were stepping on and, oh yes – what happened to Padre? There was a small crowd of onlookers on the beach curious about this family of five and especially, the very blond haired children whose hair they were not shy to touch. Our kids were not sure what to think about being touched like this. Padre walked right past us caught up in the moment as people were genuflecting and kissing his outstretched ring hand, and he disappeared into the dark night.

The welcome committee had obviously not gotten the memo about our arrival. Where was the chief saying: "Welcome to Punlap, Buckley Family, follow me to your home by the beach." Not expecting my Peace Corps type of welcome, but I wasn't expecting Padre to just abandon and forget us on the dark beach of a strange island. Suddenly, out of the darkness, the first friendly voice we had heard, said in perfect English, "Can I help you?" Yes, yes! A very nice young man who was leaving on the ship the next day to go back to the University of Oklahoma said he was told by Seles to show us the way to our new home.

We were led in the dark to a kerosene lamp dimly illuminated interior concrete structure which was crowded with adults and small children. Seles was there pointing me to a homemade ladder that would take us up to our new home. In the dimly lighted concrete interior, we carefully climbed up a thrown together ladder with uneven and crooked steps to a one room dark storage attic. With a floor to ceiling window at one end, I was afraid the kids could easily tumble out. It looked to be a storage loft for bags of copra and already occupied by coconut rats. We could see and hear the strangers downstairs through the large gaps between the hand- hewn floor boards that provided some light. Definitely, this not the enticing home Padre had written about, and that we were expecting; but it was the house Seles had described on board the ship. Safe living conditions by any measure for my family would not be available in this attic- especially fire, sanitation, access, and privacy. This was a bad dream that was very real and came true when we woke up.

It was an embarrassment for me to have put Donna through so much and to leave a beautiful home in Vail, Colorado for a confined attic space accessed by an uneven and thrown together scrap wood ladder. Donna gave me a thousand yard stare which didn't need an interpreter. GOOD GRIEF! We were expecting to live in the home that Padre had described to us in his invitation letter, but this was not it. You could hear every whispered word down below, and I presumed every word we whispered in the attic could be heard downstairs.

Padre's actual lack of concern where we would sleep or if we had anything to eat or drink or if our accommodations were comfortable or if there was anything he could do to help make us comfortable, shocked me! NOTHING! He just vanished not to be seen from again that night. Not a good sign! This was not the reception I had on the Namonuito Atoll. Donna, Brian, John, and Amanda, and myself had come to help the people of Punlap build their church, and nobody offered us a coconut to drink or any food for my children. There was no "feito monga," from the outer islanders' friendly instincts to share their food. Unfortunately, I knew right away that there was something very strange going on here on Punlap!

If you needed to go to the bathroom at night, forget it! Besides you would have to climb down in the dark on a makeshift ladder, stumble through the living area below stepping on who or what, and the children and Donna didn't know the language to say "excuse me."

Luckily Donna had a can of Coke and a half a bag of caramels in the children's back pack to be shared for our, "Welcome to Punlap feast." So we just snuggled together to keep warm, and the children were so tired they fell asleep quickly. Later that night, the young teenagers who were leaving on the ship the next day to attend high school on Ulul went around from house to house singing. I needed to talk to Padre first thing in the morning before any of our many boxes were off loaded from the ship. The next stop for the ship was Ulul Island where Lucia's brother and my friend, Leon married his sweetheart that we visited years ago when we sailed there with Santiago from Piseras. I knew Leon would help us. We were family and friends when I lived on Piseras Island 13 years before arriving on Punlap Island-nice to have a backup to Padre.

Leon whose older sister was Lucia, my host mother, was married and living on Ulul. Picture was taken on Piseras.

Maybe we could teach in Ulul's high school or grade school, but one thing I knew for sure, we wouldn't be spending another night in Seles's house, not to be ungrateful, but I would rather sleep on the boat and leave for the Namonuitos. I knew I needed to have a conversation with Padre and hopefully with the chief. What kind of a priest just walks away from his invited construction helper, his wife, and three young children in the pitch dark on a strange island after traveling thousands of miles to help him? I was chagrined but more than surprised!

Early the next morning and still dark in the house, I slowly climbed down from the attic and carefully stepped over and around the family below, and went exploring the island in the growing light of dawn looking for Padre. Walking up the main island path, I came to a clearing where to my utter surprise there was an existing white coral block church with Padre's tall concrete foundation wall on one side and wrapping around to the back. I just stood there in the dawn gaping in disbelief and with a sinking feeling and beginning to grasp at why it had taken 4 years for Padre to build just a quarter of the foundation of a church on Punlap.

There was more than one *why* to be asked. The first was *why* was Punlap replacing this existing white coral block church with another, and obviously planning on demolishing the coral block church? And *why* not just add an addition if you needed more space? But for now I needed to know whether I was offloading my box of supplies or keeping them on the ship and taking our chances moving up to Ulul uninvited and not learning the answer to my *whys.* I found Padre's small house next to the church and knocked hard on his door. I needed an answer now whether Donna, Bob, Brian, John, and Amanda stayed or moved on later that day with the ship.

Hopefully the house of Lambert's would be available, and if not, was there another? Padre said he would go and meet with Seles and get this worked out. When I got back to the attic Donna and the kids were not there. She would have taken far fewer than *16 ponies* in a trade for me that morning after spending the night in the one room attic with only a few caramels and a Coke to share for our dinner. She and the kids also had risen early and went for a walk on the "pretty" beach having many island children helping them in collecting sea shells and were unaware of their father's challenge that morning, just happy walking the beach with other happy island kids.

Meeting with Padre, Donna and I learned that he worked something out with Seles who would be moving back into their own house with their children's family. Lambert's mother and Seles had moved into his house because she enjoyed the night sea breeze which made it more comfortable for her to breathe and cooler and quieter for sleeping suffering from tuberculosis. If anyone should be entitled to use Lambert's house, it was his ill mother. What a horrible position to be in as a guest on an island with young children and a wife and to be asking Seles to move his wife who had TB. What was Padre thinking? How could Lambert have ever agreed to loan his house to the Buckley family.

Seles said he would build a new wood frame house for her next door to Lambert's house near the beach. It sounded complicated but the Buckley family would be moving into Lambert's house after all. I just did not have the heart to pull the plug at that point after all that we had to go through to get to Punlap. **I really did feel like a rewan** having to move an elderly, overweight, woman with tuberculosis! If Donna and I had any advance knowledge of this complication, we wouldn't have come. And to be honest we both were very tempted to just get back aboard the ship and spend the year in Hawaii. But we learned that this was not God's plan this first day.

It was time to have our supplies off loaded from the ship and carted over to what would be our new home for the next year. And Donna and the three children and I walked alongside the men carrying our supply box to see the house for the first time. And it wasn't very long that very morning that one reason for us to have sacrificed and worked so hard for the family to journey all the way to Punlap Island was to be revealed in a most amazing coincidence or my thinking- a miracle.

A young father with two small sons introduced himself, as we were moving our bags into Lambert's home, and brought us fresh coconuts. While I was thanking him, I customarily asked him, "How are you feeling today?" He answered: "Not that well. My wife will die before sunset!" At first I may have misunderstood him, since I hadn't spoken his language for thirteen years. So I asked him to repeat himself. I understood him perfectly. Fresh from ski patrolling in the winter, I was confidently heading out on another 10-50 and told him to take me to see his wife.

We hurried over to the other side of the island to a traditional village of coconut thatched houses, where his wife was located. Stooping low, I entered into the dark interior with him and sat by his prone wife. She looked to be in shock. She had been vomiting and having severe diarrhea for most of the night and morning, obviously exhausted and dehydrated. After taking her vitals , I told the couple that I would return soon with medicine!

Running back to my new house at full speed, I grabbed Dr. Doug Canham's canvas medicine bag. Next stop was the island radio which I used to call the Stanford doctors and relay to them the woman's symptoms. As I guessed, she was most likely suffering from the last stages of severe cholera. The doctor wanted me to immediately start an IV of Ringers Solution to quickly rehydrate her and administer a very strong antibiotic drug from the canvas bag. Seles arrived and had already hooked up the IV with Ringers to run fast. As the doctors ordered, I inserted the prescribed medication into the IV line's needle port and prayed that the IV and antibiotic would work. Later, I reported back on the radio to the Stanford doctors who said they would have the ship, which departed earlier in the morning, to turn around when it got back to Moen- assuming she would still be alive when I radioed back in to them.

Three days later the ship did return and picked up a very much alive young wife and mother likely saved by antibiotics and IV of Ringers Solution. Without the IV and antibiotic medication, she very probably would have ended up buried in Punlap's cemetery joining the too many other cholera victims.

Vail Valley Medical Center and Dr. Doug Canham's canvas medical bag was instrumental in the last minute saving of a life faraway from Vail, Colorado, There was no better reason for the Buckley Family to have traveled halfway around the world to Punlap Island. What an amazing miracle. It was always God's plan. Now I knew the reason for the persistent whispering in my heart to return to Micronesia with my family. It is certain that Donna and I will remember that day on Punlap!!

Soy bottles stuck in the ground mark some of the graves in the Punlap Cemetery.

CHAPTER 17
German Chocolate Cake

Unbelievable all of the luggage needed for a family of five for a year that was packed to live on Punlap Island, and it took us the better part of two days to unpack. Donna had even brought along a fold up table that you screwed the legs into that she had seen in a catalogue. When I was in the Peace Corps walking into the houses on Ono, Onari, and Piseras in less than ten minutes, I unloaded my toothbrush and opened my small bag carrying all my earthly belongings and tacked my ski poster on the wall.

Our blue and orange tin house had windows built at floor level propped open to allow for ventilation were handy for the children of Punlap to sit in and watch everything that was going on inside the house. The kids would have stood at the doorway, except those front row seats were taken by the curious adults. It wasn't long until the curious bystanders rescued our seven year old son, John, who learned that he could climb up a coconut tree but not down.

Lambert's house had a tile floor making it easy for Donna to sweep up the sand that the kids drug in from the beach. And the house had a sink in the kitchen area with running water from a tank that collected the rain water off the roof. Rain water needed to be boiled before drinking it- to kill squiggly critters swimming in it. Roosters perched on the roof at night and awakened everyone in the house at dawn letting us know it was time to get up! The same loud church bells rang out loudly if you missed the roosters' cock-a-doodle-doo! I'm not sure which was more annoying, Padre's loud bell, the roosters crowing, or the clumsy house rats scurrying along the shelves and counter top.

It didn't take Donna long to get us organized and comfortable with our futon couch/beds and mosquito nets hung by string from the walls and that could be let down at night. We found we also had our own king sized rats at night that were looking for leftovers and knocking over everything left on the counter. We moved our food into large trunks which ticked off the rats but not the ever present micro-sized ants that took up residency in the trunks. At night I sometimes heard snickering and whispering from the floor level windows which didn't last for too long, as we were really quite boring and not that entertaining and I had learned a few tricks for the renakirh (peeping toms). A well- directed and sudden beam of my flashlight and a loud hissing sound nearly always worked to hear a sudden scrambling and stumbling of feet, but the sneaking up from behind and scaring the children half to death stopped it altogether!

After finishing up with unpacking and getting the house set up, Donna and I and the kids began to explore our surroundings and meet our neighbors. Donna made the comment to me that our small village looked like a movie set with its thatched houses, the large thatched canoe house (oot) overlooking the turquoise waters, outrigger canoes pulled up on the white coral sand beaches outlined with coconut trees, and women walking around without tops, and men wearing loin cloths. She kept looking for Marlon Brando (Fletcher Christian) in the movie *Mutiny on the Bounty*. You knew that you were somewhere very different and very special and very beautiful.

The children began making friends, and Donna was approached by the principal of the elementary school about teaching an hour long English speaking class to the 8th graders early in the morning. In all the excitement, somehow we lost track of John and Amanda when they came running back breathless all the way from the main village. The two had secretly launched their tiny inner tubes into the lagoon outside of our house for a test run, and the current swiftly carried them beyond our house and out to the outer reef on their way to the open ocean. At the main village beach, some of the island children spotted them and swam out to the outer reef rescuing the two frightened wide- eyed children saved from floating away never to be seen again! Thank God we didn't lose them, and how in the world did we miss the launching of their big adventure? Obviously Donna and I had to be more watchful, especially when the moments were filled with so many distractions! My heartfelt thanks go out to the children of Punlap who rescued them from being castaways on the open seas of the Pacific, and saving us from never knowing what happened to them.

Donna and I awoke and at first bell and organized everyone to go to church. The Mass was difficult to understand and unfamiliar from what we were used to back in Colorado, or even on Moen at the church in Tunuuk. Padre's sermon in Lagoon Trukese was spoken with a New York accent. The people on Punlap seemed to understand him, but even for them it must have taken some time and patience.

Talking to Padre after Mass, he made it clear that he thought little of the Catholic reforms of Vatican II stating that, "When Pope John opened the window of the Church to let in some fresh air, the **devil** rushed in the open window, instead!" Change can be difficult; Padre was an older man set in his ways who thought he knew everything and strutted around in his pith helmet having the people genuflect before him and kiss his ring. He had the, "Bully" pulpit and didn't want to share it with deacons, readers, or Communion distributors! He was a pope.

After holding a meeting that morning with his construction workers to let them know that he was moving back down to Puluwat Island for a month and the construction on the new church would begin anew with my supervision. Later that day, before he left for Puluwat, I went over to Padre's small wood frame house to look at his construction drawings of the church. **He didn't have any construction plans**???

Unfortunately his legacy might be that some of his churches were falling apart at the seams. Maybe that was because he didn't accept help or hire an architect or a structural engineer. The church roof overhangs on Puluwat had to be propped up by long two-by-fours nailed together to make poles and the sides of some windows were simply crumbling and falling apart.

He left the next morning after Mass for Puluwat Island on a sailing canoe to carry him back to Puluwat, probably to try and repair the church and his home headquarters.. walking over to the construction site, I looked to join the workers to get started for the day. There were no workers! I waited around until Roman, who was Padre's catechist and construction foreman, came by to tell me that there weren't going to be any workers coming to work on the church. No workers were going to be available to work on the church for me anytime. Now that had me scratching my head! What the fokuun fiti- go-go(craziness) was going on here- no construction plans now no workers?

Roman explained to me that it took the island over twenty years to build the coral church, and the chief and the islanders did not want to demolish it. That's why there had been so little construction progress on the new one. The island treasured their coral church. Rough large coral heads had been leveraged from the outer reef and transported back to the island on specially built canoes designed to carry the heavy load. Men spent painstaking hours chiseling the rough coral heads into square blocks. All the the roof timbers were hand-hewn from breadfruit trees grown on the island. Punlap Islanders were not against building a new church but were hoping that the coral church wasn't slated to be destroyed by Padre. This church was important to them because of its history of hard work ,and that it cost two lives and twenty years to build.

Now I knew the answer to *why* the construction was so slow and *why* my family was shoved up into an attic upon arrival on Punlap without anything to eat or drink. Now what? It finally dawned on Padre that I might be a threat to him. Not only had I been educated at a Jesuit University, but I was also fluent in Weito and could talk to Roman.

I never questioned for a minute the Jesuit priest's invitation. I had **assumed** Padre was totally honest and could be trusted! Sadly, it wouldn't be the last assumption about him that was totally wrong!

What was I thinking to not have at least checked with the priest on Ulul who Padre had disparaged as being old and senile? But really what was Padre thinking? Why did I simply trust him just because he was a priest? No, that was why I trusted him! It was time for Donna and me to go and pay a visit with Punlap's chief whom I hadn't yet met. After finding the chief's thatched house, we met his wife outside the low entrance. She was a real talker who had her ear lobes stretched to open a big hole that could display flowers or store a pack of cigarettes.

She invited Donna and me into her home to join the chief who was sitting on a pandanus mat in the house and drinking from a glass jar filled with coffee and smoking a cigarette. The chief was very friendly and finally welcomed us to his island. An older silver haired man, he beckoned Donna and me to join him and offered us a jar of instant coffee.

The chief of Punlap Island and wife, note left ear lobe, outside their home after Donna and I met with them and a rooster.

I thought he was possibly in his mid-seventies, but it was difficult to say after asking him how old he was when he said, "He didn't know because they didn't keep birth records when he was born." I then asked him about the church project and why didn't the men of the island want to work with me? Just then a redheaded rooster happened to strut in the open entryway and was pecking up and down all around us on the mat. The chief shooed it out the opening and with a wide smile and chuckle he commented that, "The chicken listened to him better than Padre!"

He said he wanted to save the coral church and unsuccessfully offered to give Padre another piece of ground, but Padre didn't want that. The chief said he also went in and talked to the Bishop in Ruuk(Truk) and the bishop didn't listen either. I had found the three chiefs I worked with on Ono, Onari, and Piseras were always truthful with me. This chief seemed to be telling the truth. The Bishop in the Punlap chief's story was also hard of listening and good at rationalizing re-wan behavior.

The Utes of Colorado in 1879 had warned Nathan Meeker that they didn't want to move the reservation buildings to their winter horse meadow and have Agent Meeker plow their horse racetrack. Ute Chief Nicaagat even traveled all the way to Denver from the White River Reservation to meet with Governor Pitkin to complain about Agent Meeker and was laughed at and ignored. The governor was elected to office by whites and the Utes were not voters so understandably the governor served the white newcomers to Colorado who wanted to farm and mine on Ute lands, including Governor Pitkin, who had mining interests on Ute land.

Rationalizing that the Native Americans were not white made it easier to steal their land rather than make long term fair payouts- like a long term loan.

The chief of Punlap went to Truk to complain about Padre and was ignored as well. Who was the new church being built for anyway? What were Padre's motivations? And why did he have to destroy the original church which he claimed didn't belong to the people of Punlap Island who built it. I wondered if I could come up with an alternative plan that could please both the chief and Padre. I worked on different schemes thinking that Padre might see as an attractive option to the Island's and the chief's frustrations. No wonder the progress was so slow and no wonder the men wouldn't work for me. The chief was very unhappy and for good reason!

What kind of a nightmare had I gotten Donna and our children into? Not respecting an island chief went completely counter to everything I knew and experienced in the Peace Corps. Padre had his way in the outer Islands. I wondered how and why he was so powerful?

Donna and I took the kids out of school and disrupted their young lives, as well as my career, and we left a life and community where we were comfortable. I was really unsure what to do next! The cards were to be dealt when Padre returned back from Puluwat in a month. Kenny Rogers sang in the *Gambler,* "You've got to know when to hold 'em, know when to walk away, know when to run!"

Padre finally returned to Punlap on an outrigger sailing canoe from Puluwat and he came directly to my house to talk about the church. He demanded, "Why wasn't there any construction progress?" I explained to him that there weren't any men on the island willing to work on the church with me! I then offered up some alternative ideas how he could incorporate the existing church into an expansion, including all the work Padre had already completed. Another idea was that he could build the new church alongside the old church and with a concrete roof addition to the coral church; it could have a dual function as a typhoon shelter and extra space for the church. His quick response was, "No! No! NO!"

Telling him of Donna's and my visit and conversation with the chief, I questioned Padre as to why he hadn't taken the chief up on his offer of another piece of land for building the new church. Padre said that didn't work because, "He wanted to destroy the existing church in order to erase the memory of Peter!" Peter was a former catechist of a prior priest and had supervised the building of the coral church. "Bob you should have known Peter, he was a devil!"

I had seen Peter's tall engraved headstone and well-tended grave in the island cemetery. I told Padre, "Peter was not going to be forgotten by the people of Punlap by knocking down the church." Padre finally came to the bottom line. I don't want the coral church to be available for "The Protestants who would move into it. The old church must be demolished." Furthermore, he said, "We white men have to stick together on this!" I was astonished by Padre's comment! I told him, "No! I can't support you on this!" I remembered sitting around my Piseras family's cook fire drinking falluba and hearing the stories of Japanese racist abuse during WWII.

Padre looked at me in shocked disbelief! No wonder the old chief said, "A chicken was a better listener" as he refused to consider any of my compromises. Padre stormed from my house, and the church bells soon began ringing! Maybe an hour after the bells tolled, my children were running back to the house out of breath from playing with their friends in the central village and excitedly told me the white church had just been knocked down! I slowly walked into the village with Donna and the kids and saw the large coral block walls of the church all pushed to the ground and the roof was in a heap in the middle of the jumble of coral blocks. The bells had tolled for the white coral church! Men and women were slowly picking out pieces of the hand hewn lumber from the heap and carrying them off. All coral blocks, beams, and posts had been hand carved and hewn! Punlap had lost their struggle with Padre and a treasured part of the history of Punlap Island. The church was more than just a building to Punlap's chief and the Islanders who were picking out reusable relics of the roof.

Many of the squared blocks were nearly three feet long and sixteen inches deep and wide. What a monumental effort it must have been to have wrestled this coral from the sea, transported the heavy rough coral heads onto the island, and hand chiseled them into square blocks, and then hoisted them up on the tall walls. Now all that had just been shoved to the ground. Padre came over by me and said, "The church hadn't been consecrated by the Bishop, so it was not a problem to demolish the church." What a rationalization by you! No, I thought, but it had been consecrated by the blood and sweat of the people of Punlap! Ignoring the chief of the island and refusing his offer for another piece of ground to build his new church were too much for me. If I hadn't spoken the language and heard the workers and the chief with my own ears and seen with my own eyes, I wouldn't have believed it. Sadly the story became even more oppressive. Padre was standing nearby talking to a group of men telling them that the wood from the roof was Church property and sternly ordered them to return it. The next morning the church bell was tolling again. What was it this time? It wasn't long before I smelled smoke and saw a huge gray plume rising over the island. Padre had demanded that the men return all the hand hewn timber from the church's roof. Now the tall pile of boards and beams was a huge bonfire. The smoke was literally in your face. What took Peter and the people of Punlap Island twenty years to build with hard labor and the loss of life, Padre ordered to be destroyed and burned!

How did Padre exert so much power over the people of the Western Islands? Meeting Padre by the bonfire, I calmly told him that Donna and I had talked it over the night before and decided to leave on the December field trip ship. I was sorry, but I was finished working on the church! And without anger or spite and like Kenny Rogers in the song *The Gambler*, we knew when to "walk away!"

Donna and I had seen enough and knew we were not alone in making this decision. We both were uncomfortable with Padre who seemed more interested in exerting his unbending will and in-your- face power, which to my mind was just another form of arrogance and false pride destroying the old church on Punlap. Why? To achieve the honor of being the church building priest of Truk? For whatever reason, he had disrespected the wishes of the chief and people of Punlap to bend and find a compromise that would have saved their coral church and still build a new one. Padre was very much like the hard of listening Prefect of Discipline at Regis High School. My parents sent me to Regis High, not only to be educated, but also for the discipline. I was sent to jug. Padre knocked down Punlap's church!

Fifteen years earlier, I was sitting around a table with other Peace Corps Volunteer trainees drinking coffee. We listened to Clark Graham comment on how much he enjoyed his visits with the German Liebenzel Lutheran Pastor and his wife- timed to when he smelled her baking a German Chocolate Cake.

Too bad, too bad, too bad that Padre didn't have a wife to bake him a German Chocolate Cake!

Donna baked cake in a navy biscuit tin set on top of a kerosene stove. Once, when Donna was baking a cake, Roman smelled it from his nearby thatched hut and knocking on our door said, " I like cake."

The apostle Peter had wife to bake a cake for him, and she and Peter were crucified together in Rome because of their love for Jesus Christ.

Brian is in cook house getting out of the rain.

John flying a kite from the dock

Amanda

Punlap Island main beach

Coconuts brought to Buckley Family

Roman blowing on a conch shell

Hand hewing a beam is a slow-painstaking job

Plucking a chicken

John and Amanda almost floated away in their tubes
to be rescued by the children of Punlap.

Brian, John, and Amanda study hard despite loud noise coming from Seles's house construction in front of the door. Halloween decorations were hung before storm scared us all on Halloween night!

Copra drying

Recess on Lino's canoe

Lino is sitting with his mom, Trinitas, and younger brothers

There is no recess for mom and no washing machine.

and no dryer!

Outrigger canoe (wa)

Donna on Punlap Beach

Island students are thanking their teacher

New church construction and what's still left of coral church inside to be
hauled away. The people of Punlap deserve a beautiful church to replace the
coral church which Padre ordered demolished. Island boys celebrate
Christmas with traditional stick dance below.

CHAPTER 18
Miracles

School finally started for the children of Punlap and for the home schooled Buckley children. Donna was set up to teach an eighth grade English language class at the first morning hour of the island elementary school. While she was off teaching, I took the kids swimming or we walked the beach picking up seashells until Donna returned home to teach the Buckley children's home school class. She had the two smaller children sitting on short beach chairs around an improvised table made of painted plywood placed between our two steamer trunks. Brian had his own little desk and chair we borrowed from the Punlap elementary school. One of the first of many lessons to be learned was not to turn down a gift of a kitten from one of the young island boys who took the rejected small kitten and smashed its head against a coconut tree and flung it into the ocean. Another new experience was learning to go to the bathroom at night in a red bucket half filled with sea water to also be flung into the lagoon to quickly float away in the current. It fell to me to empty the bucket every morning. That wasn't half as unpleasant as coming back one morning from a meeting in the village to pick up what appeared to be a half full can of Coco Cola and take a big gulp. My son John had used the can to urinate in and had set it on the counter! I learned a lesson that day myself!

I didn't feel guilty for not answering the call of Padre's work bell. My reputation traveled far and wide as an Emergency Medical Magician, following the antibiotic magic trick with the lady whose husband had summoned me on our first day on Punlap! My reputation spread to nearby Tamatam Island when two young men also summoned me to take a look at their rapidly failing father.

Since it was the weekend, I thought Donna and the children would like to go and see the neighboring island, if just for the day. Donna put some snacks in a backpack, and we accompanied the two sons over to Tamatam- an Island I wanted to see. Now I had the chance to go over there with my family, and hopefully find out what was ailing the man. Not knowing what to expect, I packed along the big canvas duffel bag and enough fresh loin cloths and tea shirts for several days. Just in case I needed to stay overnight!

When we arrived on Tamatam, it was again like the circus had come to town. People crowded around the children touching their heads to see if their blonde hair was real. Immediately the brothers took me to see their sick father, while Donna and the kids walked the beach again looking for sea shells and toured around the island. I was occupied assessing the sick man. The beachcombers were excited finding many small pink and purple sea shells. But the younger kids were beginning to be frightened and annoyed by the curious people constantly touching them, as if they had just landed from another planet.

I took one look at the sick man and knew he was indeed circling the wagons! His extremities were so swollen that he looked like the Pillsbury Dough Boy, and he complained of chest pain and shortness of breath. I was having a difficult time finding his pulse in his swollen wrist and had to use his carotid artery in his neck. After taking the man's vitals, I asked to use Tamatam's solar powered radio close by to call the doctors on Moen. They instructed me to immediately insert an IV in the man and start him on a diuretic drug which would make the man urinate and relieve some of his swelling. Also they ordered me to insert in the IV port emergency heart medications that they knew to be in Dr. Canham's canvas bag of medical magic. I had already learned on Punlap that antibiotics worked like magic, and I was hoping that the heart drugs would do the same on Tamatam! The Stanford doctors asked me to stay over on Tamatam with the patient monitoring him and reporting back to them on the radio. They would send the ship out to pick him up, if he was still alive the next morning!

The children and Donna were very uncomfortable being circus attractions and wanted to return back to the comfort of our home on Punlap. Telling the sick man's sons that I would stay with their father, I asked them to return my family back to Punlap. Suspecting that the seriously ill man might die at any moment, I told Donna I would probably rejoin the family the next day. If he pulled through the night there would be a ship sent out to pick him up. Too many times heart attack victims on Vail's slopes didn't make it off the mountain alive. But with my training, the canvas bag of medicine from the Vail Valley Medical Center, and the Stanford doctors' direction we just might be able to pull off another miracle save for a middle aged man. I sure was going to give it my best effort and pray what I always sang quietly to myself every time I left ski patrol headquarters headed to a serious 10-50 (accident), "God is love, and he who abides in love, abides in God, and God in him!" I was always quieted and confident that God would hear me. I knew he would hear me even on Tamatam Island in the remote Caroline Islands.

Three days later, just as with Punlap, the ship arrived off the beach of Tamatam to take the heart patient back to Truk and to the two Stanford doctors at the Hospital. Wondering at the time when Dr. Canham was pointing out to me the contents of the emergency room's medical supplies would the sophisticated heart medications ever be used? This seriously ill man used them and thankfully they worked for him surviving long enough to be picked up by the ship. I was now able to return to Punlap and rejoin my family, but before leaving I paid a visit to a beautiful small church Padre had built and to thank God for His help in answering my prayer for this emergency on Tamatam and that this church was in good shape.

Back on Punlap, Seles's construction project on his new house was in full swing. I already told him that we were only going to stay long enough for the scheduled December Field Trip Ship to pick us up. His sick wife was really suffering in the heat over at the other house, and I was very sympathetic for Seles's urgency knowing I refused to live there and wasn't suffering from TB. Seles had tried shoving my family in the upstairs attic which would have been even more unbearably hot, but Seles was consoled somewhat by the knowledge we were leaving at Christmas. The best Christmas present we could have given him! I couldn't blame him for his concern for his TB stricken wife who was having breathing difficulties.

The location for his new house was literally just a few steps out the door where Donna and the children had set up their home school and where Donna was trying to conduct her class. The noise from Seles's radio and the construction was very distracting! I spoke to Seles about turning the radio down which was met by a half-hearted apology. But I understood his irritation for being moved out of Lambert's home with a desperately sick wife! I couldn't imagine that I would have done the same as Seles, for any reason and move out.

The children were developing some nice friendships with island kids their age. One boy in particular by the name of Lino would hang out at the house with Brian and John and brought us island food which his mother had prepared special. Lino's family took Brian on outings to a nearby uninhabited island to fish and gather coconuts and make copra. The three Buckley kids could be found often with Lino out paddling around in the lagoon in his paddle canoe. And Amanda was also making friends and hanging out with the little girls in the village. And I was becoming very popular with everyone who had a headache and was looking for an aspirin or an Advil or needed a band aid.

One morning the chief's wife banged on our door and upon Donna opening it, she promptly fell into the house and passed out on the floor. After getting a cup of sugar laced coffee from Donna and two aspirins from me, she was cured of whatever felled her. The children were more surprised by the chief's wife wearing cigarettes in her ear lobes.

Seles delivered a clear message with the construction noise and smoke just five feet away from Donna's home school. He didn't like having to move or happy that the chief's wife came to me for medicine. Clearly my desire to come to Punlap was not to replace Seles as the Health Aid on Punlap Island. When Padre, less than welcoming or cordial, left my family hungry and thirsty that first night on Punlap, the two of them made it clear they wished that we would move on with the ship.

Lambert wasn't going to be happy with this new building blocking his view. He had been very successful with a high paying government job responsible for the Field Trip shipping in Truk and wasn't afraid of sharing his money improving his home Island. He built a concrete pier on our beach which the kids loved to run full speed and jump into the turquoise waters of the lagoon. He built a generator powered walk-in-freezer to foster a fishery business on Punlap, selling frozen fish to the ship's stores. And he had a television and VCR set up to show videos to the island children when the freezer generator was running.

One night while the children were sleeping, a particularly strong Pacific wind and rain storm hit our side of the island which was so strong that Donna and I were afraid that it might be a typhoon. We made preparations to retreat into the main village to ride the storm out in the school. Luckily the wild storm abated, and we could put back our last minute emergency bag that we packed with our passports, snacks, flashlights, and Donna's last emergency Coca Cola. The kids didn't even wake up!

But on another night, John. our 7 year-old son, woke up and calmly awakened me with a chilling alarm, **"Dad I have a centipede on my arm."** I jumped up from sleep and grabbed a towel and my flashlight and walked to the back room where the two boys slept beneath their mosquito nets. I lifted John's net and seeing him sitting up and calmly staring wide eyed at a three inch long and a quarter inch wide slithery centipede. Quickly snagging the venomous arthropod in the towel, I tossed it out the door. (*When John was three years old, he broke his leg skiing with his mother one morning on Vail Mountain. While I was at the Far East patrol facility at the top of chair 14 and the top of China Bowl* *on the backside, I received a call from one of my ski patrol friends who had responded to the 10-50 which was my three year old son. The patrolman splinted John and was transporting him down the mountain to an awaiting VVMC ambulance. Frank McNeil informed me on the radio that John was being taken down off the mountain in a toboggan and going to the hospital as just a precaution. He laughed and said he didn't think John had a fracture as he was soundly sleeping in the toboggan and he hadn't made a peep when Frank splinted his lower leg. Donna knew otherwise, as she had originally straightened his leg which was 360 degrees spiraled out of place telling from the crease in his ski pants. He was crying before Donna had put John's leg in an anatomically correct position. He didn't cry after it was in proper alignment causing Frank to think that John may have just been scared. Donna was afraid to tell Frank that she had earlier realigned John's leg, but she insisted on getting an X-ray at the Medical Center")!* So I knew that John was a tough kid and why he hadn't panicked. If he had seen my Peace Corps training advisor's swollen face, he might have had a different reaction to the large centipede crawling on his shoulder. If it had bit him, I guarantee he would have been screaming!

One early afternoon, John and I were taking over to Padre a freshly baked loaf of bread from Donna's biscuit tin oven sittingt on the top of our kerosene burner. Knocking on his wooden door a couple of times, Padre shouted to us to come in joining him as a group of very young girls quickly exited his house. Shirtless and wearing shorts, Padre was sitting in the back of his hot darkened house. He explained that the small children had just dropped off **spiders,** and that he liked spiders in his house whose webs trapped the mosquitoes. Seeing a large spider crawling on a boy's arm, John couldn't escape Padre's house fast enough......with me following closely behind?

We had finally drained the last drop from Donna's last coke, and there was a young man who had a small Island store which only opened up upon request. He had a very limited inventory of mostly canned mackerel, soda pop, and candy, and unfortunately he was out of any rice or flour. We first noticed the small store proprietor at church and that he was always alone with two young toddlers. We spoke to Roman about him and were told that his wife had died earlier in the summer from the cholera epidemic on Punlap Island.

We were getting low on all of our food supplies; so it was nice to learn about the small store where we could at least buy some canned fish, candy, and pop. But we now knew why the nice young man was taking care of his small children alone in church. I was all the more appreciative for Dr. Doug Canham supplying his large canvas medicine bag which had already saved another young mother on our first day on Punlap from the same fate as the store proprietor's wife.

Donna couldn't believe that we had almost gone through all our large bags of rice and flour and were nearly out of food. The food problem on Punlap Island was caused by all the able-bodied men preoccupied building the church. The men were not having much time to go fishing or climb the breadfruit trees to harvest the primary staple of the island. I couldn't imagine why the men were now so dedicated to working on the church when I couldn't get even one to help me. Padre must have given one heck of an inspiring speech to the men of the island, but he was without a doubt the poorest Jesuit speaker I had ever heard. Or did he have another method of persuasion that men would allow their families to go hungry to work on the church??? It was so unlike the steady supply of island food on Ono, Onari, and Piseras even when we were at the busiest in building the dispensaries. Punlap was a starving Island!

We attended a special celebration at the Punlap public oot, which Padre had simply appropriated after knocking down the church, for his faithful altar boys who were being rewarded with jars of Padre's jelly. He told Donna and I that the glass jars of jelly had been on his shelves for years and had spoiled, and it was time to get rid of them. Padre seemed to have lost all touch of common sense. He had no idea how inappropriate it was to gift rancid jelly. Knowing from my experience the effects of loneliness and isolation after just two years in the Peace Corps, Padre had been out in the Western Islands for well over thirty years.

The church authorities in Truk had to have some reason for keeping him isolated in the far flung outer islands by himself, but I couldn't figure it out knowing how the Peace Corps operated out there. The Jesuit Bishop may have felt that Padre was indispensable and some kind of hero for his long dedicated service there. After personally witnessing Padre on Punlap, he was more than eccentric. But who was I to judge who is normal, I spoke to Johnny Kruger, my friend on the Winter Park Ski Poster, for two years on Ono, Onari, and Piseras Islands!

One morning after greeting Padre, he blurted out of the blue, "Did you know that the "Holocaust was exaggerated by the Jews? Yes! There some killed, but not the millions that the Jews would have you believe." Why was Padre saying this to me now out on Punlap Island. What a strange answer to my, ". Good morning, Father." It was not unusual for Padre to make troubling statements to me like his statement on Vatican ll or his stating, "We white men have to stick together on this." This was just one more outrageous statement from him.

His fellow priests back in Truk must have experienced his outbursts when they were dining or playing bridge with him. Just like a leopard doesn't change its spots, neither does a disturbed person control their outbursts. The Holocaust was all too tragically real and impossible to keep secret with a staggering 6 million innocent Jewish men, women, and children exterminated. But it didn't always connect at more than past history with me, until I personally heard and felt the stories of Dr. Charlotte Donsky, my college French professor, fellow coucilman Dr. Tom Steinberg, and Vail's Fr. Tom Dentici.

My first experience with the Holocaust came with Dr. Charlotte Donsky, my French professor at Regis, who could set Padre straight. He was fond of saying, "Too bad, too bad, too bad." It was too bad he hadn't seen her uncontrollably trembling in fear or heard her softly crying, after she had over-heard an angry conversation between two German language instructors speaking loudly in German. She had experienced a flashback to an unfathomable and gut -wrenching time of terror when being a Jewish child and living in Leon, France. Over 100 members of her extended large family had been seized by the Nazis and and were shipped off to Nazi death camps- never to be heard from again. Christians like the famous Evangelist, Corrie Ten Boom and her family sheltered Jews in the Netherlands during World War II. Corrie's book the _Hiding Place_ tells how her family hid entire Jewish families in their home and how she and her family were eventually caught by the Gestapo. Corrie's father, Casper, told his daughter, "I pity the poor Germans, Corrie. They have touched the apple of God's eye." Corrie miraculously survived but her sister, Betsie, died in Ravensbruck Concentration Camp December 16, 1944 and her father, Casper, died in Scheveningen Prison near the Dutch Hague.

Another witness to the Holocaust was a Vail Town Council person when I served on the Council. I was privileged to know Vail's first perma nent physician and one of the original founders of Vail's Hospital, Doctor Tom Steinberg. For forty years after World War II Tom said nothing about his experiences as a young American infantryman serving with the 42nd Infantry Division of the Seventh Army, not even to his wife or children. But after history revisionists began saying that the Jewish Holocaust was a **hoax,** Tom felt compelled to break his long silence about his buried war experiences. Tom would annually make a public statement about when he was involved in the liberation of Dachau, the Nazi's first concentration death camp near the end of World War II. The articulate and usually calm doctor unsuccessfully attempted to fight back against crying telling his long suppressed story of his 42nd Army Division taking the South Gate of Dachau. He was just a young American infantry soldier seeing the horrors that no young man should ever personally witness. It was such an emotional moment when Dr. Tom Steinberg spoke that there wasn't a dry eye in the Vail Town Council chamber. He is one of Tom Brokaw's, "Greatest Generation" whose personal eye witness at the South Gate of

Dachau must not be forgotten. Historian George Santayana warned, *"Those who cannot remember the past are condemned to repeat it."* It was noticed that the Jewish Star of David was accidently still hanging over the altar and not replaced with the Christian Cross at the start of Mass in the Vail Interfaith Chapel. Father Tom Dentici said it was very appropriate hanging over the altar and for the ushers to leave it instead of exchanging it for the Christian Cross, "Christians sit on the shoulders of the Jewish Prophets and our Jewish brothers and sisters. Any anti-Semites who are offended are now asked to leave the service!" Usually at the beginning of Mass Father Tom would always ask for a show of hands of anyone from Brooklyn, obviously with his strong accent you knew where he was from! When he saw a few hands he said with a smile, "I give you my personal dispensation to go skiing!" He was not your usual priest! Celebrating his 50th anniversary as a priest and then living at Holy Family Catholic Church in Steamboat Springs he told the congregation how he received his vocation.

"As a young man-about-town he was out dancing in Manhattan and having a great time with friends and when later that night returning back to Brooklyn on the subway, he heard a loud voice say, 'Tom, I want you to study and become a priest.' He looked around and asked his friends if any of them had heard the loud announcement. 'What announcement? We didn't hear anything!' Again he heard loudly, 'I want you to study and become a priest!' He again was the only one hearing the loud voice. Thinking that he was a most unlikely candidate for gaining entrance to a seminary having not gone to Catholic Schools and having his father opposed at the time, he turned to his devout Catholic mother who had connections, if you know what I mean. She had a very deep prayer life. One of her daily prayers had been for a seemingly an impossible religious vocation for her son and now he had heard directly from God that he was handpicked for this calling. Finding a seminary was a piece of cake for God!" Father Dentici was now a big believer in miracles. He commented that, "it was a miracle I was accepted into a seminary." He also said that,

"Miracles happen all the time. People just don't recognize them."

In my own life "The Steamboat Bike Shop Miracle," as our family has dubbed it, gives me hope on even the most hopeless of days. It was Father's Day 2011. My wife had given me a neon green bike jacket as a gift. Very nice, but a little tight! We were going to church that morning, and as the ski shop she purchased it in was just around the corner from the church, we decided to take it along and exchange it after Mass. She rewrapped the jacket in the tissue paper, put it back in the gift bag and stuck it in the car. Nothing extraordinary so far! After Mass we grabbed the bag from the locked car and walked across the street to the bike shop.

As we entered the shop we were greeted by an employee and we told him we would like to exchange the jacket for a larger size and my wife pulled the jacket from the bag still wrapped in the tissue paper. Donna un-wrapped the neon green jacket from the tissue and was holding it up to the cashier when he told us that we cannot exchange it since it had something all over the back of the jacket! "What are you talking about!" Donna answered, "The jacket was absolutely perfect when I put it back in the bag!" And furthermore, there was nothing on the tissue paper or anywhere in or out of the bag. Yet all over the back of the jacket was a fresh red substance that was definitely wet and dripping. At this point we are not thinking, "Miracle!" We were just so amazed and unbelieving at what we were seeing. The employee brought Donna some paper towels and with a little rubbing Donna was able to wipe off the red substance and there was no stain left behind. The shop still was not interested in taking the jacket back and so we left still perplexed by this whole situation. "What had happened? How did it happen?" This was no ordinary event. That jacket was in perfect shape when we put it in the bag and yet when Donna pulled it out the entire back was covered in wet red. It certainly wasn't jelly or juice or ketchup. Could it have been **blood?**

Donna had jokingly commented to Father Tom after his 50th celebration that she never seemed to recognize any "signs" in her life. She guessed she would need a neon sign! Could the neon green jacket with the **"blood"** on the back be a sign she had asked for and God had answered?

He was right there with her and could change things in the blink of an eye. Just coming from Mass and receiving the **Jewish** Blood of Christ in the chalice and having this experience was humbling. The neon green jacket has become our "miracle jacket" and the message was not lost on us. You are not alone. God is with us every moment, can change your life in an instant and performs miracles in our lives! I am reminded of this story when thinking about Padre's comment to me about the Holocaust!

The Buckley family was staying on Punlap Island only until the end of the school semester at Christmas. Donna was enjoying teaching the eighth graders and didn't feel right to just abandon the school or the kids who were making real progress. But we were still anxiously waiting for the Field Trip Ship to arrive on Punlap so we could resupply our empty food stocks. We had run out of our supply of rice, flower, and cases of can goods. Donna didn't know what she was going to feed the children for dinner that night, when we heard a knock on our door. A big bowl of fresh hot breadfruit was dropped off that very night when we were out of food to feed our children! We ran out of caramels in the attic on our first night on Punlap!

The word from our island radio was that the ship had stopped on its way out to Punlap when one of its crew members had suddenly died of a heart attack. The ship delayed four days trying to figure out what to do and finally arrived off Punlap Island. All of a sudden there was loud wailing and keening by the women as the dead crew man was unloaded on his home island. He was a young married man with small children looking forward to seeing his family at home on Punlap. The mourning went on for two days with nightly loud wailing by the women. His body had been laid out in the middle of the oot surrounded by his wife and children and other family and friends filling the oot with their loud wailing. Donna and I brought our children to the oot that night to see their first sight of an island funeral, and show the Buckley family cared for them in their time of sorrow. I was asked if I had any medicine that might bring the dead man back to life. I didn't have any medicine that strong in the canvas bag. I then was asked if I had any medicine which could help to preserve his body so his family from the outlying islands could attend his funeral. I again answered that I didn't, but I suggested that the body be put into the big fish reefer. No was the quick reply! Nobody would buy or eat any fish stored in the same freezer where a dead person had been preserved. The power of superstition and *anumaumau* (strong ghost or curse) was real and powerful. And either translation works!

The ship surprised Punlap Island again, but this time not bringing another Punlap Islander's body, but only just for one day and night quick surprise by the Education Department of Truk. It was carrying a very special friend of Punlap and former Peace Corps Volunteer from years earlier. Dr. Chris (Kit) Lorentz and his wife were hoping that they might be able to catch a ride on a ship to Punlap and have an opportunity to spend a night with his Peace Corps host family. Donna and I were surprised seeing this American couple walking on the pathway by our house in the morning on their way back to catch the ship after spending the night with his host family. As we introduced ourselves, a medical emergency came unexpectedly. A frantic mother and father were carrying their bleeding four year old daughter who had ripped and torn her small vagina slipping off a coconut tree ramp onto a sharpened support stake. The naked little girl was bleeding profusely. She was lucky that a shark hadn't attacked her in the lagoon.

Our house was turned into a temporary operating room for Kit who calmly washed the wound and numbed the torn flesh with pain killing shots. Seeing the crying and bleeding child getting shots was too much for the wide eyed Buckley children and Donna removed them from the house. Kit had his medical bag with him and his emergency instruments and carefully operated on the small child and then stitched the anesthetized wound. That was the first and only time I had met Kit, but I will never forget his calm superb medical care rendered to this beautiful little four year old child. After cleaning up from just performing a skillful operation, he and his wife had to quickly leave to catch the ship before its departure from the Island, but not without leaving his instructions for the follow up care and the removal of stitches.

Never doubt that God made a way for a skilled physician to be available in a remote corner of the remote Western Islands. This was a **miracle** that had so many puzzle parts that it still leaves me without words and can only say, "Ah! Ah!"

Obviously on Punlap they didn't celebrate an American style Halloween with haunted houses and trick or treating, but for us Halloween on Punlap was the scariest one ever. Donna and the kids had decorated the little house with cutout orange pumpkins tacked to the wall above their school desks. Brian and John had been over in the village at Lino's family's large thatched house watching the roasting of a pig, which was a huge event and meant that for the first time in a long time there would be meat on the table. With no weather forecasters, weather just showed up and had to be dealt with. That night a major Pacific front blew in with high shrieking winds and blinding rain. Donna and Amanda and I were worried that the two boys might have difficulty finding their way back in the raging storm and the approaching black night. I grabbed my flashlight and was ready to venture out when we heard Brian's loud cry and knew surely the boys were in trouble! I headed out into the blinding storm with the wind screaming loudly through the trees with rain and debris flying sideway so hard that I could barely see the pathway with the flashlight.

The wind had actually blown rain through the flimsy walls of the house and Donna's only mirror blew off the shelf it was sitting on breaking it into tiny pieces of glass. For the next two months there was no checking yourself out in a mirror. Amazing how Donna depended on this simple act.

I stumbled and swayed blindly along the path following Brian's continuous loud crying and finally came upon my two young sons off the path huddled together lost inside the forest and sheltered behind a bush. Thank goodness Brian was so loud! He had dropped the treasured roasted meat that Lino's family had given to him for celebrating All Saints Day, and he couldn't find it on the flooded forest floor. The violent storm continued to strengthen sounding like a freight train roaring loudly through the woods. Donna and Amanda were greatly relieved when the three of us soaking wet stumbled back in the door. I was so proud of all three of our young children, and my sons bravely trying to bring food to our hungry table. And I was especially proud of Brian protecting and keeping his seven year- old brother at his side all the while that terrifying Halloween night! There were many tricks that Halloween, but thankfully some treats as well. As superstition goes, Donna's broken mirror probably meant seven years of bad luck. But God's plan will conquer any curse or broken mirror and take you into His prepared blessings and, especially when no storm can *shake* your *inmost calm* when your family survives roaring wind and rain, crashing trees, and flying branches. *How can I keep from singing? (Enya, Irish Musician)*

As Christmas approached and the end of the island school's semester, the principal and the eighth grade class held a surprise feast for Donna in appreciation for her hard work. It was quite a tribute for how much Donna meant to the young girls who had made significant progress speaking English. We were also surprised to see an outrigger sailing canoe arrive on the beach in front of our house **from Tamatam**. It carried the two grateful sons of the sick man who returned back to Tamatam from seeing the Stanford doctors and was happily on heart medications and doing just fine.

They brought with them from Tamatam a hand carved replica of their sailing outrigger canoe, including the traditional woven pandanas sail. What a gift! It meant a great deal to both Donna and I that our efforts to come to Punlap and Tamatam were appreciated. With all the negatives in connection with the building of the church and with Padre, it just went to show that whatever we thought our plans and goals were for our trip to Punlap God had other reasons for our going to Punlap. After a rather dubious greeting our first day on the island, with God's help we had saved lives, improved others, and stretched ourselves in directions we had never imagined.

They are good, strong, grateful people and it was a privilege to get to know them. And yes, thank you Padre for inviting us to Punlap Island, even though it was for another reason than helping you build the church. God had a more compelling reason for the Buckley Journey to Punlap!

CHAPTER 19
"Don't Be Afraid"

With the Field Trip Ship imminent passage back to Moen, Donna was thinking that it might be a an educational opportunity for Brian's friend Lino to go back to live with us for a year and go to school in America to improve his English language skills. I wasn't totally sold on the idea at first, but encouraged Donna to see what his parents thought. His mother, Trinitas, who was related to Lambert saw how education had opened doors for him and was very supportive to give it a try for a year. The decision was made to talk to Lino about such a major change in his life and he was very excited about the opportunity. Donna and I were thinking that since we had our house rented out in Vail that we should try living in Hawaii for the next six months until the lease was up on our house. It would be an easier transition for Lino than renting back in Vail which receives about 300 inches of snow in the winter. Donna had also become accustomed to the weather in the South Pacific and was not in favor of going back to Vail and the cold and snow in the winter. We would be running low on funds but not Trust.

We packed our clothes and passports and left all of our household belongings with Trinitas, and Seles and we said our goodbyes and along with Lino boarded the ship taking us back to the Truk Lagoon. Only the weather was not like the summer weather in which we had travelled out to

Punlap. The trade winds were blowing strong in late December and the ride proved to be very rough and trying for the kids and Donna who were seasick once again.

I was approached on the ship by a man who wanted to speak to me in private about Padre. This man's Island will remain unnamed for reasons you will probably understand by now.

His story began by going to Confession to Padre several years earlier and had confessed that he had sexual relations with a married woman on his outer island. For his penance he said Padre ordered him to go and tell the husband. But he refused absolution from Padre because he was afraid that her husband would cut the woman's nose off!

Jesus, when confronting the zealous mob wanting to humiliate and stone to death the woman caught in adultery, said to the mob, "Let the one among you who is without sin be the first to throw a stone at her." The mob drifted away leaving Jesus alone with the woman. Then Jesus said, "Neither do I condemn you. Go, and from now on do not sin anymore."

Asking Padre for another penance, the penitent was refused! So the man said that he was going go into Truk on the next Field Trip Ship and find another priest on Moen for Confession. As his account was related to me, when the next Field Trip ship arrived Padre spoke to the captain of the ship and told him not to allow the man to ride on the ship back to Truk. "Padre had asked the captain, if he had heard the Bible Story of *Jonah and the Whale.*" The penitent confessor was not allowed to board the ship. Again the story was told to me by someone who sought me out on board the ship and another cry for help!

I hoped there was an **expiration date on curses**! Having lived and worked and sailed with a palu who had abandoned the many taboos that went along with being a navigator, it was inconceivable to me that a missionary would be using anumaumau to control the behavior of the islanders. Originally, it was Spanish Catholic missionaries that suggested to the ron palu (navigators) that their taboos were meaningless superstitions. Having no bad repercussions from venturing forth on the open seas without their preliminary taboo precautions, pragmatic strong navigators abandoned the superstitious taboos. Now I know how Padre had the power to have the people of Punlap knock down their *Treasured* coral church, and it was a concerned father that moved his daughter to another Island when Padre desired spiders for his mosquito webs!

When we dropped anchor on Moen Donna and the children, except Lino, were green with sea sickness. I had to find a place now for six people to stay on Christmas Eve! I knew that our little teacher's house at Xavier was occupied and I wasn't in the mood just then to talk to anyone about our experiences on Punlap. But we needed a comfortable bed for Donna and the kids to recuperate. We piled into a taxi and headed down to the Continental Hotel, like the one I stayed when on Peace Corps vacation, owned by Air Micronesia on the south end of Moen. I was able to secure two adjacent rooms for a fairly reasonable rate and everyone was happy to spend the night anywhere that was not moving. This was Christmas Eve and my present to the family!

But we did have to educate Lino how a toilet worked. At first he thought you sat Island style with your feet planted on the rim. I was able to join up with a friend and former Micro 7 Peace Corps trainer Clark Graham and meet his beautiful Chuukese wife and see his beautiful children. Clark developed a successful diving business on Moen scuba diving on the Japanese wrecks in the lagoon and is still very active as a leader on the island. It was great to see his friendly face again and hear how he was going to teach his son how to "slam dunk" a basketball!

Donna and I visited the Truk Hospital after Christmas to thank the Stanford doctors for their support, and by the Grace of God and Dr. Doug Canham we had just the right medicine and the doctors had the right diagnosis. I hadn't been Padre's answer to his slow construction on his church project on Punlap; if for no other reason, God had uniquely placed us on Punlap Island. The concerned young father brought the first friendly faces and coconuts to the Buckley family on that first day on Punlap Island and the first of many miracles. The doctors gratefully accepted the remaining ample supply of needed drugs for the Hospital on Truk. We were surprised to see some people from the field trip ship fresh from Punlap at the Hospital who were suffering from malnutrition, a direct consequence of Padre pushing the construction workers on the church.

Donna also noticed the many cockroaches scurrying on the floors which we barely avoided squashing underfoot.

We next went to the airport office of Air Micronesia to book our flight back to Hawaii. I already had pre-purchased tickets back to Colorado through Hawaii for our later date, and was going to use that portion of the tickets for my family. I also needed to purchase another ticket to Hawaii for Lino. Donna and I waited our turn in line to meet with a ticket agent and we walked up to the busy counter to a young Micronesian agent dressed smartly in his Air Micronesia uniform and who spoke very good English. We explained our situation that we also needed to purchase an extra ticket for Lino. He looked at me inquisitively and soon said in Weito that he needed to talk to me. I was worried that he was about to tell me that we couldn't change the dates on the pre-purchased tickets. "OK, what do you need to talk to me about?"

"Come with me!" He closed his ticket station and led me outside about fifty yards from the terminal where we were alone and nobody could overhear us talk, "I have heard about you; I am from a Western Island (to be left unnamed) and I need you to go to the Bishop and have an anumaumau removed that Padre placed on my family! My sister tried to get into the Catholic girl's school and was turned down because there wasn't room, but she was accepted into the Micronesian Lutheran School. Padre had placed a curse on my family if she attends the Lutheran School." I assured him that I would try to speak to the Bishop.

The Bishop was unable to meet with me and Donna, but a meeting was set up for us to talk with the Jesuit Superior who was quite cordial but was very careful in his response to us and very non-committal. I learned later that Padre remained for another 8 years. The white Bishop informed him in writing sometime in the early nineties that he was being sent back to New York. The grandson of a former chief of Ulul shared this with me, "For me superstition and Padre.....are synonymous. Only when I grew up and joined the Jesuits did I understand what a crock of bull..... his brand of Catholicism was in those islands-especially his overuse of the threats of anumawma. It was all meant to control the people." Padre died in 2005, and is buried in the Jesuit cemetery in Auriesville, New York.

On June 6, 1995 Bishop Amando Samo succeeded the white Bishop as the Ordinary Bishop of the Caroline Islands. Bishop Samo was Chuukese and knew the language and the customs of the Western Islands of Chuuk. The chiefs in the Western outer islands of Chuuk now had someone who wasn't hard of listening, a native Ronmetau (a person of the sea). A Jesuit priest friend of mine at Regis University, after hearing my story about Padre asked, "Do you know the best thing that happened to the Catholic Church?" What, I asked? He replied, "**The Protestant Reformation!**" I think that Lydia and Elvin Ranke, Donna's late Lutheran grandparents who helped to raise Donna when her father was killed when Donna was only three days-old, would have been happy for Donna hearing what Fr. Bob had said to us!

Martin Luther had tremendous courage standing up to the 16th Century Catholic Church that Donna and I witnessed on Punlap Island. Sadly Padre wasn't too different from Shoichi Yakoi, the Japanese holdout who hid out for 28 years on Guam because of the fog of war. Padre was a priest in the Western Islands of Truk and was also abandoned there for nearly forty years. But his Jesuit Superiors knew the Prefect of Discipline was there.

Donna, Brian, John, Amanda, Lino and I were able to celebrate New Year's twice, first in Truk and then crossing the International Date Line in Hawaii. Please look at my friend Clark Graham's Chuukese youth foundation at www.ship-hoops.org and please support his effort at improving the education of the children of Chuuk (Truk). You will also see pictures of Clark and his beautiful family and the stories of two genuine heroes of Chuuk. I didn't hear whether Keitani could slam dunk, but he sure made a lot of people proud in Chuuk and Hawaii, wrestling in the 2012 Summer Olympic Games. Clark probably still likes freshly baked German Chocolate Cake-timing his visit to the Lutheran Pastor when smelling a cake baking in the oven.

It was New Year's Eve in Truk and we were booked on Air Micronesia to fly to Honolulu. For Lino it would be his first plane trip. Actually, this would be only one of many "firsts" for him. For our family it would also be a first. This would be the first time we had ever experienced two New Year's Eves in one year. Traveling from Micronesia to Hawaii we were crossing the International Dateline. We left on 12/31/83 and arrived in Honolulu on 12/31/83. The ultimate New Year's Eve! Alas, with four children and the time change we kept the celebrating to a minimum, found a good hotel to stay in on the beach and watched a few fireworks from our room. Donna and I wanted to quickly make a move over to Maui, where we were very familiar, and try to rent a house for a few months until the end of the lease we had signed with the renters of our Vail house. Dream on! This was high season in Maui. We were able to rent a condominium there for one week thinking that would give us enough time to find a rental home. This turned out to be a mini vacation for the children and Donna while I scoured the entire island for a house rental. Like any popular resort locale, prices were high and last minute comers were going have to pay a big price for absolutely not what they were looking for. I should have known that Maui would be just like Vail. We needed to have found something months earlier, but this was not part of the original plan.

Finding absolutely nothing suitable and affordable for my family on Maui, and for reasons I could not explain, I had been thinking about a Vail couple, George and Jeannine who shared a friendship with me and a Regis College Jesuit priest. Out of the blue I gave them a call and our mutual Jesuit friend was spending the night with them and going cross country skiing on Vail Mountain in the morning. I told the priest my challenge of finding a home to rent in Hawaii and he said to call a priest friend of his at Malia Puka O Kalani (Hawaiian for, *Mary Gate of Heaven)* Catholic Church in Hilo on the Big Island of Hawaii. What did I know about the Big Island? Nothing! What did I have to lose? Nothing! I gave Father George a call and he told me to get on an inter-island plane the next day and he would meet me at the airport and we would go house hunting.

Donna's strong instructions were to find a house that was furnished and had a dishwasher! We were now a family of six so that sounded reasonable. Father George and I spent fruitless hours looking at houses advertised in the paper and for much the same reason as on Maui, found nothing. Father George inexplicably decided to drive up Wailuku Drive in Hilo and swiftly turned into the driveway of a home after seeing a man in the window sweeping his floor. He knocked on the door, the man answered and Father George asked him if the house was for rent? "How did you know? I was just going down to the paper to put in an ad." We found a house. It wasn't furnished or have a dishwasher, but it had beautiful landscaping, a great view of the volcano Moana Loa in one direction and the ocean in the other, and a great price! And I was Irish and rented it on the spot. Father George drove me back to the airport and as he dropped me off, he said he would pick us up in his station wagon when I returned with the family.

Thankfully Donna was just as impressed with the small three bedroom house as I was. It had Chinese cherries and coconut trees, no rats, and no construction project going on three feet from the front door. Instead, our next door neighbor was a cardiologist with a wife who Donna instantly became friends with and a young daughter Amanda's age who actually played with dolls.

We quickly and sparsely furnished the little house with second hand furniture and settled in on the Big Island – although Donna was back washing dishes by hand. But we didn't have to worry about boiling our water to kill the cholera bacteria and squirming worms, we had modern plumbing and chlorinated city water. We were in Hawaii! Our landlord let us use one of his extra cars which Lino immediately proclaimed as "*expired*" surprising both Donna and I as to where he had learned this word. He didn't have many English words, but he knew that the car was falling apart. I must admit that every time we drove down Wailuku Drive I wasn't sure the car would make it back uphill to home, at least in one piece before more rusting parts would fall off.

Sunday rolled around and the Buckley Family went to Malia Puka O Kalani to Mass. It was a very old white church with Hawaiian greeters at the door. Father George, at the beginning of Mass, introduced the Buckley family with Aloha to his mostly Hawaiian congregation. It felt like I was back on Ono Island where Chief Sak had embraced me and I was welcomed by dancing and singing. What a difference from Padre's Punlap! The traditional Hawaiian music during Mass was accompanied by a traditional hula dancer. At the embrace of Peace one large Hawaiian woman actually lifted me off the ground. No tepid handshake here. Upon leaving at the end of the Mass, we found a pickup truck filled with papaya. Each and every parishioner was welcome to take as many as they would use. This was a weekly event we really appreciated and Mahalo to the farmer who was so generous. What a special place to be after coming from the land of fear, curses, and paranoia. One Sunday we arrived at Malia to find Dateline NBC reporters there to do a story on Father George and his Hawaiian parish.

Our children enrolled in the local school and Amanda officially became a first grader, John was in second, Brian was in 4th grade, and Lino became a 5th grader in a Hilo elementary school. It was an experience that allowed three "Haole (white) Kids" and a Micronesian to learn not only their A-B-C's, but also some Hawaiian history and culture. I decided to return back to Vail where I could work on the ski patrol to earn some immediate money to help pay for our new unexpected expenses. A good friend, and an assistant Ski Patrol Director, graciously put me up in a spare bedroom in his house where I lived while Donna and the children lived in Hawaii. Two months later while watching the late news on TV, I was stunned to see that the Moana Loa Volcano had erupted above Wailuku drive and where Donna and the kids were living!

Thinking of my wife and children living on the flank of Moana Loa, I immediately called Donna who seemed to be very calm and said she wasn't going to get worried until she saw the next door neighbors beginning to pack up their belongings. All the news reports were warning residents to prepare for a permanent evacuation. There would be no coming back to get anything as the lava would destroy everything. Since the neighbors had all their possessions to pack up, she was not going to panic about a few second hand store things. Just grab the kids, the clothes and leave. Donna told me not to worry that they were doing fine for now and that most likely the TV reports were exaggerating the situation. Normally you could see the top of the volcano from the house, but since the eruption began it was shrouded in smoke and clouds. Nevertheless, I could not just sit in Vail and worry, so I booked a ticket back to Hawaii. Now April Fools' Day, just like the previous Halloween, and the two New Year's would be forever memorable. I called to Hawaii and Brian answered. I told him I was on my way and to tell his mom to pick me up at the Hilo Airport. When she picked me up, instead of being like, "Oh my hero! I'm so glad you're here to save us," I got, "What are you doing here?" Not the reaction I was expecting. My human worries were for naught, but at least our family was all together again.

Brian, John, Amanda, Bob, and Lino at Hawaii's Volcano National Park

We sometimes find ourselves in places and circumstances which are not comfortable and we don't know what is going to happen next. We all live on borrowed time, and each human being in each age is faced with a world full of change and challenge! But we are not alone and always can reach out to our Savior for help, *"Get up! Don't be afraid!"* (Matt. 17:7) All things are possible with our God who is bigger than any myriad of diseases, violent storms, avalanches, volcanos, sinister rogues (some are fish), even curses (anumaumau). His light and hands are always stretched out to His beloved children! Jesus, our **Easter Shepard**, said to the women rushing to tell the disciples of the Lord's empty tomb "**Do not be afraid!**" (Mt.28:10).

"It might seem there's an ocean in between. But He is holding on to you and me. He is with us. He is with us, always. We can trust our God. We are not afraid. He is with us. He is with us always, always. God is with us…We are not afraid." (He is With Us. Musical Video on You Tube by Love and the Outcome)

BOOK FOUR: SKIING MADE ME DO IT

Amanda at Volcano National Park in Hawaii

CHAPTER 20
Donna's Dream

Nothing changed. Donna always wanted to live in Hawaii! Our little rented home on Wailuku Drive was a dream come true for her, even without a dishwasher. Reading a book in a backyard filled with bright red Poinsettias growing on bushes, red Anthuriums growing in the gardens, and purple Bougainvillea flowers climbing on trellises was Donna's idea of a dream come true. There were macadamia nut trees, banana trees, and two small coconut trees. Chinese Cherries were hanging like red and yellow lanterns from bushes on the side of the house. Sitting quietly enjoying the beauty of the garden and the serenade from birds of every color, her Hawaiian joy was broken by a mongoose racing through the green grass. Her youthful dream of attending the University of Hawaii, instead of SUNY Oswego with snow levels coldly blowing high up to her second story dorm window, had come true without the classes, late night cramming for tests, and day-old pizza!

After sleeping the first night on cold floors, our very first purchases were air mattresses. The little house was built on stilts and the cool January night air flowed beneath the wood floors. Starting at sea level, Wailuku Drive steadily climbed up the flank of the Mauna Loa Volcano finally reaching the new Buckley home way up high next to the last house on the block where, "Bluebirds fly." With the air mattresses it was very comfortable sleeping in the cooler air, almost like being back in our own beds on Bald Mountain Road in Vail, Colorado. Many days rainbows often painted the Hawaiian skies. The Micronesian palu (navigators) for thousands of years believed *Anumwerici*, the Spirit of Flowers, lived in the rainbows. One of my favorite songs is <u>Somewhere Over the Rainbow,</u> sung by Hawaiian Israel "IZ" Kamakawiwo'Ole.

All four young children, Brian, John, Amanda, and Lino, our Punlap Island adventurer, were enrolled in the nearest Hilo grade school. Amanda and Dewi Lim, her next-door new friend, playmate, and also first grade classmate looked forward to sitting together on the school bus which stopped for the kids right in front of our house. Although called "Haole", a word in the Hawaiian language aimed at white people, Brian, John, and Amanda were welcomed into their respective classes. Lino was right at home with everyone and everything. The boys were each other's best friend.

Hawaii is truly a melting pot for all of the Pacific Islanders and Lino was the most at home of all on the Buckley Family Journey. Even his lack of English language skills didn't handicap him since most Pacific languages have many similarities from their common root language called, *Apai n' lamalam,* now only spoken by the Micronesian navigators, or *'Olelo Hawai'i* spoken by Native Hawaiians. Latin is the root language for many of our European languages now mostly spoken by Catholic Priests. (*Angnus Dei qui tolis peccata mundi, miserere nobis, Angnus Dei qui tolis peccata mundi, dona nobis pacem.* Lamb of God who takes away the sins of the world, have mercy on us. Lamb of God who takes away the sins of the world, grant us peace.) Pounded taro is called "po" on Punlap Island and called "poi" in Hawaii. The word for canoe is "Wa" on Punlap and "Wa" in Hawaii. On Punlap *Olela* means goodbye.

Most foods that Lino was accustomed to eating back home on Punlap were available in our local grocery stores; and some were growing in our own garden and swimming in the nearby ocean around the Big Island. Lino felt very comfortable at Malia Puka O Kalani Catholic Church with its Hawaiian hula dancing and natural harmonized singing in the Hawaiian language. Happy and joyful people and music filled the small white church. We all enjoyed the papaya offered freely by generous farmers who parked their pickups in the church parking lot, their truck beds filled with fresh papaya. Hawaiian life was going well, but what is life if it doesn't have a few surprises. And the dreams that you dream come true!

Never in our wildest dreams did we ever think we would get to experience one volcano erupting, let alone two! Retold stories of a family journey filled all of us with awe at experiencing first-hand the eruptions of both the Moana Loa and the Kilauea Volcanoes. It was a once in a lifetime opportunity that hadn't happened in over one hundred years. For the most part, you didn't feel the powerful impact of this except when you would hear the announcement on TV and Radio that if you were ordered to evacuate you should prepare for a permanent evacuation. Most probably, there would be no returning back to your current home. The red lava flow was visible zig-zagging down the slope as we drove up Wailuku Drive to home. The biggest thing standing out in my mind about my time at Colorado School of Mines was an inspiring Geology professor, Doctor "Lett" Leroy and his lectures on volcanoes.

Arriving back to Hilo from Vail, Donna really surprised me with her, "What are you doing here?" More expecting to hear, "My hero is here to save us!" No! She wasn't going to be worried unless she saw our neighbors packing up all their belongings. At least Dr. Leroy would have been proud of my not missing the opportunity to witness one of nature's greatest fireworks shows, two volcanoes erupting simultaneously. This was way more spectacular than Vail's annual famous Fourth of July fireworks show. The four children were standing with Donna and me in the middle of a quiet Wailuku Drive, on a memorably first crystal clear night since the eruption, viewing red glowing lines of molten lava slowly flowing towards us.

Kilauea was, hopefully, drawing down some of the explosive angry energy from the Moana Loa Volcano because Moana Loa could blow us all to kingdom come, or bury us in its toxic ash. "There's a fanfare blowing to the sun/ There was floating on the breeze/ Look at Mother Nature on the run/ In the Twentieth Century," harmonized by Emmy Lou Harris, Linda Ronstadt, and Dolly Parton on the *Trio ll Album.*

Another example of "Mother Nature on the run/In the Twentieth Century" was just about a month after the lava stopped above our home on Wailuku Drive, astonished renters back in Vail called telling us that mud slides were threatening our home. One slide already glanced off the Nott house just hundreds of feet from our home on Bald Mountain Road. Another mudslide blocked nearby Booth Creek, and another hit at the end of Bald Mountain Road. Our renters, along with other Vail neighbors, were ordered to evacuate Thankfully for my family in Hilo, the lava stopped before smashing into Donna's dream-come-true just below Moana Loa and forcing a permanent evacuation for our wonderful neighbors.

An important gentleman's agreement with a fellow Vail Associate Real Estate broker to service my real estate clients in my absence was sealed with just a handshake. My returning in January to the Vail Ski Patrol to help with our unexpected expenses, Craig Denton handed me a nice check. The money was burning a hole in my pocket.

I beelined to a local jewelry store where the wife of the attorney who rented our house in Vail was smiling at me from behind the jewelry case. When proposing years earlier to Donna, a young ski patrolman simply asked, "Will you marry me?" And she replied, "Yes!" An appreciation ring was overdue for both Donna's breathtaking reply and for making our journey to Punlap Island possible!

CHAPTER 21
Mahalo

Leaving Hawaii is never easy! With the children out of school for the summer vacation, packing up and moving back to Colorado was the last thing on Donna's to-do list. She was happy living in Hawaii! Kids are out of school and time for the bread winner to start winning again.

Living in Hilo, Hawaii for six months was a great start for Lino's year of education in America. He knew that he could survive in Hawaii and fend for himself if needed. Learning to speak the English language was the emphasis for those who didn't. Hawaii had a program called ESL-teaching English as a Second Language. Most Hawaiian children studied the more conventional courses of reading, writing, and arithmetic. Our three children were also picking up Hawaiian pidgin along the way. "Eh haole, howzit?"

Lino's memory always impressed me but wasn't surprising to me. While serving in the Peace Corps on Piseras, the island children memorized, word for word, the entire movie dialogue from Padre's old movies. "My name is Stryker, Sgt. John M. Striker…" (John Wayne in Sands of Iwo Jima). For thousands of years, Pacific Islanders in the outer Islands of Chuuk were crafting time tested and proven designs for their open ocean outrigger sailing canoes, without engineering degrees.

The superior trees for the canoes were thought to be found on Puluwat Island, and therefore the best canoe builders and navigators (palu) were found there too. The Western Caroline navigators developed a sophisticated and complex dead-reckoning navigation system that utilized what nature provided-just some of what nature offered to the navigators were visible stars and planets, ocean currents, wave patterns, wind directions, cloud formations, flight directions of Terns, weather cycles and the Trade Winds, and use of known back sights for setting a course. Micronesian and Polynesian outrigger sailing canoes ventured far and wide between the islands of the vast Pacific Ocean for thousands of years before Captain Cook's voyages of discovery.

For many thousands of years navigation and canoe construction methods were acquired and passed down by word of mouth. Craftsmen canoe builders and the experienced navigators utilized hands on training, stick charts, and musical chants in the ancient language to pass on their lessons. Lino had descended from a uniquely proud and accomplished culture. But people of the Western Islands of Chuuk would be considered poor by U.S. education standards.

(The East is a Big Bird by Thomas Gladwin)

Scuff marks from Donna's shoes might still be visible on the tarmac at Hilo's Airport. But the Buckley family's continuing journey was finally flying back to Colorado. Her biorhythm chart, purchased in a vending machine, was plunging while the four happy children and I were enjoying the flight! Lino had a smile from ear to ear that would have pleased his mother back on Punlap.

Meeting us in Denver's Stapleton Airport was once again my mother who was anxious to see Donna and her three grandchildren and to meet Lino. After my ignoring her warning about taking my young family on a risky journey, she had the added natural worries for her three grandchildren and Donna. All, including me, were in her prayers. "You Can Always Tell An Irishman But You Can't Tell Him Much"was written on a small green pillow Donna bought for me on the rare occasion her driving directions were right and I turned left. My mother's misgivings were well founded, but I ignored them relying on a powerful tugging in my heart that there was a compelling higher reason.

John and Amanda are alive today, I think, because of my mother's worried prayers, Jesus answering them, and the alert children of Punlap swimming out to the barrier reef to rescue them. Jesus was also kept busy when a young wife and mother was kept alive by a brown duffel bag of medicine, not coincidentally, arriving on Punlap from Colorado.

This was not my first time to face life and death emergencies. Earlier in my ski patrol career, Diver and I were together on top of Vail Mountain. Super Sweep duty meant that we were the last of the patrol to stay on top while the sweep was moving down the front side of Vail Mountain insuring the public was safely off the mountain. A call came in to us by a lift operator skiing down on Git-along Road who came upon an unconscious man behind the bottom of Chairlift 4. We grabbed the heart kit and oxygen and skied down to the victim. Diver first did a quick assessment and then we started CPR. It had to be at least 5 degrees below zero. Tasting frozen hot chocolate while doing mouth to mouth CPR resuscitation, I knew the elderly man had recently been warming- up in near-by Mid Vail.

The Ski Patrol Director, in the LPR (lower patrol room) at the bottom of the mountain sent us a patrol doctor up from the LPR on a snowmobile. Diver had been a specialized medic who served in a US Army Surgical Hospital in Japan. Some severely wounded soldiers from the Vietnam War were daily flown to Japan for surgery. Diver was calm, cold, and collected. The doctor halted CPR while he examined the elderly comatose man. We quickly resumed CPR until a haul cat arrived. At which point, in the dark, the doctor re-examined the elderly man and made the call to halt the resuscitation efforts. Diver and I were both freezing and exhausted as we loaded the man's body into a toboggan and covered him with a sleeping bag for the trip down in the back of the haul cat. There was only one of us in the bed of the cat that was shivering on the cold ride down with snow from the cat's tracks kicking up cold snow on us. Diver had skied down ahead in the dark to the waiting ambulance. Thinking the deceased stranger in the toboggan may have friends or family in town worrying about his whereabouts, we soon would know his name at the Clinic to give to the Vail Police Department.

Arriving at the Vail Clinic, we were greeted by an ER doctor stunningly shouting at us, "You killed him. Why didn't you answer me on the radio?" Mountain Manager, former Army Commanding Sergeant, William Brown grabbed him by the back of his hospital gown and pulled him into a nearby exam room.

You could hear Sarge shouting through the closed door of the exam room. Bill knew his team of cold and exhausted Vail Ski patrolmen had given their best effort to save the man. The next morning the Vail Ski Patrol learned why we didn't hear the ER doctor's transmissions-he forgot to depress the transmit key on his radio. On another day, riding with Sarge on Chairlift 1 carrying us above the ski trail *International*, he told me about the time when a famous World Cup Downhill champion jumped off the same chairlift in front of him. It seems the racer wanted to re-examine something more on the race course. This was a violation of basic common sense and United States Forest Service Regulations. Having caught up with the offender a few minutes later, Sarge told him, in no uncertain terms, what he thought of his jumping off chairlifts. Forest Service didn't look kindly on jumping off chairlifts, neither did Vail Associates!

Responding disrespectfully, the World Cup Alpine hero didn't, obviously, know who he was talking to. He was disqualified from the race, and It could have been much worse. Sarge knew how to key his radio to transmit to a Town of Vail policeman to make an arrest for violating a Forest Service Regulation. The World Cup champion hadn't won Olympic Gold but was lucky that gruff Sarge Brown had a heart of Gold.

Bill, like everyone, had his detractors. He was a real stickler for skier safety and details. At all times he carried a black notebook filled with his inspection notes on boundary closure ropes needing to be raised or lowered, fallen bamboo hazard markers, rock on the runs, grooming, and anything out of order. Army standards ruled on Vail Mountain. Not only was Sarge concerned with the grooming of trails, but there were strict employee grooming standards. Bill was known to drive employees over to Leadville for haircuts.

Once he sent a Vail ski patrolman, working inside PHQ on phone duty for the day, home to shave. The patrolman hung up more than just the phone and didn't return. That former patrolman, now a retired contractor and proud grandfather, wears his salt and Pepper beard with pride.

A Sarge alert would be sounded by the bottom Chair 4 lift operators whenever Sarge boarded the lift headed to PHQ. The patrolmen on phone duty sounded the "Seven Oh" (70) alarm", Bill's radio call number. The urgent signal warned patrol to immediately start vacuuming the thin carpet, clean the tables, wipe clean the com-room window, and clean the basement public lunch room. Brown's favorite inspection target was the refrigerator which often he declared a "Disaster!" There was no doubt that PHQ, Vail Mountain, the Shop, and his employees were spit- polished and groomed to army standards.

One summer, Sarge asked me to take a ride with him to meet one of his retired 10th Mountain officers, a Colonel Hanson, who was in need of advice on his golf course frontage home in West Glenwood Springs, CO. While Bill was talking to his wife, his commanding officer took me aside and told me a story about Sarge, who had been left for dead on a battlefield for three days until a fierce battle was over. The cemetery detail went to retrieve Bill's body. Colonel Hanson commented to me that, "Bill Brown was simply too stubborn to die. He is the finest man I know and just as tough as leather." Jesus is tougher than Hell and Bill proved that he was as well.

Decorated with 5 Purple Hearts, 2 Silver Stars, and 3 Bronze Star medals Commanding Sergeant William Brown, originally from McCall, Idaho, lived to retire shortly following the 1989 World Ski Championships in Vail and Beaver Creek.

Sarge Brown always placed safety and training a high priority in his budgets! He deserves some of the credit for saving the young woman's life on Punlap Island and the man on Tamatam Island. Likely he should be given another Purple Heart. "Management needs to be concerned about the safety of its customers and employees as much as the safety of their checkbooks." Steve Hyland, former Mgr. of Vail and Beaver Creek Lift Dept. and close friend of Bill, would know first- hand.

CHAPTER 22
I Had Help!

It was the original plan to move back into our Vail home on August 1, 1984 per the terms of the lease. There was just one small glitch. Mr. "I am a lawyer" said he wasn't honoring the lease expiration date and couldn't move out on time. "The law in Colorado is on the side of renters and would be months before we can be evicted." After talking to his gracious wife, the nice clerk at the jewelry store, who sold me Donna's ring, we moved back home per the year's lease. It proved that Mr."I am a lawyer" had -married up- to a very strong and beautiful wife.

Travel East

Travel West

after all

Home's Best

A needle point message, framed in my Aunt Eva's house in Silver Plume, best describes the Buckley family's feeling upon first entering our home on Bald Mountain Road for the first time in a year. The renters had returned the furniture to its rightful place! The home was clean as a pin. All of our close neighbors and friends welcomed us home, but the welcome of Dennis and Sheila Linn especially stood-out in my mind. They were walking up Bald Mountain Road accompanied by Dennis's brother, Father Matthew Linn, S.J. who I had met before at the Vail Interfaith Chapel.

A later visit with Fr. Linn proved to be very healing, especially then. He was the first Jesuit priest that I had talked to since Donna and I had our conversation with the Jesuit Superior on Moen Island in Chuuk. After relating the experiences on Punlap Island and our encounters with the Jesuit Padre's powerful and frightening use of superstition and curses (Anumaumau), Fr. Linn said an exorcism prayer for me, just in case I needed one. He took very seriously what Donna and I had personally witnessed. It wasn't, from all appearances, that important to the Jesuit Superior in Chuuk. Being grateful for Fr. Linn's obvious concern, the prayer should have been directed towards Padre and those that allowed for his situation to exist. My confidence didn't rely on an exorcism prayer, my confidence arose from the following story:

On a weekend when some Loveland, Vail, and Breckinridge Ski Patrolmen were involved in the famous Shot Out at the Gold Pan Bar (Corral) in Breckinridge, I was one of the few Loveland patrollers who wasn't at the mayhem- only because I wasn't old enough to drink. Finding myself holding down Loveland's Lift One station by myself, the call came in that there was a very seriously injured man on Mambo, a green run.

No wonder! He had a badly displaced fractured femur. While unpacking the toboggan to secure a first aid splint, a mysterious stranger suddenly appeared OUT OF NOWHERE to help me splint this difficult and painful fracture! And did I need this Stranger's help! The injured skier stopped screaming at His first calming touch and soothing voice. Skiing the toboggan slowly down Mambo, normal breaths came easier for me and the victim. The standard procedure was to place a half-ring splint on this type of fracture in the controlled environment of the patrol 1st aid hut. An ambulance then would transport the injured skier to Dr. Fowler's office, in Idaho, Springs. But Rich Lane, the Patrol Director, said, "Let's get him moving now!" Looking at me later, Rich said, "Great job, Bob, splinting that femur fracture on Mambo." Still shaking I replied, "Thanks Rich" but knowing I had help!

Before Christmas working at Loveland as a T-bar lift operator at the top isolated station, my only chair was a carpenter's saw horse. During a cold wind driven blizzard and sitting on the saw horse, I became aware of an overwhelming and comforting sense of Peace. It completely displaced my feelings of claustrophobia and disorientation in the isolated confinement. I knew I was not alone! "It is I, do not be afraid." (John 6:24)

The Buckley family quickly settled back into our home and Lino seemed to have a thousand questions about his new surroundings in the high Shining Mountains of Vail. I was constantly busy as his sole language interpreter. Vail was nothing like living on Punlap Island or Hawaii, and he instinctively knew he couldn't survive in this new environment without a crash course. There was no coconut, breadfruit, banana, or pandanus trees. There wasn't an ocean to catch octopus, lobsters, or needlefish in the lagoon currents, nor turtles at night laying eggs on the beaches. He was wondering what people did to make food in Vail. This environment was totally foreign and very scary for young Lino. He couldn't fend for himself like in Hawaii. He was totally dependent on the Buckley family.

My returning to work after a years absence was challenging for me with the changes at Vail Associates Real Estate. There was a new broker, a very nice fellow, but I had so much that had happened in the past year that I wasn't ready for this change. One thing that I realized soon after returning home was that my career working at Vail Associates Real Estate and being a Vail Ski Patrolman (VSP) was going into my history book. The following story is one of the retold stories from my career as a professional ski patrolman that is one for this book, maybe even the ages.

Mike Beckley, VSP (Vail Ski Patrol) sent his well told remembrances of a unique accident we handled together. Mike, later in his career with Vail Associates was the Director of Mountain Operations at Beaver Creek, wrote the following: "I remember you and I were manning the 'Taj' (Top of Golden Peak Patrol Facility) and I was dispatched to a vague accident somewhere around the creek at the bottom of Golden Peak. I skied down and didn't see anything. Fortunately, I glanced over the edge of the drop off into the creek and saw our victim lying semi- conscious in the middle of the creek. I kicked off my skis and slid down the edge of the embankment. It was obvious immediately I had to wade into the water to help him, and the water (because it was flowing and couldn't freeze) was well below 32 degrees! I waded in up to my thighs and reached the victim who was not alert and conscious. I made sure his head and airway were above water and did the best quick "head to toe" I could do. It was obvious he had at least a fractured femur and probably a chest impact injury. He was in obvious respiratory distress, in addition to his many orthopedic injuries. I grabbed the radio and called you and…..I began listing the equipment I wanted you to bring….A rig, some rope to pull us up out of the creek, extra manpower, a backboard, oxygen, a half-ring,…….at this point I realized we were going to need everything (in terms of emergency equipment) the "Taj" had to offer……I rolled it all into one statement, 'Bob….BRING IT ALL.' With that I did the best I could to just keep the victim's airway open and maintained and waited for you to arrive. In what seemed like no time at all you arrived, literally COVERED in equipment! You had every piece in the "Taj" draped off your body and you were peering over the embankment looking at me with your eyes as big as dinner plates!

It took you half a second to totally assess our situation and the next thing I knew you had slid down the embankment with all the equipment and waded into the stream. The next few minutes were a study in emergency medicine (which the guy later thanked us for saving his life) where we applied a half-ring to his fractured femur, a backboard under his broken ribs, a neck collar to his possibly unstable neck, and oxygen to supplement his labored breathing. That was still a problem as we were still under water in the creek????? Right then I heard a snowmobile and Bill Bird stared over the edge of the embankment. He had arrived at the scene with a snowmobile. Somehow, we took a rope you brought and tied it to the backboard, threw the other end to Bill Bird who secured it to the snowmobile and we then towed the 10-50 up the embankment where he was loaded into a toboggan where other patrollers (who'd arrived to see this epic accident) ran the toboggan to the waiting ambulance. You and I (soaked to the skin and freezing) expected to go to the Lower Patrol Room to change to warm, dry clothes, and punch out…..EXCEPT the accident had so depleted the manpower on the mountain, the dispatcher asked you and I to ride back up Chairlift 6 and perform sweep of Golden Peak. It, undoubtedly went down as one of the most epic wrecks in Vail Mountain history and it was an honor to run it with you."

Donna's comment to me later that night after sharing with her the events of the day was almost laughable, "You have to be kidding me! What kind of crazy ass sport is skiing anyway?"

Let me tell you about another epic wreck for the Vail Mountain history book and in my book now!

Frank McNeil and I were sitting in the Eagles Nest Patrol room and monitoring a wreck over the radio on Upper Lionsway and the intersection with the bottom of the Cold Feet Catwalk. An out of control skier had flown off the Upper Lionsway's downhill embankment hitting a tree and was unconscious. The two patrolmen were struggling in waist deep powder snow tending to the victim and loading the unconscious victim into the toboggan. The patrolmen side-stepped a path through the deep powder and up to the catwalk so their sled could be pulled up to the waiting haul cat. The trees almost always win, unfortunately, and the victim died from his injuries. Fatalities haunt me!

The next day I skied down to the accident site below the Upper Lionsway embankment to view where it happened myself. Not wanting to hike back up to the catwalk on the same path the patrolmen had packed, I skied downhill into the trees and easily reached Git-along Road several hundred yards below. What were the odds that lightning strikes the same spot twice in a week. Not very high I would bet.

The emergency call came into the dispatcher that there was a profusely bleeding unconscious skier that hit a tree below the Upper Lionsway Catwalk at the Cold Feet Catwalk. This had been a busy day for wrecks and Chris Brewster, a Vail Host, was dispatched with me to the accident. We took a backboard, Oxygen, and my special prayer with us to the tree. Assessing that the victim's injuries were life threatening, Chris and I quickly packaged the victim into the toboggan and were able to follow my old tracks down to Git-along Road. We met the ambulance in less than 10 minutes. My prayer, "God is Love, and he who abides in Love, abides in God, and God in him," was answered. Our 10:50 survived. Returning to the site to fill out my accident card, I scraped the end of his nose off the tree trunk.

Donna finally gave up skiing altogether, most likely because, as she thinks, of the stories her husband brought home after work. But before giving up on skiing, Donna was always on the verge of being seasick, especially for the three days journey out to Punlap Island. She always rides in the front seat of an automobile preferably driving, otherwise she will get car sick. Dramamine is her best friend on a boat, a ship, in a car, or on a chairlift. My stories were not exclusively to blame for her giving up skiing.

Another skier hit a tree and sadly lost his life on a beginner run on the frontside of Vail Mountain. Not just any skier, but a long time local and friend of many in Vail. The Vail Ski Patrol always benefitted from his sharing gourmet left-overs from his many picnics on the PHQ sundeck. The expert skier and sailor was eulogized at the top of the mountain by a long time, close, and loving Vail friend who told humorous stories sailing with his close friend and their families off the coast of Norway and sharing much laughter.

This expert skier was likely over-confident and distracted looking backwards over his shoulder skiing fast on the beginner Swingsville ski trail.

Another well- known person hit a tree while throwing a football while skiing down a run on Aspen Mountain. The collision with the tree killed this young man, another over-confident expert skier, who was distracted when playing a football game while skiing. It's like texting on a smart phone while driving a Mercedes. The fault does not lay with the sport of skiing or driving a car. Too many times it is not a pine tree that is smacked into by the distracted or speeding skier.

Other skiers were often involved in collisions with distracted or out of control skiers who are much more vulnerable than a pine tree. The victims often have serious injuries left for the ski patrol to pick up the pieces. And that was the reason that the Vail Ski Patrol called the lower Ramshorn and Swingsville intersection, "The BONE YARD" and not "The LUMBER YARD." Now The Colorado Skier Safety Act makes it possible to sue the distracted or out- of- control skier, and that is why so many times they flee the scene.

CHAPTER 23
Micronesian Snowball

Donna and I built our house in the Booth Creek Subdivision in East Vail when in our twenties. I was blessed with good fortune in my real estate sales business and had accumulated just enough money to buy Lot 7 on Bald Mountain Road. It was a steep lot on the north side of the narrow valley facing south to the sun. Even at that early time in Vail, land was scarce-and expensive! We would have preferred a flat lot which would have been easier to build on for first time home builders. But our lot had amazing views across the valley to the steep colder north facing slope that had less to no sun in the winter months. But it had abundant pine and spruce trees, waterfalls cascading down into Gore Creek, and treeless avalanche paths onto the Vail Golf Course.

The view of one of the water falls, directly from our living room windows, was one famous to the many ice climbers in the winter. *The Rigid Designator* scared even Susan Nott, one of the leading female climbers in the world lost on Mt. Foraker in Alaska in 2006. She was the beloved daughter of Bob and Evie Nott and was loved by her sisters Sara and Karen. The Notts were our neighbors on Bald Mountain Road. But much more, Bob was my mentor at Vail Associates Real Estate, and Sara, Karen, and Susan's babysitter on occasion was Donna when they were just cute little girls. All of Vail mourned the loss of our most famous female climber and

325

tears will flow from the Rigid Designator forever in memory of Susan Nott! The Nott family was flown to Alaska to aid in the search for Susan by Mike Shannon, a former President of Vail Associates, whose daughter lost a dear friend- as did so many in the Vail Valley.

Looking East towards Vail Pass, we had a postcard view of the Gore Range boldly rising five thousand feet above the valley floor to over an impressive thirteen thousand feet above sea level. There was our very own hiking trail directly in the back of our house on Forest Service land leading to the Booth Creek Falls, conveniently out our kitchen door. Not the trail everyone in Vail is familiar with, but a horseback trail from the old Mahaney Ranch torn down when the Booth Creek Subdivision was built. To the West and also on the northside of the valley, we viewed the ski runs on Vail Mountain from our breakfast nook. The three-story Buckley home was tucked in and around aspen trees with tall windows opening to the sun and the mountain views. This was all amazing, if you hadn't grown up on a remote tropical island in the Western Islands of Chuuk not used to frequent bear and elk encounters in the back yard.

Living your entire life on Punlap Island, with the roar of the ocean waves crashing on the nearby reefs, Lino's immediate family lived and slept in a one- room thatched house. The nearby benjo overhanging the lagoon was the nearest bathroom. The kitchen was a separate thatched cook house, and food was kept fresh and living on trees or swimming in the ocean. And because Lino would be sleeping on the bottom floor of our house, he would be all alone at night instead of sleeping next to his brothers and mother on the same pandanus mat. Something Donna and I were aware of when bringing Lino to our home in the mountains. The culture and lifestyles were so different. But Lino sprung from a strong, a resilient, and a very proud tradition. He quickly adapted to the changes, and the four children enjoyed a very special rest of the summer in Vail. School was fast approaching and Donna and I visited the Middle School in Minturn which Brian and Lino would be attending in just a few weeks. Explaining the situation that Lino was just learning English, the teacher understood her challenge. Not like in Hawaii where there was an ESL program, Eagle County Public Schools at that time didn't have an ESL program. However, the teacher was young, idealistic, and eager. Youth and enthusiasm hopefully could find a way to teach someone who was just beginning to learn English. Donna, being a teacher herself and my being fluent in Lino's native language, thought we could contribute in making this a positive educational experience for Lino. Next task was to outfit him for snow country. And does it really snow in Vail, Colorado! Lino was beyond excited experiencing his first snow and snowball fight.

Dressed in the necessary warm ski clothing and wearing one of Brian's racing warmups, a Vail Snow Pig wool hat, ski gloves, and goggles, Lino was camouflaged but betrayed by his wide smile. When entering Patrol Headquarters on top of Vail Mountain with me, he was an immediate celebrity receiving high fives around the room.

He remembered Didi Haskins from her visit to our home in Hilo, Hawaii just a few months earlier. Didi already met Lino when staying with us last May for a few days when escaping the marathon snow year patrolling on Vail Mountain. Vail Ski Patroller Frank McNeil's wide smile was almost as big as the one on Lino's face! Frank was the patrolman who rescued my son, John who broke his leg skiing with his mother. Lino and his friends also rescued John and Amanda from the outer reef. There was an instant bonding between Frank and Lino and two parents thankful to the both of them.

The only recognizable feature on the short snowman at the bottom of Vail's famous Riva Ridge was a wide toothy smile emerging from underneath a snow- covered ski patrol wool hat.

There wasn't anything that the boy from Punlap was afraid to experience. His ice skating style at Dobson Arena wasn't quite up to Scotty Hamilton's Gold Medal form at the 1984 Sarajevo Olympics. But he wobbled around the hockey rink like he owned it. For the laughing Buckley cheering section, he did! When skating off the ice with Brian, Lino gamely flashed his smile and gave another loud, Wi-yo!

Christmas marked the end of the first half of the school year. Each of our parent and teacher conferences were being scheduled. The conferences for the three Buckley children went well enough. But Lino's teacher dropped a Christmas surprise! Not a good one like the U.S. Airforce Christmas drops of food and presents onto the typhoon ravaged Namonuito Atoll Islands during my Peace Corps Service. Lino was progressing with speaking English, but he wasn't performing on tests for the more abstract lessons- like reading, writing, and arithmetic. His teacher thought it was time for him to return to his own school system and culture where teachers could communicate with Lino in his own language. Donna knew that her students on Punlap learned by listening to her speak English, and not diagraming sentences on a blackboard.

We did not blame Lino's teacher. She was just being honest and wanting to do what was best for Lino. East is a Big Bird/ *Navigation and Logic on Puluwat Atoll* by Thomas Gladwin, explains the cultural challenges of inner- city education using the Westen Island of Puluwat as a model. There is a oneness of human experience across the world and important lessons can be shared between our cultures to improve education.

I wrote Lino's uncle whose house we lived in on Punlap. His main house was on Moen where he was in charge of the shipping in all of Chuuk, and Lino could stay with Lambert until the next ship was going out to Punlap Island. Not once did Lino ever cry or complain about being so far distant from his home and culture. His was the attitude of his palu ancestors exploring the unknown.

The Buckley family learned just how remarkable was the world that Lino shared with us. Nobody will believe the stories we have to tell. My then 10 year- old son Brian could tell of the time that he sailed on an outrigger canoe from Punlap with Lino and his family to a nearby small uninhabited island. Brian had gone on camping trips back in Colorado. What Brian experienced was unique!

The weekend campers smoked tree crabs from old hollow standing breadfruit trees, speared fresh lobster, and parrot fish from the reef, and captured large seagulls from the tops of coconut trees- all barbequed on the hot coals of a cook fire and served with pounded breadfruit (po) wrapped in large banana leaves. These two young friends learned quickly to communicate with newly learned words, gestures, and smiles.

Lino's subsistence culture was closely related to that of the early Hawaiian and Native American. Those native peoples, living on remote Islands and Native Americans living on the edge of American Frontiers, had too often been victims of predators beyond the laws of man, not God's.

The early miners to Colorado originally settled on the Cherry Creek and Platte Rivers in an existing Arapaho Native American Village. Chief Left Hand (Niwot) did everything possible to live in peace with the White intruders. "Big Phil the Cannibal aka Charles Gardner led a group of drunken whites over to Left Hand's camp near Cherry Creek. They forced their way into Arapaho lodges and raped a number of Arapaho women. One of the victims was Left Hand's sister MaHom, as well as possibly his wife, and nine-year-old daughter…When Left Hand returned and learned what happened, Beckwourth convinced him to take no revenge."

(Forgotten Heroes and Villains of Sand Creek by Carol Turner) Chief Left Hand was killed and mutilated at the Sand Creek Massacre.

"Another chief, White Antelope, ran towards the commanders, a scout named James Beckwourth later testified, "holding up his hands and saying 'Stop! Stop!' He spoke it in as plain English as I can." As the firing intensified, according to Cheyenne and Arapaho stories, he folded his arms and calmly began to chant his death song, "Nothing lives long, except the Earth and the mountains." Shot through with bullets, he died and was mutilated in the creek bed. (A Massacre in the Family, by Mike Allen WSJ)

This is a great WSJ article written by the great-great grandson of William M. Allen who had enlisted in the Third Colorado Cavalry Regiment and participated in the Sand Creek Massacre. He had not only participated in the fighting but also the desecration of bodies, including one special.

Even now writing about sending Lino back, I am feeling such a sense of failure…..I knew Lino was disappointed. Brian, John, and Amanda were heartbroken. But Lino's storytelling could be told in both Appai en Weito (Outer Island language) and in English. Donna and I received a letter some weeks later from his mother, Trinitas who was very thankful for our investment in time, money, and love to help educate her son about the world. I'm sure she was both relieved and happy to see her young world traveler.

Lino said to us, "No one on Punlap will believe my stories." Things we take for granted were mind blowing for him. Really, how do you describe to people who know nothing except life on an island what it is like sliding down snow on skis, or gliding on ice skates, riding for hours on a jet plane, or standing on Wailuku Drive seeing a volcano spewing lava. These were just a few of the stories that Lino would be describing to his wide-eyed mother, brothers, and friends sitting around cook fires or on long outrigger canoe journeys to other islands.

John wrote a paper his freshman year at Lewis and Clark College combining his experiences on Punlap Island, mine in the Peace Corps, and photos from both. His Professor was so impressed by his paper he thought it should be submitted to the National Geographic Magazine.

Lino will always be loved by the Buckley family. Brian, John, and Amanda love Lino as a brother! Donna and I love Lino as a special son loaned to us by his brave mother. We went with him as far as Honolulu and were relieved to hear from her that the rest of his trip went well. Many thanks to Continental Air Micronesia for their helpful consideration caring for the young teenager flying from Hawaii to Chuuk for his first solo journey across the wide Pacific in a big bird. Lino's ancestors sailed the Pacific following the "Big Bird," Altair, east in outrigger sailing canoes. (East is a Big Bird, by Thomas Gladwin)

CHAPTER 24
It's a Deal

The Buckley Family Business Charter (Book One pg.65) states, "Obey the ten Commandments, always." And Article 3 states, "Speak the truth in even the smallest matter, so you can look straight in every man's eyes with your chin up."

This is what Vail Associates and the Town of Vail expected from a respected engineering firm that had completed a boundary survey for them. Their substantial billing reflected the import of just such a survey. My VA crew was surveying the road center-line for all of Booth Creek, Filings 1, 2 and 3, Town of Vail. After attempting to close out the loop on our work to another known government survey pin outside our private land, I couldn't believe my eyes. We missed closing the loop by over 300 feet at the end of what would become Bald Mountain Road. Waiooo! Where was our mistake? I spent a full day in the office rechecking the math for every angle turned on our instrument and every distance pulled on our chain. The survey crew spent another two days back out in the field double checking our work to find the mistake.

We then researched the original survey book from the last century and backtracked the latest boundary survey and found the mistake. The surveyors from the firm in Summit County missed a corner that had been chiseled into a red sandstone outcropping and provided another false one that missed the chiseled mark. It was just above our home that Donna and I built years later for my family. Often when hiking up to the top of Bald Mountain and proudly checking out the corner long ago chiseled in the red sandstone flat outcropping, Ute arrowheads were found on the hillside along with herds of elk and deer. Our home was built on a favorite Ute hunting camp likely of the White River Band pushed out of Colorado at about the same time the original corner was chiseled in sandstone.

The engineering firm that performed the boundary survey didn't close the loop on their work. A good surveyor knows to check work completed within a large private boundary with other known government survey reference points. Just closing a loop within the given project could mean, with obvious exaggeration, that the loop closed within itself might be in a checkbook. Or a large water tank, on a very steep mountain side off the property, was built on a shaky foundation of "a 300 feet mistake." My survey crew found that the tank was not built on Vail Associates property but on Forest Service land bordering the Gore Range Wilderness Area.

Later that summer my survey crew was given the assignment to verify a critical boundary survey on a Beaver Creek ranch being purchased by Vail Associates from Willis Nottingham and his wife, Willie who purchased and consolidated the ranch properties back in 1950. The 2200-acre cattle and sheep ranch was chosen to become the base for the 1976 Winter Olympics Alpine Events. Vail Associates was going to close on an option in August of 1972 and before the closing, needed to verify the boundary corners and place a reference pin in the middle of what would become Beaver Creek Village. Pete Seibert, from his experience, knew the importance of 'chattin' with the proud ranchers

Early every morning before driving up into the ranch, we would stop and have coffee with Willis and Willie Nottingham. By this time in his life, Willis was so crippled up from cattle ranching that he walked stooped over from the waist. Always welcoming, "The chattin' wasn't put on, with genuine 'sittin round' their table. One year later Donna and I were sent to Craig, Colorado to close on their ranch house, the last piece of Vail's $4.4 million purchase.

As Peter W. Seibert wrote in his book, **Vail**/Triumph of a Dream, March 26, 1976 was the day of the tragic Lionshead Gondola Accident. "In September 1976, less than six months after the gondola cars fell, the Vail Associates board fell too. We sold the company to board member, Harry Bass, a Texas millionaire….A couple of days after he took over, he asked me to lunch… 'You know what git-along means, Pete?' I shrugged and said nothing."

'Git along means you got to get along, Pete. You got to get a long long way from here. Goodbye.'

"As he got up from the table. I wished him well and said that I hoped he'd take good care of Vail." Peter Seibert, like Sarge Brown, was another 10th Mountain sergeant who bravely defended our freedom in WW Two and returned home terribly wounded.

Peter is a hero of mine, and I was blessed to call him one of my most cherished friends. At the 10-year reunion of Vail Pioneers, every speaker was lauding him with praise for his accomplishment. When it was his turn to speak, he brushed all the accolades aside, and he gave credit to all in the Marriott ballroom saying, "Vail wouldn't have happened without each and every one of you."

Peter was also a hero in Georgetown and Silver Plume, Colorado rebuilding Loveland Basin into a favorite Regional Ski Area. One day when one of my cousins was bulldozing the parking lot out of steep mountain sides, a dynamite blast almost took his life with boulders raining down all around him and smashing into his bulldozer. Storming after the careless bomber with a large wrench in his hand, his swinging arm was stopped mid- swing by Peter Seibert. My uncle Ron wanted me to shake a can of beer and spray it in his office when applying for a job at Vail Associates for Pete doing the same in the Buckley Store.

Taking many trips to prospective new ski area opportunities with Pete in Canada, Colorado, Vermont, Idaho, and even to the Dominican Republic's Casa de Campo, he always kept me laughing at his New England humor and quips.

Harry Bass didn't expect most of Pete's crack executive team to resign losing almost all of those involved in the early planning of Beaver Creek.

He will always be remembered for marrying Betty, his lovely wife, their amazing 3 sons, Pete Jr. (who was a fellow Vail Ski Patrolman), Brandt, and Calvin, and all of Peter's and Betty's amazing and special grandchildren. Pete's many friends around the world are also thankful for his lifelong dream of building a European style ski resort in Colorado. Harry Bass may have told Peter Seibert to, "Get-along." But Peter got the last laugh writing in his book, "February 12, 1989, the final day of the 1989 FIS World Alpine Ski Championships, when the prize ceremonies were coming to an end, George Gillett turned to me. "What a day!" he cried. He then looked me in the eye, grabbed my shoulders in a bear hug and shouted, "Pete! When are you coming back?".... "Coming back?"

"Back to work for Vail Associates. We need you fella."

"I'd been waiting quite a while for something like this to happen. I laughed and said, "Sounds great. Let me think about it. I'll get back to you soon, George."

"I paused for a full five seconds while George frowned slightly." Then said, "Okay, it's a deal? Where's my office?"

(**Vail**/Triumph of a Dream by Peter W. Seibert)

After my year dealing with anumaumau (curses) and sending Lino back to Micronesia, working for and with old friends would be comfortable transferring down to Beaver Creek Properties.

Just newly settled in my Beaver Creek office, I received a phone call from Ron Allred, the developer of Avon just below Beaver Creek. His Benchmark Company purchased part ownership in the Telluride Resort. Dr Ron Allred, DDS offered me an opportunity to join him and be part of making his vision for Telluride happen.

Thanking him for the opportunity, my "no thank you" wasn't the last time I would hear from Dr. Ron Allred.

CHAPTER 25
Poker Face

A couple of years earlier, Donna and our three children and nephew, Todd Kaiser, had been camping nearby to Telluride. A close friend of Ron's and Vail's Bob and Diane Lazier (the family Donna worked for at Vail's Tivoli Lodge), was having lunch at the Floradora Restaurant. Totally engrossed in our two -sided conversation over lunch and rudely ignoring a bored Donna and the kids, the two "chattin" friends missed my family's desperate departure. Out of breath from running down the sidewalk and catching the car, I could see Donna's evil payback smile in her review mirror. I saw the same similar smile when we were newlyweds and her almost locking me outside our first home. Donna's exasperated look showed me then that I better make a desperate naked run to safety. My crime was innocently setting a plastic cup of water on a partially opened bathroom door for an early morning surprise. Back then her payback smile was on her face through the house front door window- realizing the flaw in my escape into the freezing Minturn dawn just in the nick of time.

Once again Ron Allred wanted to meet with me. It had been a week earlier when I turned down his offer to join him in Telluride. What does he want now? Ron had to possess the best poker face ever facing me across a conference table, later confirmed by his lifelong friend and Grand Junction High School football teammate. "When our team was travelling by bus to a distant road game, Ron would always end up with every dollar from his teammates pockets. Only fools play poker with him." Ron had a plain yellow pad in front of him and with a poker face, he began by telling me that he had dinner with a former President of Vail Associates who told him that he had been upset with me. Bob Buckley, a Vail Ski Patrolman, was making more money than him. "Bob, I want you to make more money than me! What will it take to get you to Telluride?"

Ron wasn't the only one with a poker face, plus I was holding aces! "Do not be afraid" (Matthew 28:10). And "God is love, and he who abides in love, abides in God, and God in him." (Clarence Rivers on You Tube)

Ron dealt the cards down on his yellow pad. He was setting up a Corporate Sales Division and wanted me to be the vice- president of this special Division. He would permit me to hire a small team to help me with securing immediate important corporate goals. These included, but not limited to, finding a partner to buy out the original Telluride owner and now a partner, a hotel developer for his new Mountain Village, assist in finding a Fixed Base Operator for Telluride's private and commercial airport, also assist TD (TouchDown) Smith, Telluride Real Estate Corporation (TREC) broker in the sales of commercial and residential lots in the exciting new Telluride Mountain Village. The impressive brochure looked very promising and exciting.

The compensation package had a cherry on top. Donna and I would have the pick of any new residential lot at a "price we couldn't refuse!" Ron wisely knew that both Donna and I needed to see his project in person before signing up. The best poker player on the team's bus knew a signature would need Donna's approval! A tour was arranged to meet him in Telluride for his personal tour on the weekend. Looking at my cards, I bumped the ante on the override and said, "Donna and I will see you in Telluride."

We arrived late in the day to the condominium in Telluride that was provided in our itinerary. Arriving after the six- hour drive from Vail tired, sweaty, and hungry, we quickly freshened up and walked downtown for dinner. The next morning, we met Ron and Joyce Allred at their beautiful

Victorian home just a short walk up above Main Street and enjoyed breakfast in their charming kitchen. Then off we went for an epic tour of historic Telluride in Ron's new Jeep Grand Wagoneer. The setting for the Town of Telluride cannot be duplicated for its 360 degrees of dramatic San Juan Mountains scenery. The Town is set in a box canyon with tall mountains and dramatic scenery in every direction.

The 19th century mining town captures the essence of the Wild West. Butch Cassidy robbed his first bank on Main Street Telluride and rode off to his hideout in the twisting canyons of the LaSalle Mountains with his famous Hole in the Wall Gang. Ron was a great tour guide filling us in on the remote town's early colorful brothel history and the still standing "cribs." Each call girl had her own small crib (house} now worth a small fortune. The entire town is in a National Historic District with exacting strict building regulations preserving authentic architecture of the early Colorado mining era. Ron pointed out his vision for new lifts and trails to connect over to the Mountain Village from town. His concept was build a three-stage gondola connecting the historic mining town to the new Mountain Village. The final stage would then connect out to a parking structure on the outskirts of the Mountain Village. While making his comparison to Beaver Creek's massive urban style bus system, Ron raised the ante knowing he held a winning hand! Riding his gondola beat my hand of cards holding crowded diesel buses carrying many thousands more of passengers. That was Ron's reason he raked in all the chips- winning that hand against my checkbook mentality.

Telluride would never be a Colorado Front Range crowded ski resort. Living in the narrow Vail Valley and with I-70's constant roar of traffic and overflowing very expensive parking structures, Telluride was sounding better to me by the minute. And Donna probably was missing the point and road noise already after our most recent quiet isolation on remote Punlap Island.

Next on our Ron Allred road tour was the Mountain Village which was in the very early stages of infrastructure construction with heavy equipment digging rock and dirt everywhere, cutting trees, bulldozing roads, and hauling gravel, rocks, road base, and all manner of pipe. Smoke filled the air from burning slash. All the while Ron was driving wildly on mostly potholed mining and timber roads sliding in mud up to his axel. Soon his Jeep was stuck up to its high running boards. Walking through the mud and the forest, he returned as promised leading a D8 bulldozer that wasn't the first time used to pull Ron out of the deep mud. With a friendly wave of thanks, we were once again on our way. Ron led us through the rough dirt to admire, "The See Forever Plaza." Standing at the edge of a steep drop-off, he told the story when he climbed up the huge fir in the foreground partially blocking the jaw-dropping view to the valley below. "Oh my goodness, Bob and Donna, what an amazing view" looking beyond the big tree. Straining my neck to see the top of Mt. Sneffels above the tree, I knew this development was very special.

Pete Seibert was the founder and visionary for Vail and Beaver Creek Resorts. He was also the Chairman of the Board until Harry Bass uprooted his life dreams. Ron Allred was the visionary for the Telluride Mountain Village and hadn't been kicked in his groans!

He told Donna and me a story when his partner, and Chief Financial Officer, had entered his office in a fit of frustration taking a phone call from a sales manager at an auto agency. The manager was wondering why Benchmark Company's name was on the title of a car a prospective purchaser was using for a trade- in on a new car. Ron picked up the line and spoke the words that drove his financial officer even crazier! Go ahead and make the sale! We both laughed at the story until my side ached! It was our mutual friend, Mickey, who gave Donna heartburn while we were just 'chattin' in the Floradora Restaurant.

Surviving the tour, we were treated to a very special cocktail and dinner party back at Ron and Joyce 's restored Victorian. The dinner guests included the Telluride Company's senior brass and local friends of the hosts. It was really wonderful meeting with former neighbors who had lived in Booth Creek. We met the editor of the Telluride Times and his wife, and the Mayor of Telluride. Great poker players know when they hold a winning hand. Ron placed his winning hand on the table and Donna threw her hand high into the thin air of Telluride conceding another move was in the cards for the Buckley family and realizing that, "Here we go again!"

Our old Vail neighbors had heard that the former owner of the Bank of Telluride was looking for a renter for his house. This was a very special home set back in a large meadow with the view of the most photographed mountains in Colorado filling the living room and kitchen windows. You might have seen Mount Wilson and Wilson Peak in a Coors Beer ad on television with Peter Coors extolling that Rocky Mountain Spring Water is the most important ingredient in the Golden, Colorado brewed beer. Mt. Wilson is 320 miles by car from Golden, Colorado.

Unique to Telluride a comprehensive plan was approved including the entire region, not just the Historic District of the old Town of Telluride or the new Mountain Village. Densities were allocated to the many open ranch parcels, as well. One of the features of the planning was that no dwellings were allowed to sit on top of ridges or mountain tops to spoil the views from the valleys below. The Mountain Village had ski runs and lifts running magically through it. Every property was practically on a ski run with ski-in and ski-out access with views in all directions. Ron took the planners and architects to Europe with him to inspect towns and ski resorts in the Alps. Mostly senior management was invited at Vail for trips which amounted to holidays. The results in Ron's planning exposed the difference.

Ron confidently raised the ante. Matching his bold move, I instinctively knew not to walk away. Donna knew, "Here we go again."

CHAPTER 26
Deer in the Headlights

(Psalms 22:1) For the leader; according to, "The deer of the dawn." A psalm of David.

(Psalms 22:2) My God, My God, why have you abandoned me?
Why so far from my calls for help,
From my cries of anguish?

(Mark 15:34) Eloi, Eloi, *lema sabachtani*? (Aramaic)
(Mark 15:34) My God, My God, why have you forsaken me?

These were the last words Jesus cried out from the cross! The Utes need look no further than to a crucifix to know there is another Who hears their cries of anguish and calls for help! "He's been there." (Pulpit Resources: Year B March 18, 2018 by William H. Willimon)

Donna and I were riding over the Dallas Divide on our way back to Vail when we saw hundreds of deer in the headlights that early awakening dawn.

This scenic drive under God's dramatic mountains, passing by Ralph Loren's Ranch, the winding Uncompahgre River, and passing the Ute Museum before Montrose, Colorado reminded me that not so long ago all this magnificent land was taken from the Utes with every broken treaty signed. "They divide my garments among them and cast lots for my clothes." (Psalms 22:19) A suffering and naked Jesus nailed to the cross knows how all Native Americans also feel.

Our three young children, Brian then 11, John 9, and Amanda 8 years old were mostly excited to move to Telluride because of the promise of a new Golden Retriever puppy. Barley had passed away prior to our family journey to Punlap Island and was buried in our backyard. We found "Bo," the pick of the litter in Arvada, Colorado.

The timing was excellent tendering my resignation to the broker at Beaver Creek Properties as my license had just recently been moved there from its parent company, Vail Associates Real Estate. He requested that I make an announcement to his sales group in the small sales room theatre. With that done, I was free to start to assemble a team. Don McLean, a friend originally from the ski patrol, asked to be considered for a job. He had been honored recently for being the top lot sales agent for the year in Beaver Creek and he would be the first candidate to fill the bill for Corporate Sales.

As well as two experienced top producers from Vail, Robby Robinson and Gordon MacGregor, agreed to travel down to Telluride and meet with Ron. Robby had worked successfully with many Vail buyers, interesting to me were his many clients from Mexico. He also was my mentor on the Vail Ski Patrol, close friend, and fellow sales agent for Vail Associates Real Estate. Gordon was a successful agent for another firm in Vail and my neighbor on Bald Mountain Road. Before moving to Vail, he and his wife Patsy were friends with George and Rose Gillett in Chicago who now were prominent home owners in Vail. All three were potentially great fits working in Corporate Sales.

Then presented to Ron was Joseph, "Just call me Rocky" Quatrocky. In my meeting with Ron the following week in Telluride, my primary selected candidates from Vail and Beaver Creek met with his quick nod of approval. But a quizzical look over his reading glasses, Ron pointed out that, "Rocky doesn't even have a Colorado Real Estate License. He sells cars." This was true but Rocky sold expensive Mercedes Benz cars to some very wealthy clients in Phoenix and Scottsdale, Arizona. Yes! Rocky needed to get a Colorado license. Promising Ron that Rocky would prove to be invaluable bringing in quality prospects from the Phoenix area. And also assuring Ron that Telluride would become the Mercedes Benz of ski resorts in Colorado, the team was approved by him and we all moved to Telluride, including Rocky.

We met weekly with Ron receiving our marching orders. Gordon invited George Gillett to Telluride to meet with Ron. George disclosed to Ron that he was actively pursuing an acquisition of another ski resort while driving back together to Vail.

Don McLean, before the dust settled on his career in Telluride, personally executed over 120 lot sales in the Mountain Village and developed his own successful projects in the Mountain Village.

Robby and I worked diligently to attract our Mexico City clients to Telluride from Vail with some success. One was however almost my last. A Vail developer team, TD Smith, and myself flew to Houston to meet with a Mexican client who was meeting with us to secure a joint- venture in a Mountain Village Plaza Development. The closing went well, but the flight back to Telluride easily proved to be the second scariest private airplane flight of my life!

Rocky proved to be invaluable bringing in qualified candidates for many of Ron's important projects. One of Rocky's major contributions was to introduce an owner of the Scottsdale Biltmore Resort to Ron along with one of the largest land owners and fruit growers in the Phoenix and Scottsdale region. They were very impressed with Ron and his vision for Telluride and became valued friends and eventually bought partnership interest with Ron in the Telluride Ski Resort. The visionary developer, with his still active dental license, no longer had to pull more teeth to move Telluride forward or quizzically look over his reading glasses.

The three young Buckley children and puppy loved their new home with its mountain meadows in the front and back- where grazing herds of elk were seen almost daily feeding in the tall grass. While jogging on a road to the west of the house, a large herd of elk suddenly surrounded me. The experience might have been more dangerous in the fall hunting season, but to my sweaty relief the huge animals slowly drifted away. The views were really spectacular from our home, but the children being less than interested could be found with Bo, playing in the acres of wilderness that served as our backyard.

One morning they were playing war when Brian caught a bb in the stomach. That's when mom showed John a red card and promptly took Brian to a doctor. Another time John was practicing casting with his flyrod with fly attached to the line and hooking Bo in the mouth. The startled puppy put up a good fight when reeled in and pinned down to remove the barbed fish hook. Both Donna and her red card were increasingly wearing thin.

The MacGregors weren't so lucky with their rented home in Telluride's Ski Ranches. Every time it would rain, water gushed down into the living room from the sloped windows. An added positive feature to the house that the landlord forgot to mention to Patsy who wasn't happy seeing her couch soaked like a wet sponge!

When Patsy was not happy, Gordon wasn't far behind. Their daughter Erin at nine had been a classmate with John at Red Sandstone Elementary in Vail and five- year old Michael was doing his five- year old thing in Telluride. Before moving to Vail, Patsy and Gordon had a much better rental experience. They had rented a guest cottage from George and Rose Gillett when Gordon was working in Chicago. A friendship developed and the two couples remained on a first name basis after George and Rose purchased their Forest Road vacation home in Vail. Gordon and Patsy lived just a few houses from us on Bald Mountain Road. Neighborhood barbeques were the best in both Vail and Telluride at Gordon and Patsy's house. Gordon was a man of many talents and one was definitely aiming to be a chef in his own restaurant.

Robby and Kathy Robinson were very happy in their quaint home in the Ski Ranches. Eight-year-old daughter, Sara had her best friend, Amanda living just down the road. And five-year old Christopher was flexible and enjoyed life with a smile for everyone. All three Vail families were fortunate to be living nearby and often would dine together not only sharing food and drink but also our problems- just like before in Vail.

Rocky and Don were both bachelors at that time and found homes down in the Old Town of Telluride. Every morning they would show up early for work with wide smiles on their faces and hearty good mornings. The day and night of a bachelor in Telluride would make a best seller book or movie. Don's Vail Ski Patrol nick name was, "The Dazzler." He was better known as just, "The Daz." He earned his nickname in both Vail and Telluride. Rocky was Rocky. When walking the sidewalks of Telluride with my team, smiling pretty girls of all ages always called him just, "Rocky." I called him, "My Hero!"

Telluride Elementary was a highly rated school that opened its arms wide to our children. Even on opening day many students congregated around our children to welcome them and show them to their classrooms. The student to teacher ratio was so low it could easily be mistaken as a private school. The quality of teachers attracted to live and teach in Telluride were young and some of most qualified in the country. The school building was new and well equipped. Although one school bus driver was a little forgetful in the early morning. Once he was backing down the driveway with three kids sitting with fastened seat belts, I remembered forgetting my brief case in the kitchen. Driving back to the house, with the garage still open, hurriedly the driver retrieved his briefcase and met Amanda running into the house. Eyes as wide as saucers, frantically she blurted that the roof of the house was laying on top of the Jeep. With my shoulder pushing against the garage center post, the roof and children were quickly restored to their proper positions. Who leaves a Grand Wagoneer Jeep running and still in the automatic's _Drive Position_? The other challenge the driver faced was Lawson Hill in a winter storm. Even when traffic was stopped, the Jeep with new studded snow tires, was no match for the slippery steep incline where ashes, not sand, were spread.

There was an event the entire elementary student body of maybe 100 kids will never forget. Every class in school was assembled in the gym to watch the Space Shuttle Challenger Launch on January 28, 1986 carrying

Christa McAuliffe, a high school teacher from New Hampshire and the seven NASA astronauts. Suddenly just 73 seconds after liftoff, the Challenger Shuttle exploded killing all eight people on board in the tragic disaster.

Can you even imagine being those Telluride teachers who were just as shocked as the assembly of children? Johnnie Stevens, Telluride's Vice-President of Mountain Operations, and I heard about the tragedy inspecting the new high-speed Vista Bahn Lift in Vail. Following is a lighter story!

Back in the days when men were men and loaded with testosterone and too much beer overriding any brains they had, Johnnie Stevens may have met his match. Having "a drink" at the local Sheridan Bar, he was challenged to a race down the Plunge on the front side of the Telluride Ski Mountain by a champion female speed skier. How could he say, "No"? Yes! He accepted- this was a much younger Johnnie Stevens than the future Telluride Mountain Manager, Chief Operating Officer, and Colorado Ski Hall of Fame hero. From the top of the steep Plunge, skiers can see the Town of Telluride 3200 feet below their trembling legs. The race quickly developed into a "Kentucky Derby" type event in this small mountain town with the betting line favoring the speed skier. Details of the top-to-bottom race, including the setting of a fixed date, were memorialized on a napkin. There was no backing out now for Johnnie, who had nothing to gain and a lot to lose. The betting began by those witnessing the "highly spirited" discussion. Many people from the starting gate at the top of the mountain to the finish line at the bottom of the Coonskin Lift discovered that day- never underestimate Johnnie Stevens nor bet against him. It may not have been pretty, but Johnnie found the finish line first.

Brian, John, and Amanda have fond memories skiing with the Telluride Alpine Racing Team (TART). They also raced around the snow- covered meadows at the house on a small snow-mobile with Bo joyfully post holing closely behind.

Dave and Sherry Farney owned the Skyline Ranch just a few miles up highway 145 from our home. Vail friend, Brian Rapp, now President of the

Mountain Village Homeowners Association, treated me to dinner at the guest ranch and introduced me to Dave and Sherry. We joined a group of business executives and their wives and children for a dinner of hearty ranch fare. Dessert was moved outside to a small pond under the Colorado star-filled night. As Dave launched paper sailboats brightly lighted with small candles, the children of the guests were in charge of making the s'mores by roasting marshmallows on a fire to be smooshed hot between Hershey bars and Graham Crackers. Dave played his cowboy accordion and remarked loudly that this is, "Mountain Joy!" And that was what my three young children were feeling racing down the steep face of the Plunge.

Telluride was noted for many things including the Grateful Dead concert in the Town's park. The Bluegrass, Film, and Jazz Festivals were some of my my favorites. During the Jazz Festival two of my close friends in Vail came to Telluride to stay with me and tour the Mountain Village. Chupa Nelson was a Master Vail Ski Patrolman and a very successful contractor always on the lookout for a good real estate investment. The other was former Vail Ski School Supervisor, Don Welch, who after a whole year unsuccessfully trying to sell his house with another company listed his house with me, and amazingly one of my clients bought it the next week. Don wanted to know why it took me so long!

These two old friends are really special in my life. Chupa and his wife, Liz, introduced Donna to me on a blind date. Don and Shirley and their three children were very close to all of the Buckley family. Promising to treat the two of them to dinner after their tour of the Mountain Village, a twinkle in Chupa's eye betrayed the small price to be paid for their long drive from Vail to Telluride, my windy pitch, and Chupa's introduction to the love of my life.

The three of us accidently bumped into Barry Stott, a renown Vail photographer, and friend. Chupa invited him to join us for dinner. He also put in the wine order for expensive champagne, followed by more bottles. Chupa likes to live well!

A former Vail ski instructor and the Director of the Jazz Festival and his staff were celebrating their last successful night at the next table. Don

Welch knew him well from Ski School. Magnanimously Chupa ordered champagne for their table. I wasn't keeping track, but I knew the bill was going to be a whopper! When the bill was delivered to me, the Jazz Festival Director grabbed it out of my hand.

Yes! There is a God!

Another goal was met when I introduced a friend and a fixed base developer to the Telluride Airport Authority. He would build the commercial terminal and set up the fixed base operation (FBO) for the highest commercial airport in the nation. Bumping into the Airport Authority's lawyer outside of my office in Telluride, she offered to let me ride along to the Eagle Airport. Conveniently Donna and our children happened to be spending the week in our home in Vail. I could ride back to Telluride with them instead of driving two cars back to Telluride after attending a hospital board meeting where I had intended to resign after 5 years of service and now living in Telluride. Her plane picked us up at the Telluride airport but had to put down shortlyafter takeoff at the Montrose Airport because of strange engine noise emanating from a magneto.

An hour later with repairs finished, we took off again for Eagle. When nearly topping over McClure Pass, our engine coughed and the propeller stopped turning. Banking sharply, the pilot calmly commanded us to look for a clearing in the timber covered hillside to land. Sitting alone in the back not only looking down for a landing spot on a steep mountain side, but also starting to pray knowing this was how I was going to die. The engine sputtered briefly and just as quickly died again with the propeller spinning slowly. The pilot said he thought he just might be able to glide back to a single unmanned runway in Paonia, Colorado. That sounded a reassuring note since I didn't see any other clearings out my side window. Some hair-raising moments later, we slowly glided onto Paonia's only runway. Our prayers were heard and the Colorado mountains missed swallowing us whole like the two huge blue sharks missed swallowing me whole off Onari Island. (pg. 162)

There was a pay phone at the Paonia runway for the pilot to call Aspen to send a plane to pick us up. Arriving back home in Vail and telling Donna all about my harrowing flight, we had a long discussion concerning the fact that Donna's friend Patsy MacGregor had called it quits after year of unhappiness in Telluride. The Robinsons had also waved a white flag and returned back to Vail. And Donna was now showing me her red card. She really missed the reassuring road noise from I-70. What she was really saying was that she missed sleeping in our own bed at our home on Bald Mountain Road. My close call almost crashing on McClure Pass was the end of my Telluride dream. Donna deserved to live where she was happy! If mama's not happy, you can bet papa is miserable!! knowing that I could resume my real estate career with almost any real estate company in Vail, maybe I could return to Beaver Creek Properties. The last few years had simply worn Donna out. Later attending the Hospital Board Meeting instead of resigning, I asked Larry Lichliter, Hospital board member and VP of VA's Mountain Department, if he would accept me back on the Vail Ski Patrol for next season. "Not a problem!"

Returning back to Telluride and expecting to turn in my resignation, Ron, and Joyce were taking some well-earned time off. Ron did call in and it just wasn't my style to resign over the phone. We did talk about his Benchmark Partner who also managed both the accounts for the Avon Project and Telluride, blow a gasket over a Corporate Sales expense item. Jim's a great guy but keeping up with Ron had to create unbelievable pressure, especially with a Denver Bank always looking over their shoulders. The scary expenses of building a Ski Resort are just unimaginable!

Just shortly thereafter, I received a call from Larry asking me to return to Vail and meet with Mike Shannon, the recently named President of Vail Associates. Mike wanted to meet for breakfast in the Lodge of Vail. Asking Larry, "Why Is he interested in talking to someone who only wants to be a Vail Ski Patrolman?" Larry simply replied, "Just show up!"

George Gillett and Mike Shannon had already met with me earlier in the summer. Gordon had set up a meeting between Ron Allred and George Gillett concerning Ron's search for another partner. And wanting to meet George myself, Gordon also set up a later meeting for me. I had first surveyed in Beaver Creek, knew the perspective of customers buying property in Beaver Creek, and had been privileged to have Pete Seibert share his vision for the entire Vail and Eagle River Valleys. Arriving at the appointed hour at George's house in Vail, his father greeted me at the door and said that George was going to be late. At that time little did I realize the real importance of my visit was to be an extended conversation with Dr. George Gillett Sr. The surgeon led me through a very detailed discussion on late term abortion surgery. He finished his description with a question, "Do you know what this is?" Dr. Gillett answered his own question, "Murder!"

George Gillett, Jr. and Mike Shannon finally arrived and we also had a detailed discussion about Vail and Beaver Creek. At the conclusion, George offered me the position of President of Beaver Creek. To George's surprise, I gratefully declined. Really enjoying my work in Telluride, I was looking forward to building on the lot that was part of my compensation package. With Mike Shannon and George Gillett, I knew Vail Associates would be in good hands. We had a good conversation. The two men were very smart and not "hard of listening."

Walking into the Wildflower, Mike was waiting for me at a table. He couldn't have surprised me more when he offered me the position of Vice President of the Real Estate Division, "Let's bring the Buckley family back home to Vail." I agreed! When Ron returned to Telluride, we met and he was very understanding saying to me, "Either the wife loves Telluride or hates it, no in-between!" One evening Donna and I had been guests at Ron's high school friend and football teammate's house to watch the Colorado Buffs and the Nebraska Cornhuskers play football. Having gone to dental school in Nebraska, Ron became a lifelong Cornhusker fan. Joined by Ron and Joyce Allred, who held hands throughout the entire game, Ron left no doubt that the licensed dentist, successful Vail developer, and Telluride visionary loved his wife. You could see in their easy affection for each other that their marriage was one of the most important blessings in their lives. Their example of 1 Corinthians 13:1-13, was their real, "Cherry on top" in Telluride.

Mine was forfeited with my resignation.

Both Donna and I are looking forward to more stories in the Buckley family journey. My landlord was not as amenable! He was holding me to the year's lease that I had just recently resigned and renewed for another year. In the Fall, I returned to the house to retrieve some of my belongings and spend the night after the long drive facing the blinding sun and the many bugs dirtying my windshield on my Jeep. Lights were on in the house as I drove into the driveway, and people were sitting in the living room. Instead of using my key to open the door, thankfully, I decided to knock instead. With a quizzical look on my face, they explained that they had the house under a purchase contract and were paying rent until the closing. Asking in disbelief, "Who is your real estate agent?" They answered my inquiry. Shaking my head, the drive down to the broker's office in town seemed really unbelievable and surreal.

After explaining my dilemma to the broker who said for me to go have dinner. Both the landlord and the broker now had time to sweat, while I was pondering over dinner whether I would accept a check to reimburse my previous rent payments. What would be a poker player's best move holding a winning hand-possibly up the ante, or call the bet, or the police? I knew that the mayor was an honest broker and likely helped me in securing the FBO for The Telluride Airport Authority. After dinner, he wrote a check for what had been paid on my new lease in my supposed empty rental.

On my drive down from Vail following the Colorado River, my windshield was covered with smashed bugs from the evening hatch. The bright

last rays of the evening sunset exposed the multiple splatters and dark smudges on the glass.

Knowing the windshield of my soul when exposed to the Light of the Son would also do the same. I humbly and gratefully accepted the large check the mayor handed to me. After driving almost all day and night, the lights were off returning home.

What some people won't do for money?

CHAPTER 27
"God is Love"

The Buckley Family Journey back home to Vail wasn't just about being the Vice President of the Real Estate Division for Vail Associates? That offer came my way years before, and I had also turned it down. Harry Bass installed Jack Marshall as President of Vail Associates after acquiring the company as a result of the Gondola accident of March 26, 1986. Harry had asked me to tour the Marshall family around Vail and find them a home to buy. It just so happened that Hugh Hyder, renown owner of Hyder Construction, built two Vail Golf Course houses and had recently listed them with me. Jack and Jeannie Marshall bought the one that best suited their family.

A week later Jack invited me to his office and offered me the job. I respectfully declined. I did recommend a former friend and boss who had started a new real estate company in the Mill Creek Court Building. Jack followed my advice and rehired Bob Nott to be his Vice President of Real Estate, for his second bite of the apple.

This time I accepted Mike Shannon's offer armed with the Vail visions of Pete Seibert, recently of Utah's Snowbasin Ski Resort, and Telluride's Ron Allred. This interesting Vail and Beaver Creek story will be for another time and another book.

Dr. George Gillett Sr. was prophetic in preparing me for a further challenge on the Vail Valley Medical Center's Board of Directors, which I had nearly resigned from earlier. The Buckley family return journey to Punlap Island resulted in the saving a young wife's life with medicine prepared by VVMC. This challenge was altogether different.

Three- year- old John Buckley's broken leg in the spring of 1980 precipitated my being invited to join the Board of Directors of the Vail Valley Medical Center formerly known as the Vail Clinic. It was the first year as a full-service hospital doing 350 surgical operations and employed 25 full-time physicians. A real attention grabber at my first Board meeting, was the bond holders and creditors threatening to close down the hospital. Now I knew the reason for the hospital's cashier panicking over my paying John's bill. The main agenda item that evening was the hospital's mounting cash burden supporting Eagle County wide ambulance service. Should there be an ambulance district formed to lift this costly burden off the shoulders of the hospital? A vigorous debate ensued. A guest of Ralph Davis, Chairman of the Board, became angrily animated calling us a bunch of Communists asking the public to bear this burden. The board voted to approve pursuing this goal. A District plan was designed to include all of Eagle County, except El Jebel and Basalt. Lyn Morgan, the then experienced Hospital Director of the Ambulance Service, was to serve as the primary spokesman leading the political task of selling this to the public. Hearings were held for months with Board members pleading that the hospital was circling the drain if this vote wasn't successful.

After many long evenings of vigorous debates held throughout the defined boundaries of the District, the vote produced a successful outcome. Lyn Morgan was elected by the new Ambulance District Board to be in charge of the ambulance service, and Vail Valley Medical Center was no longer in the ambulance business. This outcome produced immediate positive cash flow to the

bottom line. But I soon learned with 25 full time doctors, there is not always harmony.

The Hospital Board began to hear complaints that the Hospital Emergency Room, that traditionally was managed by the first pioneer doctor group, had been self-referring mainly to their own group. We also learned that most hospitals were employing professional Emergency Room Groups that were trained in Emergency Medicine and referred out patients according to their medical needs. This situation would solve the self-referral complaint, if it was true, but more importantly it provided Emergency Medical Specialists trained for our emergency room.

Competition is healthier when referrals are made based on the medical needs of the patient. An advocate medical group having an apparent, if not actual, competitive edge in the Emergency Room was not conducive to harmony in the larger medical community nor in attracting a variety of specialists to the Vail community hospital.

The, "Save our local doctors" war erupted in the Vail Valley. It soon became very personal and hurtful to many board members who did actually appreciate our local doctors. We just wanted improved quality care for our patients, and a fair playing field to attract more good doctors to our expanding hospital. One of the doctors with our local doctor group joined the new Emergency Group healing hurt feelings all the way around.

The challenges that the Hospital Board faced together, forged some very close bonds of friendship between the Board Chairman and myself. One issue was brought forward to the board by some surgeons now practicing in the following recent hospital expansion. This group of

doctors were now requesting that operating rooms be approved to perform late term abortions. I didn't recognize most of the doctors, even though I had voted to give them privileges. But there was one who saved my daughter's life. Eight years earlier, newly born Amanda came home from the hospital in Denver running a very high fever. Seeing my neighbor walking a golden retriever by my house, I summoned him to look at my feverish daughter who was quickly put in the hospital. The fever was broken by his quick action. Now this friend was one of those sitting in the board meeting requesting to have the right to destroy a late term baby's life for any reason. It was already allowed to save a mother's life.

A physician board member said, "Bob you don't understand that some babies are **monsters!**" It was obvious my arguments made no headway with the board members until I told Ralph that this would be my last board meeting if a motion was approved. Ralph said he didn't agree with my arguments but didn't want to lose me on the board. The motion was tabled to the next board meeting! All of the other board members agreed with Ralph. I now bought a month to the next board meeting. It was interesting to me that the board members that were in favor of allowing late term abortions were already born. There was just one voice standing up for those children who had no vote. But thanks to Ralph Davis, I had a month.

John and Amanda were really very good at ski racing. Brian was a good ski racer but was also exceptional at hockey. He was a really gifted skater even when he was three and enrolled in the Vail Mighty Mites. There was a good children hockey program in Telluride that kept his skills at a high level. While over at Hockey practice at Dobson Arena one of the Lutheran Ministers was also in the stands watching his son. We sat together and before long we had struck up a conversation on abortion. His position was the same as mine. Before long his Gracious Savior Lutheran Church members, many had been contributors to the hospital at earlier financial crises, began inundating The VVMC Board members with letters and petitions not to allow our small private hospital to permit late term abortions. The letters numbered in the hundreds.

The last thing that VVMC needed were locals picketing outside the hospital just when it was recovering from its earlier financial crises. The next Board meeting the arguments for entering the politics of abortion were the last thing the Board wanted to consider-or any more letters from the Lutherans at Gracious Savior Lutheran Church. George Gillett Jr. was raising the possibility of recruiting his friend, Dr. Richard Steadman, the U.S. Ski Team Orthopedic Surgeon in Tahoe, CA. to the Vail Valley Medical Center.

My Aunt Ruth and cousin Marilyn did not fit the label, monster! These two were very cherished and loving relatives in my family who happened to have Down syndrome. Who are the real human monsters? Casper Ten Boom told his daughter, "I pity the poor Germans, Corrie, they have touched the apple of God's eyes" I pity the poor doctors.

Vail Ski Patrolman, Walt Olsen, introduced me to Karen Josephson who gifted me with her sister Gretchen Josephson's poems in <u>Bus Girl</u>, and <u>PEACE</u>. Gretchen had Down syndrome.

"The poems of Gretchen Josephson, lyrical, poignant and insightful, eradicate, once and for all, the misguided notion that individuals with Down syndrome have diminished capacity for creativity, imagination and sensitivity. These verses establish Ms. Josephson, not as a poet with Down syndrome, but as a poet! (Emily Perl Kingsley- writer for Sesame Street and author of Count us in)"

This is written on the back cover of <u>Bus Girl</u>.

Bus Girl

Poems by Gretchen Josephson

Opening Comment by Epic Records Country Singer, Joe Diffe, Gretchen's favorite singer:

"Tears streamed from my eyes as I read the poems in Gretchen's book. To be blessed with a Down's child as I have been, and to realize the accomplishment of achieving a book filled with abstraction and conceptualization just stunned me. God bless Gretchen for her efforts and for helping people grasp the fact that people with Down syndrome can contribute to society in an artistic capacity as well as in the labor force, and that Down's people are just that ... people."

—Joe Diffe

The following poem by Gretchen Josephson is from her <u>PEACE and other poems</u>. Christmas 1971

"GOD"

God is Love and God is Warmth

Like in a bonfire

With the lights low

And you can see yourself in a bonfire

You can see the flame

And you bring in the wood
And you hear the crackling wood in the fire
And you can see the flickering lights at night
When the lights are dim
And they shine on a lake at night, and…..
"Oh" GOD
Would you tell my Mom and Dad
I love them too much to cry for them
But they need to feel it.

Amen

"I am surely with you always, to the very **end!**" (Matt. 28:18).

Acknowledgements

In the preparation of this work I have received help from many sources. My late father Robert Buckley Sr. and the late Dave Collins shared their memories and traditional oral stories of the family and early Silver Plume. Also, my brother Don Buckley and his wife Kathy contributed much of their compiled family history and old photographs. My cousin Sharon Haskins Kennedy shared her family research and records from Ireland, the United States, and the State of Colorado. Christine Bradley, the Archivist for Clear Creek County, who has been enormously helpful writing about Silver Plume, Colorado. I am very grateful to Steve Hayden guiding me with my stories of my Peace Corps years, and Carly Britton for her expert writing advice. Polgarus Studio did the formatting and book layout. Thanks to Karen Josephson for sharing her sister's books with me.

Stan Hoig's *The Peace Chiefs of the Cheyennes,* Hampton Sides' *Blood and Thunder,* Carol Turner's *Forgotten Heroes & Villains of Sand Creek,* Simon J. Ortiz's *From Sand Creek,* Nathaniel Philbrick's *The Last Stand,* Robert Emmitt's *The Last War Trail,* and John Neihardt's *Black Elk Speaks* all provided Native American historical background. I received daily encouragement and support in this project from my wife, Donna who has rendered invaluable assistance in editing, proof reading, and endured all my musical inspiration on YouTube. My three children Brian, John, and Amanda provided technical support and love. Also, I received love and publishing and writing support from my long-time Vail friends Shirley Welch, Dave Sage, and Tom Boyd who was the editor of the Vail Trail. All gave me much appreciated guidance and encouragement! The cover was designed by Russel Davis at Gray Dog Press in Spokane, Washington.

In Memoriam to Benjamin Cherny (2002-2009) beloved son of Jason Cherny and Amanda Buckley and fun older brother of Colin and Lucy.
Silver Plume Irishman Black Bob Buckley Sr,

I give praise and glory to my Lord and Savior, Jesus Christ, for bringing Light into the world and into the life of a creature made of clay who was stumbling around in darkness. (Black Bob Buckley Jr.)

"When I am afraid, it is in You I place my trust." (Psalms 56:3)

The Pandanus tree provides the palms for making Micronesian woven mats, textiles for clothing, and formerly the woven sails for the outrigger sailing canoes of the Pacific. The fruit in the above tree looks similar to a pineapple with individual fruit within the cluster. When I first arrived in the Caroline Islands, I would see the people chewing on a sliver or spine of the yellow ripened fruit, much like chewing on a piece of sugar cane. The fibers contain sweet nectar, but the fibers are too coarse to swallow. You just bite off a sliver and chew on it like a piece of chewing gum, and when it loses flavor you spit it out and bite off another.

I hope you enjoyed reading all the stories in **Don't Get Too Comfortable.** Most of the pictures in *Book One* were taken by my family ancestors and were preserved by myself or other members of my family. Pictures in *Book Two* were taken with my own camera, while I was in the Peace Corps. And most of the pictures in *Book Three* were taken by my wife, Donna or me.

Olela me Kinnisou,
Bob and Donna Buckley Jr.

Made in the USA
Middletown, DE
13 March 2019